Brain Power

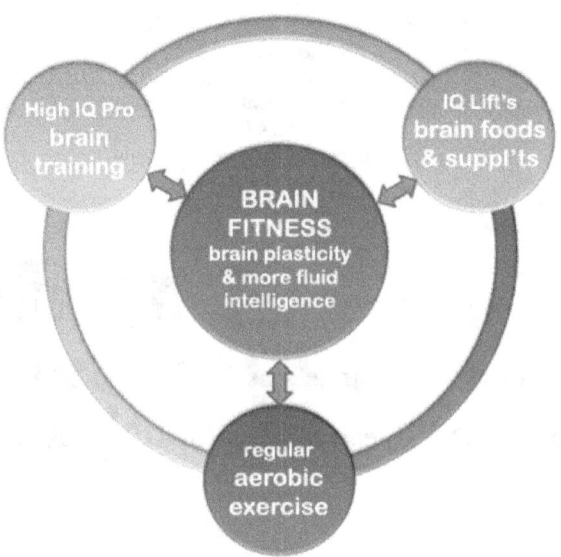

By
Luis S. R. Vas

Published by:

F-2/16, Ansari Road, Daryaganj, New Delhi-110002
☎ 011-23240026, 011-23240027 • *Fax:* 011-23240028
Email: info@vspublishers.com • *Website:* www.vspublishers.com

Branch : Hyderabad
5-1-707/1, Brij Bhawan (Beside Central Bank of India Lane)
Bank Street, Koti, Hyderabad - 500 095
☎ 040-24737290
E-mail: vspublishershyd@gmail.com

Follow us on:

For any assistance sms **VSPUB** to **56161**
All books available at **www.vspublishers.com**

© **Copyright:** *V&S* PUBLISHERS
ISBN 978-93-505707-5-3
Edition 2013

The Copyright of this book, as well as entire matter contained herein (including illustrations) rests with the Publishers. No person shall copy the name of the book, its title design, matter or illustrations in any form or in any language, totally or partially or in any distorted form. Anybody doing so shall face legal action and will be responsible for damages.

Printed at : Param Offseters, Okhla, New Delhi-110020

Publisher's Note

After a number of books on Health, Personality Development and Self-Help, such as *Improve Your Memory Power, Nature Cure, Comprehensive Memory Development Course, The Success of Failure, Success 2020,* etc., V&S Publishers has now come up with this altogether new and unique book called **Brain Power** by the well-known author, Luis S.R Vas.

It is a fact that the brain is the centre and master of the nervous system in all animals including the human beings controlling all our actions and reactions. In this book, the author has basically collected and compiled numerous methods devised by a variety of researchers to strengthen and sharpen the human brain and make it more efficient, so that it improves the overall immune system of the body and health. The techniques that have been presented in the book are in a very systematic manner so that it serves the purpose of one and all, irrespective of one's age, sex, colour or race. Some of the salient features/aspects of the book are:

- The Seven Ways to Sharpen Attention, Insight and Creativity
- How to Reinvent Yourself – Mindfulness Meditation and Self-Coaching
- Exercise to be Still
- Two Easy Strategies to Boost Your Brain Power
- Nine Things Successful People Do Differently
- Ten Habits of Highly Effective Brains
- Meditation Makes You More Creative
- The Magic in 'Yoga Sleep'
- How Positive Thinking Re-Wires Your Brain
- Cheerfulness: A Psychosynthesis Technique
- Eight Benefits of Laughter
- Breathing Techniques
- Ten Benefits of Power Napping
- Living to 100: What's the secret? And many more...

Hence readers, it's definitely a Must Read for all of you as it will prove to be of great value in your personal as well as professional lives.

Contents

Introduction 7

1. Attention Training 10
   Attention Training 11
2. Mindfulness 24
   Using Mindfulness to Rewire the Brain 25
3. Habits 36
   Things Successful People do Differently 37
4. Meditation 46
   Meditation 47
5. Positive Thinking 69
   Positive Thinking 70
6. Memory Training 74
   Memory Training 75
7. Physical Training 88
   Physical Training 89
8. Manage Your Emotions 129
   Manage Your Emotions 130
9. Breathing Techniques 143
   Breathing Techniques 144
10. Thought Control 192
    Thought Control 193
11. Diet-Control 208
    Diet-Control 209
12. Power of Posture 215
    Power of Posture 216
13. Longevity 222
    Longevity 223

Introduction

It is well known that the brain senses the well-being or ill health of the body and tries to remedy the latter as best it can. It is less well known that you can alter the brain using several techniques like attention training, mindfulness, breathing techniques, exercise, memory enhancing techniques, meditation and diet to enhance the performance of the brain in promoting our health and well-being.

For example, mindfulness therapy is an emerging, non-pharmacological therapy that involves exercising the human brain to improve learning, memory problems, anxiety and problems with depression.

Dennis S. Charney, MD, Dean of the Mt. Sinai School of Medicine and a world expert in the neurobiology and treatment of mood and anxiety disorders, has said:

'One of the things that we have found in our research is that in general, we don't make full use of the capacity of the human brain. We identified that actually initially from hearing from a couple of the POWs [prisoners of war] when they were in solitary confinement. They told us that when they were in solitary confinement for years and all they had was the ability to think that they developed unusual cognitive capacities that they never had before when they were in solitary confinement, like they were essentially exercising their brains.

One individual told us he was able to multiply eventually many numbers by many numbers, 12 numbers by 12 numbers accurately. Never was he able to do that before. Another told us that he was able to remember to very early times in his childhood, like remembering the names of the students in his kindergarten class. Admiral Shoemaker, one of the individuals that we came to admire a lot, built a house in his mind nail by nail, cabinet by cabinet, room by room and then when he got out, he built that house, and when we met him, he was having a fight with his wife because she wanted to renovate the house and he said no way was that going to happen.

That brought home that when you exercise your brain and you don't have any outside distractions because you're in solitary, you have enormous capacities. Our research group subsequently hearing about this and others around the country have now taken a tact that through specific exercises we might be able to enhance brain plasticity, or using more of the capacity of the human brain.'

In this book, I have collected several techniques, devised by a wide range of researchers, to strengthen your brain so that it enhances the body's immune system and its overall health. The techniques are presented below so that you are able to use them when appropriate:

- Seven Ways To Sharpen Attention, Insight And Creativity
- How to Reinvent Yourself – Mindfulness Meditation and Self-Coaching
- Be Here NOW – Getting Off Your Auto-Pilot
- Exercise To Be Still
- Two easy strategies to boost your brain power
- Things Successful People Do Differently
- 10 Habits of Highly Effective Brains
- Meditation Makes You More Creative
- The Magic in 'Yoga Sleep'
- 4 Steps to oust self-defeating thoughts
- Meditation to open the Third Eye
- How Positive Thinking Re-Wires Your Brain
- 20 Memory Tricks You'll Never Forget
- How Jon Gabriel Lost 103kg! (without dieting, drugs or surgery) and So Can You
- The Power of Stretching
- Retro-walking: The Great Leap Backward
- The Qigong Walk
- Super Brain Yoga
- The Five Tibetan Rites: Exercises for Healing, Rejuvenation and Longevity
- 25 Suggestions for Living a Contented Life by Managing Your Emotions
- Cheerfulness: A Psychosynthesis Technique
- Eight Benefits of laughter
- Breathing Techniques: Three Steps Rhythmic Breathing; Be, Breathe, Blossom; Breathe Your Way to Super Health
- 10 Benefits of Power Napping
- 3 Quick Stress-Releasing Techniques for the Busy Professional
- The Light Channelling technique for Peace and Harmony
- Control Your Thoughts with Raja Yoga Intensive
- Two Minutes in a 'Power Pose' Completely Boosts Your Confidence
- Living To 100: What's the Secret?

The techniques presented here are provided merely for the purpose of enhancing the readers' awareness of their health potential, not as prescriptions for curing any specific ailment. Readers are urged to consult their doctor before using them for this purpose. Since humans differ so widely among themselves, it should be clear that the impact of these techniques on various individuals are more than likely to vary as widely.

For the readers' convenience, I have clubbed the techniques under separate sections, but they often overlap and are not intended to be treated as mutually exclusive.

I hope that whatever is presented here will prove useful to a wide section of readers.

Luis S. R. Vas
luissrvas@gmail.com

ATTENTION TRAINING

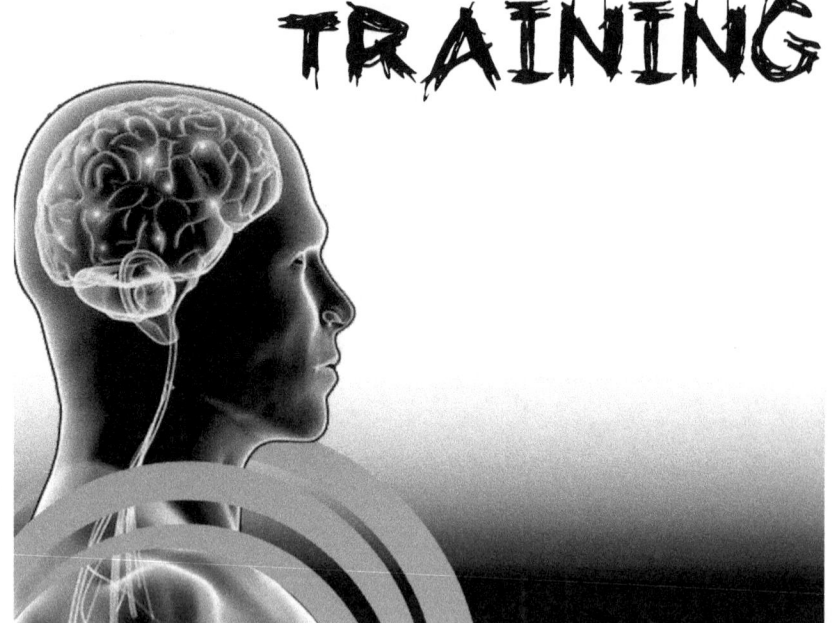

Attention Training

Seven Ways to Sharpen Attention, Insight and Creativity

Attentional Training
There's one very special thing that many do, religiously, that really helps push them over the edge from good to professional super-power good. And while many do it intentionally, far more don't even realise they do it. Or, they don't realise how or why it works or how critical it is to their success.

I wonder when was the last time you felt any of these was?
- Stressed,
- Anxious,
- Tired,
- Unfocussed,
- Depressed,
- Moody or
- Burnt-out.

Reality is, everyone experiences these on some level virtually every day, but your ability to handle, quickly recover from and master these states so often makes the difference between worker-bee and executive suite in the high stakes world of business. Think about it, what is the corollary to the above states?
- Calm
- Content
- Energised
- Highly-focussed
- Upbeat
- Even-keeled and
- Optimistic

There is a simple daily practice that has the ability to not only make the dramatic changes in mindset and operating state noted above, but alter your "attentional" abilities to literally allow you to see things others miss.

This hugely-beneficial daily practice is called **Attentional Training (AT)** and it comes in many formats, both active and seated (even lying down). Regardless of how is it pursued, though, the critical elements always include the cultivation of high-levels of sustained focus that are required either by instruction or by the intrinsic nature of the activity.

How powerful is this practice?

Done right, AT induces a psycho-physiological state where your heart-rate, blood pressure and levels of stressor hormones all drop precipitously, while your attention becomes highly focussed. And, inducing this state on a regular basis not only helps your mindset, it dramatically lowers your risk for heart-disease, diabetes and various other life-limiting conditions. It helps you sleep deeper, longer and wake fewer times at night and it can lower anxiety, stress and depression. That's where the focus has been in most of the research.

Back in 2007, a team of researchers from China and the University of Oregon, USA, reported a study that showed improvements in a person's attention and response to stress after only 5-days of practising their specialised IBMT protocol. The lead investigators wrote, "after training the experimental group showed less cortisol release, indicating a greater improvement in stress regulation. The experimental group also showed lower levels of anxiety, depression, anger and fatigue than was the case in the control group."

Want to jump right in today?

Here's a simple technique to get you started with a very basic, accessible 10-minute daily seated practice.
1. Find a quiet place.
2. Sit in a comfortable upright position with your hands on your knees.
3. Close your eyes and take 10 breaths, letting your exhale get longer and longer with each one.
4. Starting at a very gentle pace, begin to count backwards from 100 by threes, saying each number softly or just sub-lingualising them with every inhale and exhale. So, for example, inhale and think and say 100, exhale, think and say 97, inhale, think and say 94 and so on. If you get a number wrong, just let it go, say the right one and move one.
5. When this becomes easy in a few days or weeks, pick up the pace a little bit until it becomes easy again. Then, bump the top number by 25 and keep practising and bumping pace until

it gets easy again. Keep at this until the whole practice takes about 20-minutes and give it a few weeks.
6. Let go of any expectations and see what unfolds...

How to Rebuild Your Attention Span and Focus?

To get a longer attention span, don't worry about managing the information. Worry about managing your attention. Paying attention, for long periods of time, is a form of endurance athleticism. Like running a marathon, it requires practice and training to get the most out of it. It is as much Twitter's fault that you have a short attention span as it is your closet's fault it doesn't have any running shoes in it. If you want the ability to focus on things for a long period of time, you need attention fitness.

Neuroplasticity is how your brain changes its organisation over time to deal with new experiences. It involves physical changes inside of the brain based on the particular tasks the brain is asked to complete. It's why the hippocampus of a seasoned taxi driver in London is larger than average, and how a meditating monk grows grey matter. Your brain isn't a mythological deity but a physical part of your body that needs to be taken care of just like the rest of your body. And your body responds to two things really well — *diet and exercise*. Let's presume your brain, being a part of the body, also does.

Like all exercises, different kinds of workouts work differently for different people.

If you think you're having focus problems, think about setting up an attention fitness regimen for yourself instead. My general advice:

- Do slightly less than you think you're capable of
- Increase your capacity while staying under that bar (#1)
- You're not going to run the attention fitness equivalent of a marathon today. Start slow.

Your brain, like your body, is only a result of what you train it to do. Attention fitness, like any other kind of fitness, takes time even to get into a routine. But once you make it a habit, it starts to pay off.

Mental Self-Regulation for Improved Concentration

Improving concentration is learning a skill.

Learning a skill takes practice... whether it is shooting baskets, dancing, typing, writing, or concentrating. Do not confuse these strategies with medicine. When you take a medicine, it acts on the body without your having to help it.

Concentration strategies require practice. You probably will begin to notice some change within a few days. You'll notice considerable improvement within four to six weeks of training your mind with some of the skills that follow. And that's a short period of time considering how many years you've spent not concentrating as well as you'd like.

Begin by practising these techniques:
- Be Here Now,
- The Spider Technique, and
- Worry Time.

Then try any of the Other Mental Strategies that sound promising to you. Give them an honest try -- use them for at least three days. If you notice a little change, that suggests that the skill will be valuable and, with continued practice, will greatly improve your concentration. There are also Other Factors You Can Change now in your environment that may be helpful.

Be Here Now

This deceptively simple strategy is probably the most effective. When you notice your thoughts wandering astray, say to yourself **"Be here now"** and gently bring your attention back to where you want it.

FOR EXAMPLE:
You're in class and your attention strays from the lecture to all the homework you have, to a date, to the fact that you're hungry. As you say to yourself, **"Be here now"** you focus back on the lecture and maintain your attention there as long as possible. When it wanders again, repeat "Be here now" and gently bring your attention back. You may notice that your mind often wanders (as often as several times a minute at times). Each time just say, "Be here now" and refocus. Do not try to keep particular thoughts out of your mind. For example, as you sit there, close your eyes and think about anything you want to for the next three minutes except cookies. Try not to think about cookies...When you try not to think about something, it keeps coming back. ("I'm not going to think about cookies. I'm not going to think about cookies.")

When you find your thoughts wandering, gently let go of that thought and, with your "Be here now," return to the present. You might do this hundreds of times a week, if you're normal. But, you'll find that the period of time between your straying thoughts gets a little longer every few days. So be patient and keep at it. You'll see some improvement!

The Spider Technique

This is another strategy that sounds deceptively simple. But it is the basis for concentration because it helps you to maintain your concentration and not give in to distractions.

Hold a vibrating tuning fork next to a spider web. The spider will react and come looking for what is vibrating the web. Do it several times and the spider "wises up" and knows there's no bug and doesn't come looking.

You can learn that. Train yourself not to give in to distractions. When someone enters the room, or when a door slams, do not allow yourself to participate. Rather, keep your concentration on what's in front of you.

Use the "Be here now" technique to help you regain concentration when you do become distracted momentarily.

Practise this in a variety of settings, such as:

In lecture classes practise letting people move or cough without having to look at them - just let them "be out there" while you form a tunnel between you and the lecturer.

When talking with someone keep your attention on that person, look at his face, and note what is being said. Let the rest of the world just be "out there."

Worry or Think Time

Set aside a specific time each day to think about the things that keep entering your mind and interfering with your concentration. For example, set 4:30 to 5:00 p.m. as your worry/think time. When your mind is side-tracked into worrying during the day, remind yourself that you have a special time for worrying. Then, let the thought go for the present, and return your focus to your immediate activity.

There's research on this, believe it or not! Persons who use a worry time find themselves worrying 35 percent less of the time within four weeks. That's a big change!

The important steps are:
1. Set a specific time each day for your time,
2. When you become aware of a distracting thought, remind yourself that you have a special time to think about them,
3. Let the thought go, perhaps with, "Be here now," and
4. Be sure to keep that appointment with yourself at that special time to think on the distracting thoughts of the day.

Other Mental Strategies:

Tallying your mental wanderings. Have a 3 x 5 inch card handy. Draw two lines dividing the card into three sections. Label them, "morning," "afternoon," and "evening."

Each time your mind wanders, make a tally in the appropriate section. Keep a card for each day. As your skills build, you'll see the number of tallies decrease. And that's exciting!

Rest/Stretch Time. Remember to take short breaks. Lectures are usually 50 minutes long, and that's about the length of time most people can direct their attention to one task. But, that's just an average. Your concentration time-span might be less (20-35 minutes) or longer (perhaps, 90 minutes).

When you take a break, oxygenate (get more oxygen to your brain)! Get up and walk around the room for a couple of minutes. When we sit for long periods, blood tends to pool in our lower body and legs (because of gravity). Our calves serve as pumps for our blood when we walk, getting blood flowing more evenly throughout the body. As a result, more oxygen is carried to the brain and you are more alert.

Change Topics

Many students aid their concentration by changing the subject they are studying every one to two hours. You pay more attention to something that's different. And you can give yourself that variety by changing the subject you study regularly.

Incentives and Rewards: Give yourself a reward when you've completed a task. The task might be small, such as stay with a difficult assignment until you've finished. An appropriate reward might be a walk around the block, a glass of water, or reading the day's cartoon in the newspaper.

For those special projects, such as term papers, design projects, or long book reviews, set up a special incentive. Upon completion, plan to give yourself a special pizza, movie, or an evening of TV.

Incentives and rewards can be overdone. Use them for the especially difficult assignment or longer projects. When you do use them, make the rewards something you ordinarily would not give yourself.

Increasing Your Activity Level

Your concentration wanders more easily if you just read an assignment straight through. Instead, take the heading for each section and turn it into a question. For this section, that would be, "How can I increase my activity level while studying?" Then study that section to answer that question. Do this routinely. The questions give us a focus for each section and increase our involvement.

Skydivers, rock climbers, tightrope walkers, and lion tamers don't have trouble concentrating! You probably haven't done any of those. But, think back to some time in your life when you had that calm, total concentration. Close your eyes and recreate that time. Visualise it, if you can. Feel how you felt at that time. Now, when you begin studying tonight, recapture that focussed attention and see how long you can hold it. Does it feel as if that might work? If so, begin all your study sessions with the feeling and see how long you can maintain it. With practice, your concentration will get better and better.

Factors You Can Control Now

Chart your energy levels. When is your energy level at its highest? When are your low energy times? Study your most difficult courses at your high energy times. The sharpest early in the evening? Study your most difficult course then. Later in the evening? Work on your easier courses or the ones you enjoy the most.

Now that's not what most students do. Instead, they put off the tough courses until later in the evening when they are more fatigued. It's more difficult to concentrate when you're tired. Reverse that. Hard courses at peak energy times. Easier ones later. This alone can help to improve your concentration.

Light: Make sure you have adequate light. It's essential to keeping your attention focussed on what you are studying. So your eyes don't tire, use indirect lights (to avoid glare) and ones that don't flicker.

Chair and Table: Sit on a not overly comfortable chair at a table, not sprawled out on your bed. Your bed is where you sleep and dream.

Posture: Sit up straight to aid concentration rather than sprawled out in a similar-to-sleep position.

Clear away Distractions: Don't have pictures where you'll notice them when looking up from your studies. Also, put out of sight any material for other courses. Seeing it can panic you a little about all you have to do. So put it out of sight.

Signs: Don't hesitate to put signs on your door. "I need the grades. Please let me study." "Please do not disturb." "Concentrating is tough. Help me by staying away." Some inconsiderate person will interrupt. Ask them to come back later. If they don't leave, practise ignoring them (See the Spider Technique above).

Take your phone off the hook. Yes, you might miss a call. But developing your concentration skills is important. It will be useful for the remainder of your life.

Where you study can make a difference. Think about where you concentrate best. Often it's difficult to study where you live, so look for a corner in the library that's quiet and facing a wall (not a door with people coming and going or a window with a distracting view). Some students study better where they live. Find the place or places you find most conducive to concentration.

Background music: *Research on productivity with music versus without music is inconclusive.* If you think you need music, choose some with no lyrics and with relatively monotonous melodies. Baroque music is the best example. Something with words, a definite beat, a catchy melody, or one of your favourite pieces can easily divert your attention, often without your being aware of it at first.

Perhaps, you might try "white noise" -- it masks out environmental noises and helps minimise distractions. Your radio can be an inexpensive source of white noise. Switch to FM and tune to the high end of your dial. You should get a steady static or form of white noise, unless your radio is an especially good one. or keep a fan running.

Enough time for everything? Ever find your study of one subject interrupted by worries about getting assignments in another course done? Or waste time trying to decide what to study? Take an hour or so and do a little planning.

First, estimate for each course the number of hours you'll need to study each week. Then work up a flexible time schedule. Include all your obligations (classes, meetings, meals, laundry, etc.). Then allocate specific time periods for studying particular subjects. When studying one course, you won't worry so much about others because you'll know that you have time for them.

Be flexible in your schedule. If you need an extra hour on a subject, continue with it and then do a little juggling to make up the study time you encroached on. You'll probably need to modify your schedule from time to time.

If you would rather schedule smaller chunks of time, each Sunday plan the following week and change from week to week. Check to be sure you're getting study time in on all your courses.

Rewards for Concentrating: In summary, the rewards for improving your concentration can be priceless. You'll be delighted at your ability to recall information given in lectures. You'll find yourself accomplishing more in the same period of time. It can even affect your social life. Your special friend will appreciate your undivided attention and, in return, will give you undivided attention. So will the other friends. Best of all, concentration skills help your self-confidence because you will realise how much more is possible when you can give your total attention.

Concentration Exercises for Training the Mind

The Concentration Exercises:
Find a place where you can be alone and undisturbed. You can sit cross-legged on the floor if you can, or on a chair. Sit with your spine erect. Take a few calm deep breaths and then relax your body. Direct the attention to your body, and relax each muscle and part of it.

Here are some exercises to practise. Sit down to practise for about 10 minutes, and after a few weeks of training, lengthen the time to 15 minutes.

Start with the first exercise, practising it daily, until you are able to do it without any distractions or forgetfulness, and without thinking about anything else, for at least three continuous minutes. Every time, you get distracted, start again, until the 10 or 15 minutes pass away. You have to be honest with yourself, and proceed to the next one, only after you are convinced that you have practised it correctly and with full concentration.

No timetable can be given, as this may be frustrating. If for example, I tell you that a certain exercise has to completed in a week, two things may happen. You may get disappointed, if you cannot get the desired concentration within a week, or you may move on without practising the exercise correctly. Mastering the exercises successfully might take days, weeks, months and sometimes even more.

Put your whole attention into the exercises, and do not think about anything else. Be careful not to fall asleep, daydream or think about other matters. The moment you find yourself thinking about something else, stop the exercise and start again. After you become proficient, lengthen the time, and if possible, include another session in the afternoon.

Do not attempt too much at the beginning, and don't try to perform them all at once. Go slowly, without overdoing them or tensing your brain.

If you find it too difficult, or thoughts distract you and make you think about other matters, don't despair. Everyone encounters difficulties along the way. If you persevere and never give up, in spite of difficulties and disturbances, success will crown your efforts. Remember, even those with powerful concentration had to exercise their minds.

It does not matter if your concentration is weak now, it can be developed and strengthened like any other ability, through training and investing the necessary time, energy and earnestness.

In time, you will find out that you can concentrate anywhere, anytime, no matter where you are. *You will be able to focus your mind, think and function under the most trying circumstances, while remaining calm, relaxed and collected.* The reward is worth the effort a thousand fold.

Now to the exercises. Some of them may be familiar to you, and some may seem too easy to perform. Some were taken from various sources, and others were created by me.

For full benefit, it is advisable that you practise each exercise for one additional week, after you are convinced that you are practising it correctly and with full attention.

Concentration Exercises

Exercise 1
Take a book and count the words in any one paragraph. Count them again to be sure that you have counted them correctly. Start with one paragraph and when it becomes easier, count the words in a whole page. Perform the counting mentally and only with your eyes, without pointing your finger at each word.

Exercise 2
Count backwards in your mind, from one hundred to one.

Exercise 3
Count in your mind from one hundred to one, skipping each three numbers, that is 100, 97, 94, etc.

Exercise 4
Choose an inspiring word, or just a simple sound, and repeat it silently in your mind for five minutes. When your mind can concentrate more easily, try to reach ten minutes of uninterrupted concentration.

Exercise 5
Take a fruit, an apple, orange, banana or any other fruit, and hold it in your hands. Examine the fruit from all its sides, while keeping your whole attention focussed on it. Do not let yourself be carried away by irrelevant thoughts or associated thoughts that might arise, such as about the shop were you bought it, about how and where it was grown, its nutritive value, etc. Stay calm, while trying to ignore these thoughts and not be interested in them. Just look at the fruit, focus your attention on it without thinking about anything else, and examine its shape, smell, taste and the sensation it gives when touching and holding it.

Exercise 6
This is the same as exercise number 5, only that this time you visualise the fruit instead of looking at it. Start by looking at the fruit and examining it for about 2 minutes, just as in exercise number 5, and then do this one. Close your eyes, and try to see, smell, taste and touch the fruit in your imagination. Try to see a clear and well defined image. If the image becomes blurred, open your eyes, look at the fruit for a short while, and then close your eyes and continue the exercise. It might help if you imagine the fruit held in your hands, as in the previous exercise, or imagine it standing on a table.

Exercise 7
Take a small simple object, such as a spoon, a fork, or a glass. Concentrate on one of these objects. Watch the object from all sides without any verbalisation, that is, with no words in your mind. Just watch the object without thinking with words about it.

Exercise 8
After becoming proficient in the above exercises, you can come to this exercise. Draw a small geometrical figure, about three inches in size, such as a triangle, a rectangular or a circle, paint it with any colour you wish, and concentrate on it. You should see only the figure, nothing else. Only the figure exists for you now, with no unrelated thoughts or any distractions. Try not to think with words during the exercise. Watch the figure in front of you and that's it. Try not to strain your eyes.

Exercise 9
The same as number 8, only this time, visualise the figure with the eyes closed. As before, if you forget how the figure looks like, open your eyes for a few seconds and watch the figure and then close your eyes and continue with the exercise.

Exercise 10
The same as above in number 9 but the eyes open.

Exercise 11
Try for at least five minutes, to stay without thoughts. This exercise is to be attempted only after all the previous ones have been performed successfully. The previous exercises, if practised correctly, will endow you with the ability to impose silence on your thoughts. In time, it will become easier and easier.

Conscious Attention Makes Positive Change in the Brain

Your attention, when applied consciously to make the specific changes you want, can be a powerful tool of healing and transformative action. How?

- The thoughts you focus on inside expand to create a particular worldview of life around you.

Your thoughts create images in your mind that your entire body responds to accordingly. A focus on what you want or how you have overcome obstacles in the past, for example, is going to produce completely different chemical reactions inside you from a focus on what you lack or how your loved have not met your expectations.

It is estimated that you have about 60,000 thoughts a day. Many of these subconscious stirrings, by the way, are remnants of what you picked up in childhood experiences. Though you may not be aware of this inner stream of thoughts, you can be once you focus your attention on becoming aware of your 'self-talk.'

- A different focus shifts the thoughts and images in your mind.

Your beliefs are perceptions that interpret the events in your life. When you shift your perceptions inside, your outward behaviour changes, as does the physiology of your entire body.

The moment you see or hear of a person who is successful at something you aspire to achieve, such as, for example, a trim-healthy body, a prosperous business or a great mutually enriching love relationship, etc., what thoughts automatically fire inside your mind?

If you've achieved a measure of success in a certain area, your brain most likely produces positive thoughts, such as "I wonder how much work and passion went into their success?" In contrast, if it's an area you've struggled with for some time, or even worse seemingly "always," you are likely to automatically think some negative thoughts, such as, "When will I ever ... so and so?" or "Why does he get all the breaks?" or "I hate her, her success annoys me."

No doubt, these thought patterns produce drastically different behaviour patterns.

These subconscious exchanges between you and life around you are potentially life changing ... and the more aware you become of even minor inner changes you are making, the more you notice their, at times, miracle-making effect on others and life around you.

When neurons fire together, accordingly, they rewire in patterned ways.

As is often said in neuroscience since the late 1990s, neurons that "fire together, wire together." When a pair of neurons fire at the same time, they build an association or connection between them.

☼ This is what happens whenever learning takes place.

Whenever you learn something new, a new grouping of cells comes together to form neural associations between them. If you learn something new, it is because either old or new neurons are wiring together in new ways. When you hear certain words or see certain images around you, and respond to what you see and hear in different ways, for example, your brain automatically forms new associations. With repetition or practice, these connections thicken and strengthen, meaning the behavioural response is more likely to be repeated.

☼ This, by the way, is how you learnt all of what you know, even how to walk, run and ride a bike.

You are always in the process of becoming what you are most thinking. Thoughts shape your actions. You become what you do. Let your brain work for you with optimal efficiency by discovering the power of consciously focussing your attention.

MINDFULNESS

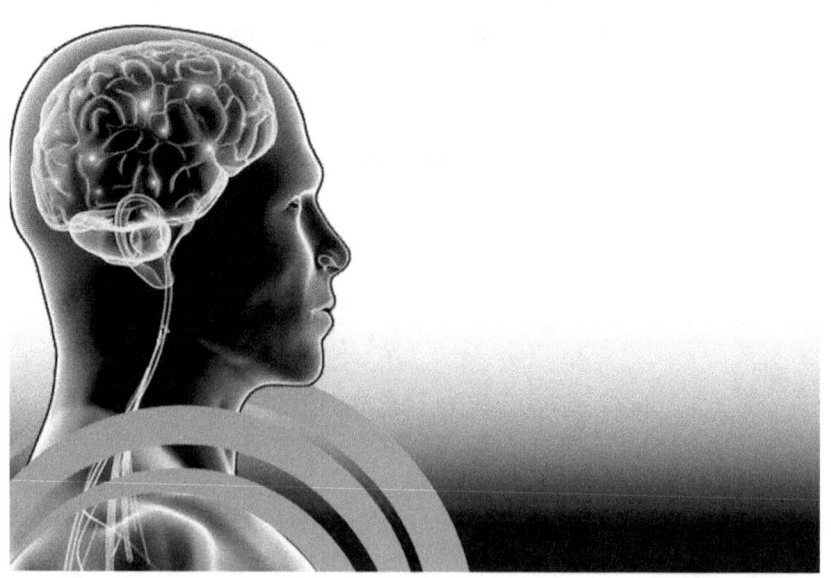

Using Mindfulness to Rewire the Brain

How the Insights of Neuroscience Can Aid Our Practice

It has become widely accepted that the brain constantly rewires itself in response to changes in our feelings, thoughts, experiences, and the way we use our body. This phenomenon is referred to as the *plasticity of the brain*. In computer language, the software and the hardware interact: the software can shape the hardware, just as much as the other way around. Neuroscience today is governed by what is known as *Hebb's rule*: "Cells that fire together wire together." The brain gets less plastic as we grow older, but the capacity for rewiring remains.

Neural pathways become entrenched, and the more entrenched they become, the more they resist the process of rewiring. The older, entrenched pathways are paths of least resistance amongst which neurons like to communicate with each other, propelling us to keep repeating similar feelings, thoughts and actions. Every time we use a particular pathway, it increases the likelihood that we will do it again.

In short, whenever we're stuck in habitual suffering, we're not just wasting our life, energy and time, we're actively entrenching this suffering in our neurological pathways, making it more likely that we'll suffer in the same way again. Suffering is not a free ride.

Mindfulness, in effect, allows us to consciously rewire our brain for improved well-being.

Mindfulness is intentional and based on our free will. Free will can be applied in many ways. An athlete or musician will construct neural pathways in his or her brain through endless deliberate practice. However, the practice of an athlete or musician will rarely be self-aware, and while it may push pathways of suffering out of sight, it won't transform them. Mindfulness may be the only state of mind that is wholly deliberate and wholly self-aware, and that is able to embrace other states of mind, transform them, and foster well-being, thereby allowing us to consciously rewire our brain.

We cannot dissolve neural pathways while firing them simultaneously. There is no way to happiness; happiness is the way. We have to step out of the stream and shine our sun of mindfulness on it. Only with the healthy parts of ourselves can we heal our afflictions.

When we're suffering, streams (or storms) of thoughts and feelings run through us; and when we manage to breathe and become mindful, these streams calm down to a gentle trickle. The suffering, the neural pathway, may still be there, but it is no longer a danger to us. It is like the mother embracing her angry child: she holds him firmly, so he can do no damage, and also lovingly, so he can come back to his true self.

Living lightly offers more freedom and clarity to practitioners and also make it possible to turn neutral feelings into pleasant ones—in other words, to turn neutral and often forgotten neural pathways into pathways that trigger well-being.

How to Reinvent Yourself – Mindfulness Meditation and Self-Coaching

Mindfulness Meditation Exercise- Creating Resilience and Well-Being
Mindfulness involves awareness, attention and energy. Learning to become more "present" will free you to be more flexible and creative. Mindfulness reduces stress and promotes resilience. You can become more resilient, enjoying better health and well-being.

1. Find yourself a comfortable position with as few distractions as possible.
2. Gently close your eyes and focus your attention inward.
3. Imagine a radiant light dissolving your stress.
4. Take a few easy slow breaths, taking air in through your nose and exhaling through your mouth.
5. Say to yourself, "Alert mind, calm body".
6. Now take a deep, soothing breath all the way down to your abdomen.
7. As you exhale, let your facial muscles, neck and shoulders relax.
8. Feel a wave of warmth and heaviness sweep down to your toes.
9. Allow the relaxation to re-energise your body and mind.
10. Slowly open your eyes, stretch, and ease back into normal activities.

Self-Coaching Questions

The following self-coaching questions can help you become more self-aware and begin to discover your true passions and identity. Engaging in fierce conversations with yourself by asking questions that interrupt long standing patterns can help you reinvent yourself. The careers of many of my coaching clients began to flourish from engaging in this contemplative practice.

1. What makes my life most fulfilling?
2. How can I live my most important values?
3. How can I spend most of my time pursuing my unique interests?
4. How can I use my talents to the fullest extent?
5. How can I make a significant contribution to the world?
6. How can I seek out opportunities to share my gifts with others?
7. How can I design my future?
8. How can I attract my ideal clients?
9. What are my life's dreams?
10. What is my life's legacy?
11. How can I live my life with purpose and vision?
12. How can I realise my dreams?
13. How can I focus on my strengths?
14. What needs to end?
15. What do I need to stop doing?
16. How can I listen more to myself than others?
17. Who am I?
18. What is my true identity?
19. What is my authentic voice?
20. When am I most powerful?
21. What are my core beliefs and what needs to change?
22. What business will fulfill my passion?
23. What are my true values?
24. How do others see me?
25. What scares me the most?
26. What have I learnt from failures?
27. How is my self-esteem and confidence?
28. What makes me happy?
29. What secrets are no longer useful?
30. How can I best make a contribution?
31. Why am I here?
32. How can I be of service?
33. What inspires me?
34. What energizes me?
35. What matters most?
36. How can I live in the present moment?

Self-Coaching Practices

1. Daily meditative practice asking yourself core questions that emerge from your unconscious
2. Diary reflecting on your personal life experience
3. Voracious reading on a number of topics including works from philosophy, religion, psychology, history, historical biographies etc.
4. Playing in nature, being mindful to pay attention and insights received
5. Fierce conversations with friends, family and loved ones
6. Personal 360-degree feedback with work colleagues, friends, family, and sometimes even critics!
7. Spiritual practices
8. Extensive travel
9. Formal "purpose" exercises, such as those in Stephen Covey's "The Seven Habits of Effective People"
10. Reading books, such as Victor Frankel's "Man's Search for Meaning" and Po Bronson's "What Should I Do with My Life"
11. Embrace the state of possibility
12. Stay in a state of gratitude and wonderment
13. Fall in love
14. Forgive fully
15. Partner with others
16. Stay conscious that life is fleeting and breathe fully into every moment

"When we are no longer able to change a situation, we are challenged to change ourselves."

—*Victor Frankel*

Be Here NOW – Getting Off Your Auto-Pilot

The 2007 study, conducted by Norman Farb at the University of Toronto showed that most of us are not consciously focussed and are on "auto-pilot" 46.9% of the time. Our minds are wandering, not attentive to the tasks at hand or on immediate outside experience, instead we're looking into our own thoughts.

So where are we when we are there – and not here?

Let's start with a little primer on the so-called mind. According to Psychology Today, the unconscious is "where most of the work of the mind gets done. It's the repository of automatic skills (riding a bike), the source of dreams, intuition and the engine of much of our information processing." It is where we store the beliefs and thoughts that are often too uncomfortable to handle emotionally.

When we act on "auto-pilot" our behaviour tends to become repetitive. On one hand, auto-pilot functioning is the brilliance of the brain at work. We don't have to learn certain things over and over again. I can type this without having to focus (much) on the mechanics of typing, rather I can concentrate on the content of the material at hand.

The down side of this smart brain functionality is that our thought patterns become hard-wired through repetition. Repetitive thinking and behaviour reinforces existing neural networks — so what we continuously do, say, think, etc. tends to strengthen (literally thicken) our brain's hard- wiring.

When we are operating with conscious awareness, we are always breaking new ground neurally because we are generally learning (even the slightest nuance) something new. We literally form new cells (neurons) every time we shift our thinking in new directions.

How We Process Experience

Reporting on the ground breaking Farb '07 study, author David Rock described two distinct systems humans use to interact with the world.

The first system, called the "default network," is the home of auto-pilots. It happens when you are mostly idle (relatively speaking) and you think about yourself. This example illustrates it well — you're sitting on a beach on your vacation, it's a lovely day and there's a nice breeze cooling you off from the sun. Nice picture, right? But for many of us, we're not sitting there in the present moment, relishing the experience, taking it in – we're off thinking about what time we should be back and how much more or less vacation time we have left.

Using Mindfulness To Rewirethe Brain

David Rocks states it well, "When you experience the world using this default (narrative) network, you take in information from the outside world and process it through a filter of what everything means, and add your interpretation. Sitting on the dock with your narrative circuit active, a cool breeze isn't a cool breeze, it is a sign that summer will be over soon."

The other way of interacting with your world is through direct experience. Studies show more regions of the brain are activated when we are in this mode. You are literally more aware, taking in a far greater range of information through your senses in real time. You are as they say — out of your head and into your experience.

When we're on auto-pilot, we can often go through an entire experience without any real recollection of how we felt or the details of what happens. We are as the term goes, "phoning it in." It's only when something out of the norm occurs that we break through auto-pilot and that often is happening externally and not of our own volition.

Being Mindfully Aware is More Than Just Being Aware

Much is being written about mindfulness these days. Several significant studies have demonstrated the positive impact of mindfulness "practice" on mental, emotional and physical well-being. Research is on-going and is trending towards revealing even greater benefits from becoming more mindful.

Take this example — Imagine that I ask you to look at your right foot. In doing this, I am essentially asking you to become aware of your right foot, which you may not have been before I brought it to your attention. In this act, you become conscious of your right foot. The question becomes what happens in your thinking when you look at your foot (or anything). Do you notice what is wrong with your foot?

When we bring mindful awareness to anything, we are in fact, aware of how we are experiencing what we see, hear, feel, etc. We are aware of the judgements — the perceptual filters — we are bringing to the experience. In doing this, we are more able to control the reactiveness of our responses. We notice what we notice. We take in a greater field of information. We are aware that we are aware. If we feel something (annoyance that our foot's not that attractive) we are aware of that feeling without being "caught" in the emotion.

Dr. Dan Siegel, Clinical Professor and Co-Director of the UCLA Centre for Mindful Awareness Research, has been a pioneer in understanding the neurobiology of mindfulness. He defines mindful awareness as "a kind of focussed attention on the workings of our own mind. It helps us to be aware of our mental processes without being swept away by them. It enables us to get ourselves off of auto-pilot and the ingrained behaviour and habituated responses, and takes us beyond the reactive emotions that we have a tendency to get trapped in."

It's estimated that we humans have about 60,000 thoughts a day. Auto-pilot works perfectly well for many of the tasks, we must carry out every day. But remember that many, if not most (depending on your level of awareness) are dredged up (automatically) from your unconscious old software. These thoughts produce feelings and behaviour patterns, some of which are unhelpful and do not support who we are today - and where we want to be in the future.

It is possible, through practice, to turn off your unwanted auto-pilot responses. You're building new neural circuitry every time you do. It takes time, especially with deeply ingrained behaviour and emotional triggers. Keep in mind that every time you do, you reinforce the new neural pathway. *That is why repetition is so important.*

A few tips....

Notice more. Set an intention, even if it is only in one part of your experience to notice more about how you react.

Notice your judgements. Notice how and what you judge, about yourself and others. Judgements are big players in the auto-pilot circuitry.

Pay attention to specific events where you seem to go on auto-pilot. Some people even brag about it, like in meetings. Auto-pilot mode doesn't serve anyone — especially not you.

Become much more aware of how your body feels. The auto-pilot mode is often associated with certain feeling states — boredom, frustration, anxiety and anger. Unless you want to keep triggering these emotional responses, bring more mindful attention to what you feel and where you feel it in your body.

Become more aware of how you are breathing. Breath is an emotional enabler. There is a wonderful quote that says — "Your breath is a doorway between your mind and your body."

Notice the stories you tell about your experience. Some people have a recurrent narrative they offer about specific experiences. These storylines are usually told on auto-pilot and are used to maintain an emotional status quo. Sometimes they are not even factual, but we come to deceive ourselves into believing they are true. Shake off the stories; find some new ones, which speak more deeply to your real and current experience.

Pay attention to the non-verbal feedback, you are always getting from others. When we're on auto-pilot, we miss valuable information from the signals people are always sending each other, usually unconsciously.

Victor Frankl's flawless quote illuminates the benefits of mindful awareness perfectly — "Between the stimulus and the response there is a space. In that space is our power to choose our response. In our response lies our growth and freedom."

Exercise To Be Still

This 20-minute exercise requires you to sit erect on the floor or a chair, close your eyes, and observe your breathing as you imagine a mountain. First, you notice small details—the trees that cover its slopes, perhaps, a dollop of snow at the peak—and eventually, you try to imagine becoming the mountain itself, feeling its strength and solidity and noticing that even when it's battered by the wind or drenched with rain, its rock-hard interior remains stable and calm.

What does experiencing the moment have to do with imagining yourself as a mountain? Think of it as strength training. By learning to quieten your mind's chatter and concentrate solely on your mental Rockies, you're gaining the focus necessary to stay present when you're not actively meditating. The point is to avoid cruising through life on autopilot, so wrapped up in your daily routine that you don't notice the world around you. "Mindfulness is about living your life as if it really mattered," says Kabat-Zinn. "If you're not mentally present in the small moments, you could be missing half your life." The body scan.

It's 45 minutes of carefully guiding your attention up and down your body, trying to home in on the sensations in each isolated part. The exercise begins with your left big toe and, unfortunately in my case, it often ends there—while, it's very difficult to learn to "fall awake" (become connected to the present moment), it's quite easy, when meditating, to fall asleep.

In 2003, for example, scientists from the University of Wisconsin-Madison examined a group that included alumni of Kabat-Zinn's eight-week course, and found that when they received flu shots, the meditators' immune systems produced more antibodies in response to the vaccine than did the non-meditators'. In a 1998 University of Massachusetts study, patients with psoriasis who meditated while receiving ultraviolet treatments for their skin healed four times faster than the control group—regardless of whether they had any previous meditation training. Researchers don't yet understand all the details of why changes like these occur, but one possible explanation is that this type of meditation reduces stress and helps people develop a more positive outlook, both of which have been shown to strengthen the body's immune system.

What's more, according to researcher Norman Farb, who studies meditation and experimental psychology at the University of Toronto, such mindfulness-based meditation can actually change the way you use your brain. As Farb explains it, most of the time, we respond to new stimuli and experiences automatically, based on how we think they'll affect us. A traffic jam isn't just cars; it's a problem that will make us late for dinner—so when we see a red wall of taillights in front of us, we become stressed-out. A pair of sneakers strewn in the doorway aren't just discarded shoes; they're an annoying obstacle. So when we trip over them, we get irritated with our husbands. In other words, we don't just experience, we evaluate—and then respond without thinking.

Farb has found that people who have completed the eight-week MBSR training, on the other hand, are able to activate an entirely different part of the brain—the insula. Located deep inside your gray matter, the insula informs you of what's happening in the present moment without connecting the experience to a specific emotion. When you're thinking this way, a traffic jam doesn't seem like a problem; it's simply a bunch of cars on the road.

The point of meditation is not to stop you from having an emotional response to what's happening in your life—it's to avoid responding purely out of habit. Every situation, if you think about it, is an invitation for you to react in a certain way, but being mindful gives you the chance to decide how to respond. Stopping your brain from thinking would be like stopping the ocean's waves. It's more productive to simply observe the thoughts without getting carried away by them—and try to tap into the calm that exists beneath the surface.

Two easy strategies to boost your brain power

No secret in the worlds of athletics and meditative arts, visualisation and reflection are two attention building techniques that date back millenniums.

Visualisation is defined as using your mind's eye to see a person, place, thing, or an experience—kind of like a movie playing in your head. Reflection is similar, but is more of a looking back on something that has already occurred. Both can be used on-the-fly, that is, while experiences are unfolding in real time.

Beyond athletics, visualisation can help you achieve the same kind of effect in a wide variety of activities—even in the world of academics, i.e. public speaking classes often tap into visualisation to help develop procedures for effective oral presentation. If you would like to try visualisation, first settle yourself down to a place of quietude. As such, you can be sensitive to the processes which allow your self-image to merge with the details of the mental picture you are about to script. Visualise a personal behaviour you want to develop (or change) and choreograph a scenario complete with characters, setting, sound and so on—whatever seems appropriate—and place yourself in it. Try to see yourself performing the behaviour from as many angles as possible: your own personal perspective, objectively, or from another person's or several other people's perspectives. Try seeing from different angles. Keep editing the scene until your responses in it are right where you want them—that is, where they are most in line with your overall goals. Then see what happens when opportunity presents itself in your daily experiences. Note: The more detailed you can script your visualisation, the better.

Reflection uses the power and potential wisdom of hindsight. For example, you may go home after a rough office meeting and try to figure out not only what went wrong, but how you can improve such outings in the future. By using your mind's eye to replay the meeting, you can identify the assets and vulnerabilities of your approach, as well as those of others. If you want to try this technique, focus on an interpersonal situation you want to improve.

Ask:

What was I trying to accomplish in this situation?

What were others trying to accomplish?

Which of my behaviour worked?

If everything matches up, continue doing things the same way.

If not, identify what didn't match and ask why?

Look for elements of the experience you feel are relevant and should be attended to and which elements you feel are irrelevant and should licit no response. Use this information to evaluate your initial responses. Then edit where necessary.

Practise your newly edited behaviour in visualisation the next time you anticipate a similar event coming your way.

Note: The more you practise edited behaviour, the more you will begin to short circuit undesired actions and replace them with more appropriate and—hopefully—more successful ones.

Visualisation and reflection can preprogramme your attentional system so that focus/execute procedures work smoother and faster when needed. They also help free up brain-space for other things. Try them out in a wide variety of situations.

HABITS

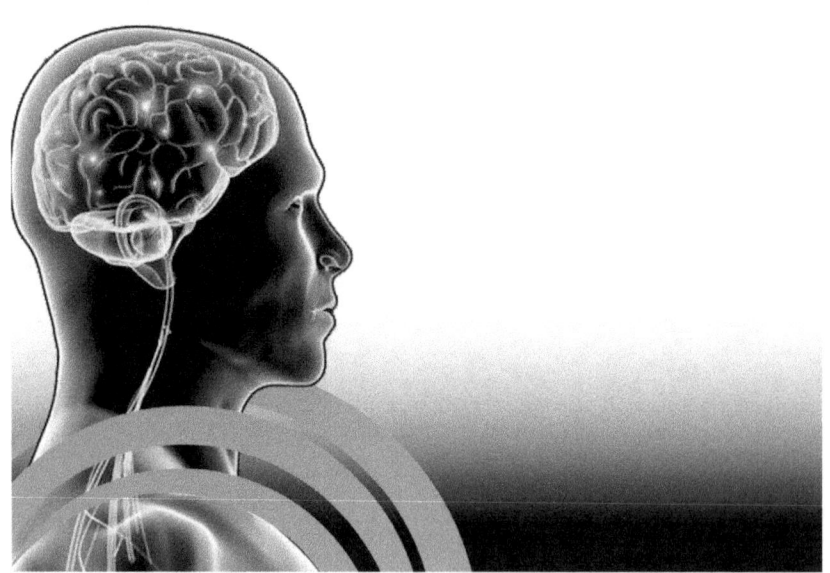

Things Successful People Do Differently

Here are three ways you can start to improve your focus.

Tame your frenzy

Frenzy is an emotional state, a feeling of being a little (or a lot) out of control. It is often underpinned by anxiety, sadness, anger and related emotions. Emotions are processed by the amygdala, a small, almond-shaped brain structure. It responds powerfully to negative emotions, which are regarded as signals of threat. Functional brain imaging has shown that activation of the amygdala by negative emotions interferes with the brain's ability to solve problems or do other cognitive work. Positive emotions and thoughts do the opposite — they improve the brain's executive function, and so help open the door to creative and strategic thinking.

What can you do? Try to improve your balance of positive and negative emotions over the course of a day. Barbara Fredrickson, a noted psychology researcher at the University of North Carolina, recommends a 3:1 balance of positive and negative emotions, based upon mathematical modelling of ideal team dynamics by her collaborator Marcial Losada, and confirmed by research on individual flourishing and successful marriages. You can tame negative emotional frenzy by exercising, meditating and sleeping well. It also helps to notice your negative emotional patterns. Perhaps, a co-worker often annoys you with some minor habit or quirk, which triggers a downward spiral. Appreciate that such automatic responses may be overdone, take a few breaths, and let go of the irritation.

What can your team do? Start meetings on positive topics and some humour. The positive emotions thus generated can improve everyone's brain function, leading to better teamwork and problem solving.

Apply the brakes
Your brain continuously scans your internal and external environment, even when you are focussed on a particular task. Distractions are always lurking: wayward thoughts, emotions, sounds, or interruptions. Fortunately, the brain is designed to instantly stop a random thought, an unnecessary action, and even an instinctive emotion from derailing you and getting you off track.

What can you do? To prevent distractions from hijacking your focus, use the ABC method as your brain's brake pedal. Become Aware of your options: you can stop what you are doing and address the distraction, or you can let it go. Breathe deeply and consider your options. Then choose thoughtfully: Stop? or Go?

What can your team do? Try setting up one-hour distraction-free meetings. Everyone is expected to contribute and offer thoughtful and creative inputs, and no distractions (like laptops, tablets, cell phones, and other gadgets) are allowed.

Shift Sets
While it's great to be focussed, sometimes you need to turn your attention to a new problem. Set-shifting refers to shifting all of your focus to a new task, and not leaving any behind on the last one. Sometimes, it's helpful to do this in order to give the brain a break and allow it to take on a new task.

What can you do? Before you turn your attention to a new task, shift your focus from your mind to your body. Go for a walk, climb stairs, do some deep breathing or stretches. Even if you aren't aware of it, when you are doing this, your brain continues working on your past tasks. Sometimes, new ideas emerge during such physical breaks.

10 Habits of Highly Effective Brains

1. Learn what is the "It" in "Use It or Lose It". A basic understanding will serve you well to appreciate your brain's beauty as a living and constantly-developing dense forest with billions of neurons and synapses.
2. Take care of your nutrition. Did you know that the brain only weighs 2% of the body mass but consumes over 20% of the oxygen and nutrients we intake? As a general rule, you don't need expensive ultra-sophisticated nutritional supplements, just make sure you don't stuff yourself with the "bad stuff".
3. Remember that the brain is part of the body. Things that exercise your body can also help sharpen your brain: physical exercise enhances neurogenesis.

4. Practise positive, future-oriented thoughts until they become your default mindset and you look forward to every new day in a constructive way. Stress and anxiety, no matter whether induced by external events or by your own thoughts, actually kills neurons and prevent the creation of new ones. You can think of chronic stress as the opposite of exercise: it prevents the creation of new neurons.
5. Thrive on Learning and Mental Challenges. The point of having a brain is precisely to learn and to adapt to challenging new environments. Once new neurons appear in your brain, where they stay in your brain and how long they survive depends on how you use them. "Use It or Lose It" does not mean "do crossword puzzle number 1,234,567. It means, "challenge your brain often with fundamentally new activities."
6. We are (as far as we know) the only self-directed organisms in this planet. Aim high. Once you graduate from college, keep learning. The brain keeps developing, no matter your age, and it reflects what you do with it.
7. Explore, travel. Adapting to new locations forces you to pay more attention to your environment. Make new decisions, use your brain.
8. **Don't Outsource Your Brain.** Not to media personalities, not to politicians, not to your smart neighbour... Make your own decisions and mistakes. And learn from them. That way, you are training your brain, not your neighbour's.
9. Develop and maintain stimulating friendships. We are "social animals," and need social interaction. Which, by the way, is why 'Baby Einstein' has been shown not to be the panacea for children development.
10. **Laugh Often.** Especially to cognitively complex humour, full of twists and surprises.

Now, remember that what counts is not reading this chapter, or any other, but practising a bit every day until small steps snowball into unstoppable, internalised habits...so, pick your next battle and try to start improving at least one of these 10 habits today. Revisit the habit above that really grabbed your attention, click on the link to learn more, and make a decision to try something different today!

Seven More Habits of Highly Effective Brains

- Have a Nutritious Diet
- Focus Sequentially — Don't Multitask
- Be Physically Active

- Participate Socially
- Sleep Well
- Challenge Yourself Mentally
- Have a Positive Attitude

10 Benefits of Power Napping

Researchers have found in recent years that the human body requires only as much sleep as the brain will allow it. In other words, so long as the brain is functioning at full capacity, there's no great requirement for sleep. The big thing is that the brain needs a rest every now and then, and apparently, the brain can refresh itself and go on "like with a full tank of gas" with just a short, 20-minute power nap.

These short 20-minute power naps for people who are really engrossed in their work, almost always provide a fresh burst of new ideas and energy. They tend to eliminate the need for caffeine boosts during the workday. And, they guarantee a reserve of energy so that the working day isn't followed by an evening in which he falls asleep on the couch watching TV or at a social event.

Here's what you need to know about the benefits of sleep and how a power nap can help you:

1. Less Stress
Curling up in a sunny patch on the floor or even lying your head down on your desk for a quick snooze brings relaxation. Research found that stress hormone levels were lower in those who took stress-reducing actions, such as **napping**. Take a break each day from the stresses and reduce your risks, find a quiet, comfortable spot and take a nap. Even a short power nap can leave you feeling refreshed, renewed, and more focussed.

2. Increased Alertness and Productivity
If you have the opportunity for a power nap, particularly after a poor night of sleep, by all means, take one. You will feel more alert and energetic afterwards, and once rested after your mid-afternoon nap, your mood, efficiency and alertness level will improve greatly. Scientists have even proven that taking a 20-minute nap approximately eight hours after you have awaken will do more for your stamina than sleeping another 20 minutes in the morning. Of course, when you first come out of your afternoon nap, you will feel a bit groggy for around ten minutes, but once your decline in motor dexterity dissipates, you will reap the rewards of being well rested and ready to go for the rest of the day.

3. Improved Memory and Learning

Naps aren't just for the very young, old, and sluggish. Daytime dozing may enhance a person's capacity to learn certain tasks. That, at least, is the eye-opening implication of a new study in which college students were challenged to detect subtle changes in an image during four different test sessions on the same day.

Participants improved on the task throughout the first session. The students' speed and accuracy then leveled off during the second session. The scores of the participants who didn't nap declined throughout the final two sessions. In contrast, volunteers who took a 20-minute power nap after completing the second practice session showed no ensuing performance dips. What's more, 1-hour power nappers responded progressively faster and more accurately in the third and fourth sessions. It looks like napping may protect brain circuits from overuse until those neurons can consolidate what's been learned about a procedure.

4. Good for the Heart

Taking 40 winks in the middle of the day may reduce the risk of death from heart disease, particularly in young healthy men, say researchers. They studied 23,681 individuals living in Greece who had no history of coronary heart disease, stroke or cancer when they first volunteered, and found that those who took a 30-minute siesta at least three times a week had a 37% lower risk of heart-related death. The researchers took into account ill health, age, and whether people were physically active. So go ahead and nap – a short daily snooze might ward off a heart attack later in life. It is known that countries where siestas are common tend to have lower levels of heart disease.

5. Increased Cognitive Functioning

In a recent study, researchers at NASA showed that a 30-minute power nap increased cognitive faculties by approximately 40 percent! Tests carried out on one thousand volunteers proved that those who continued working without rest, made lower scores in intelligence tests like the IQ test. More importantly, their capacities to work and memorise decreased in comparison to those who napped after lunch.

In concordance with NASA's work, biology students at Berkeley determined that the nap must be short in order to produce maximum effectiveness. Over forty-five minutes, the beneficial effects of napping disappear and it is therefore suggested to take a fifteen to thirty-five minute "power nap". This is the time necessary for the organism to rest and enables brain neurons to recuperate.

6. Get Motivated to Exercise

Sufficient sleep and naps help motivate exercise. Some 28 percent of adolescents say they are too tired to exercise, due to sleep. As adults, let's not let tiredness ruin our jogs. You're guaranteed to run longer, faster, more efficiently and mindfully when your body has it's required amount of zzzz's. So, store-up, shore-up and build-up your energy reserve with a power nap. It's easy (free!) and proven effective.

7. Boost your Creativity

Rest and relaxation isn't only vital to your health — it might also make you a more creative person. People tend to be more imaginative after a good night's sleep. Other experts agree that taking a nap or stepping away from a problem or project refreshes the mind and could lead to better ideas later. Power napping allows your brain to create the loose associations necessary for creative insight and opens the way for a fresh burst of new ideas. So if you feel stuck, then you might want to take a nap. Return to the problem after diverting your attention for a while. The best part is that there's no need to feel guilty, because taking some "me time," in this case, could help your business in the long run.

8. Make up for Midnight Tossing and Turning

Some of the most recent research suggests that a bad night's sleep can stress the body as well as the mind. One such study, suggests that missing sleep throws the body's metabolism off kilter. Scientists at the University of Chicago studied physical changes in 11 young men who slept four hours per night for six nights in a row. They found that sleep deprivation seemed to trigger a diabetes-like condition, harmed hormone production, and interfered with the ability to use carbohydrates.

According to some studies, power napping is clearly beneficial to someone who is a normal sleeper but who is getting insufficient sleep at night. Researchers still don't understand the underlying neurobiology, but it looks like sleep time is cumulative. They compared the alertness of people who slept eight hours a night to that of people who slept less but took a nap during the day. Both groups were equivalent.

9. Protect Yourself from Sleepiness

Scientists had also found benefits in the "prophylactic" nap for people who have to stay up late. It can protect you from sleepiness. If you have to be up all night, a two-hour or a four-hour nap does provide additional alertness the next day. Research conducted by NASA produced similar results. Naps are clearly useful for some people, including shift workers, students, and anyone doing long-haul work, such as pilots on transcontinental runs.

10. Better Health
Napping in general benefits heart functioning, hormonal maintenance and cell repair, says Dr. Sara Mednick who is at the forefront of napping research. A power nap, says Mednick, simply maximises these benefits by getting the sleeper into and out of rejuvenating sleep as fast as possible.

Everyone, no matter how high-strung, has the capacity to nap. But the conditions need to be right. Here are some helpful hints from Dr. Sara Mednick, author of *Take a Nap! Change Your Life*.

Getting the perfect nap

- The first consideration is psychological: Recognise that you're not being lazy; napping will make you more productive and more alert after you wake up.
- Try to nap in the morning or just after lunch; human circadian rhythms make late afternoons a more likely time to fall into deep (slow-wave) sleep, which will leave you groggy.
- Avoid consuming large quantities of caffeine as well as foods that are heavy in fat and sugar, which meddle with a person's ability to fall asleep.
- Instead, in the hour or two before your nap time, eat foods high in calcium and protein, which promote sleep.
- Find a clean, quiet place where passersby and phones won't disturb you.
- Try to darken your nap zone, or wear an eyeshade. Darkness stimulates melatonin, the sleep- inducing hormone.
- Remember that body temperature drops when you fall asleep. Raise the room temperature or use a blanket.
- Once you are relaxed and in position to fall asleep, set your alarm for the desired duration (see below).

How long is a good nap?

- THE NANO-NAP: 10 to 20 seconds. Sleep studies haven't yet concluded whether there are benefits to these brief intervals, like when you nod off on someone's shoulder on the train.
- THE MICRO-NAP: two to five minutes. Shown to be surprisingly effective at shedding sleepiness.
- THE MINI-NAP: five to 20 minutes. Increases alertness, stamina, motor learning and motor performance.

- THE ORIGINAL POWER NAP: 20 minutes. Includes the benefits of the micro and the mini, but additionally improves muscle memory and clears the brain of useless built-up information, which helps with long-term memory (remembering facts, events and names).
- THE LAZY MAN'S NAP: 50 to 90 minutes. Includes slow-wave plus REM sleep; good for improving perceptual processing; also when the system is flooded with human growth hormone, great for repairing bones and muscles.

Contrary to popular opinion, napping isn't for the lazy or depressed. Famous nappers have included Bill Clinton, Lance Armstrong, Leonardo da Vinci and Thomas Edison. The moral of the story: to be ultra-productive, just rest your head. You snooze, you gain. Give it a try for yourself and see if you aren't amazed at the results!

The Magic Questions

"If I did know how to easily solve this problem, how would I?"

By just asking this one question, you direct the mind to access it's vast unconscious database of knowledge. Practise asking yourself the magic question and you will quickly create a very useful new habit.

If I were to ask you who your favourite role model is or someone you deeply admire, who would be your first choice? Imagine if you found yourself in their presence being able to ask them anything you wanted!

Well you can; By using the power of your imagination.

It was discovered many years ago that looking up at a 20 degree angle turns your alpha brain wave rhythms on. In this state of mind, your left and right hemispheres are hooked up, giving you access to the whole brain.

In this alpha state, it becomes much easier to do creative work like imagining and communicating to your favourite 'genius.' With your eyes up at a 20 degree angle, picture your role model in front of you. Say 'Hello!' and ask, "How could I understand this better?" or "How could I solve problem x ?"

Thank the person in front of you for their help, just like you would a real person. Shake their hands. This, of course can help you gain even more rapport with the genius.

If you enjoy this kind of thought experiment, you may want to take it a stage further...

Noticing your role model in front of you, imagine taking their head and placing it onto your own shoulders, rather like you are wearing a helmet. You can then see through their eyes, hear their thoughts and feel their feelings.

In the world of hypnosis, this process is known as *Deep Trance Identification* and can often give you amazing insights and perspectives leading to new solutions.

Here are some useful questions to ask when you have the role models head on:

"How can I view this problem in a new empowering way?"

"How can I solve this problem?"

"What else can I learn about this?"

"What's surprising about problem x ?"

So if you've got a few minutes, why not give these ideas a go. You never know, you may discover a breakthrough solution to one of your problems, reducing stress at the same time!

MEDITATION

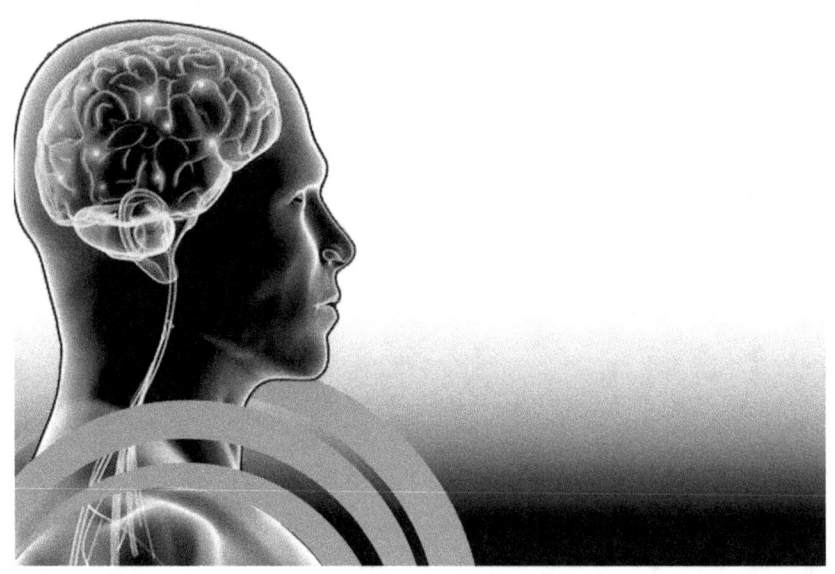

Meditation

How to Meditate

For focussed-attention meditation, start by sitting on a cushion or chair with your back straight and your hands in your lap and eyes closed. Then concentrate your mind on your chosen object — say your breathing, or more particularly the sensation of your breath leaving your mouth or nostrils. Try to keep it there. Probably, your mind will quickly wander away, to an itch on your leg, perhaps, or to thoughts of what you will be doing later. Keep bringing it back to the breath. In time this will train the mind in three essential skills: to watch out for distractions, to "let go" of them once the mind has wandered, and to re-engage with the object of meditation. With practice, you should find it becomes increasingly easy to stay focussed.

In mindfulness meditation, the aim is to monitor all the various experiences of your mind — thoughts, emotions, bodily sensations — and simply observe them, rather than trying to focus on any one of them. Instead of grasping at whatever comes to mind, which is what most of us do most of the time, the idea is to maintain a detached awareness. Those who develop this skill find it easier to manage emotions in day-to-day life.

Meditation: Stabilising and Analytical

Tibetan Buddhism speaks of two different types of meditation. One is Stabilizing and could be characterised by a type of "mindless" repetition of a word or phrase *(mantra/japa)* or by simply doing an action over and over like *yantra* (the continual gazing at an object, ie..,: a picture or statue of a deity, the symbol for *OM*, a flame, etc.). The other type of meditation is Analytical. In this form, the practitioner doesn't simply repeat a word over and over or look at a picture repeatedly. The meditator would try to understand everything they know or everything that can be known about the object of their attention.

As an example of the difference between a stabilising and an analytical meditation, let's use the word peace. You could repeat peace, peace, peace, ad infinitum and eventually, go deeper and deeper into a state of quietude that could be described as **Peace**. This is very nice but perhaps, might not be a fulfilling relative to an increase in understanding about peace. This is where analytical meditation might bring a benefit.

The meditator who is trained in analytical methodology might also start by repeating the word, peace, but once firmly concentrated on it would then proceed to analysing everything they knew about peace. They might think about the things that bring them peace like swimming, or eating, or maybe, holding a baby. They may also think about the things that make them lose their peace like their boss, or unfulfilled desires, or driving in heavy traffic.

In theory, eventually, if they kept at it, they would connect everything in the universe, because everything is in some way connected with peace (Einstein's' theory of relativity — all things are relative to everything else). But what actually happens is that the object of your meditation begins to present itself to you and you can sit back in your mind's eye and simply witness your Higher Mind reveal every aspect of peace to you.

Your inner Witness, who is your Real Self, is always receiving, knowing, and at one with everything and once, we remove the false concept that we are different (a body, a mind, an emotion, even a separate soul) from it, we will know and be at one with everything. Our consciousness awakens to its real natural state of infinite, eternal Peace, Love, Knowledge, and Bliss, and we live happily ever after. This state is known as **Contemplation**.

So, to summarise, you start by *Concentrating*, then *Meditate* by the analytical method, and then this segues into *Contemplation*. It is then when all the ???'s turn into !!!. The Tibetan Buddhists consider analytical meditation techniques to be superior to the stabilising. For you, now, it may be possible that this may bring about the result you seek.

Brain Imaging Shows How Meditation Reduces Pain

Meditation produces powerful pain-relieving effects in the brain, according to new research published in the *Journal of Neuroscience*.

"This is the first study to show that only a little over an hour of meditation training can dramatically reduce both the experience of pain and pain-related brain activation," said Fadel Zeidan, Ph.D., lead author of the study and post-doctoral research fellow at Wake Forest Baptist Medical Centre.

"We found a big effect -- about a 40 percent reduction in pain intensity and a 57 percent reduction in pain unpleasantness. Meditation produced a greater reduction in pain than even morphine or other pain-relieving drugs, which typically reduce pain ratings by about 25 percent."

For the study, 15 healthy volunteers who had never meditated attended four, 20-minute classes to learn a meditation technique known as focussed attention. Focussed attention is a form of mindfulness meditation where people are taught to attend to the breath and let go of distracting thoughts and emotions.

Both before and after meditation training, study participants' brain activity was examined using a special type of imaging -- arterial spin labelling, magnetic resonance imaging (ASL MRI) -- that captures longer duration brain processes, such as meditation, better than a standard MRI scan of brain function. During these scans, a pain-inducing heat device was placed on the participants' right legs. This device heated a small area of their skin to 120° Fahrenheit, a temperature that most people find painful, over a 5-minute period.

The scans taken after meditation training showed that every participant's pain ratings were reduced, with decreases ranging from 11 to 93 percent, Zeidan said.

At the same time, meditation significantly reduced brain activity in the primary somatosensory cortex, an area that is crucially involved in creating the feeling of where and how intense a painful stimulus is. The scans taken before meditation training showed activity in this area was very high. However, when participants were meditating during the scans, activity in this important pain-processing region could not be detected.

The research also showed that meditation increased brain activity in areas including the anterior cingulate cortex, anterior insula and the orbito-frontal cortex. "These areas all shape how the brain builds an experience of pain from nerve signals that are coming in from the body," said Robert C. Coghill, Ph.D., senior author of the study and associate professor of neurobiology and anatomy at Wake Forest Baptist.

"Consistent with this function, the more that these areas were activated by meditation the more that pain was reduced. One of the reasons that meditation may have been so effective in blocking pain was that it did not work at just one place in the brain, but instead reduced pain at multiple levels of processing."

Zeidan and colleagues believe that meditation has great potential for clinical use because so little training was required to produce such dramatic pain-relieving effects. "This study shows that meditation produces real effects in the brain and can provide an effective way for people to substantially reduce their pain without medications," Zeidan said.

Meditation Makes You More Creative

Certain meditation techniques can promote creative thinking. This is the outcome of a study by cognitive psychologist Lorenza Colzato and her fellow researchers at Leiden University, published in *Frontiers* in Cognition.

This study is a clear indication that the advantages of particular types of meditation extend much further than simply relaxation. The findings support the belief that meditation can have a long-lasting influence on human cognition, including how we think and how we experience events.

Two Ingredients of Creativity

The study investigates the influences of different types of meditative techniques on the two main ingredients of creativity: Divergent and Convergent styles of thinking.

Divergent thinking
Divergent thinking allows many new ideas to be generated. It is measured using the so-called *Alternate Uses Task Method* where participants are required to think up as many uses as possible for a particular object, such as a pen.

Convergent thinking
Convergent thinking, on the other hand, is a process whereby one possible solution for a particular problem is generated. This method is measured using the Remote Associates Task method, where three unrelated words are presented to the participants, words such as 'time', 'hair' and 'stretch'. The particpants are then asked to identify the common link: in this case, 'long'.

Analysis of Meditation Techniques

Colzato used creativity tasks that measure convergent and divergent thinking to assess which meditation techniques most influence creative activities. The meditation techniques analysed are Open Monitoring and Focused Attention meditation.
- In Open Monitoring meditation the individual is receptive to all the thoughts and sensations experienced without focusing attention on any particular concept or object.
- In Focused Attention meditation the individual focuses on a particular thought or object.

Different types of meditation have different effects
These findings demonstrate that not all forms of meditation have the same effect on creativity. After an *Open Monitoring Meditation* the participants performed better in divergent thinking, and generated more new ideas than previously, but Focussed Attention (FA) meditation produced a different result. FA meditation also had no significant effect on convergent thinking leading to resolving a problem.

Focussed Attention (FA) Meditation

A widespread style of Buddhist practice consists in sustaining selective attention moment by moment on a chosen object, such as a subset of localized sensations caused by respiration. To sustain this focus, the meditator must also constantly monitor the quality of attention. At first, the attention wanders away from the chosen object, and the typical instruction is to recognise the wandering and then restore attention to the chosen object. For example, while intending to focus on localised sensations around the nostril caused by breathing, one may notice that the focus has shifted to the pain in one's knee. One then "releases" this distraction, and returns to the intended object. Thus, while cultivating the acuity and stability of sustained attention on a chosen object, this practice also develops three skills regulative of attention: the first is the monitoring faculty that remains vigilant to distractions without destabilizing the intended focus. The next skill is the ability to disengage from a distracting object without further involvement. The last consists in the ability to redirect focus promptly to the chosen object.

Progress in this form of meditation is measured in part by the degree of effort required to sustain the intended focus. The novice contends with more distractions, and the three regulative skills are frequently exercised. As one advances, the three regulative skills can be developed to the point that, for example, advanced practitioners have an especially acute ability to notice when the mind has wandered. Eventually, FA induces a trait change whereby the attention rests more readily and stably on the chosen focus. At the most advanced levels, the regulative skills are invoked less and less frequently, and the ability to sustain focus thus becomes progressively "effortless."

In advanced practitioners, FA practices create a sense of physical lightness or vigour, and the need for sleep is said to be reduced. Advanced levels of concentration are also thought to correlate with a significant decrease in emotional reactivity. FA practices typically involve a relatively narrow field of focus, and as a result, the ability to identify stimuli outside that field of focus may be reduced.

Practice of Focussed Attention: Meditation

This type of meditation involves focussing on something intently as a way of staying in the present moment and turning off your internal dialogue. Many people find this type of meditation easier to practise than classic meditation where you focus on nothing to quiet your mind. With focussed meditation, you can choose to focus on almost anything that involves the senses, including sounds, visual pieces, tactile sensations, tastes and smells, and even the sensation of your own breathing! Here's how:

Difficulty: Easy
Time Required: 5 to 30 Minutes

Here's How:

1. Choose a target for your focus. The sound of a *metronome, the smell of incense*, or a *pleasing picture are all popular choices*.
2. Get into a comfortable position, and relax your body.
3. Turn your attention to your chosen target, and take in the sensation it provides. Focus on the sound, smell, sight, etc. and simply experience what it has to offer. The idea is not to think about it, but simply to experience it, being fully present in the moment.
4. If your internal voice starts to analyse it, or begins to rehash stressful situations of the day, worry about the future, make a list for grocery shopping, or anything else, gently turn your attention back to your chosen target and the sensation it provides. Let your mind stay quiet and clear.
5. If you find your mind engaging you and realise that you're not being fully present with the sensations of your chosen target, don't let your inner perfectionist beat you up for 'doing it wrong'; simply congratulate yourself for noticing, and return back to the present moment and the sensations it has to offer.
6. That's it. It may sound a little strange or difficult to understand as you're reading this, but as you practise this type of meditation, it will become easier and make more sense. The more you practise, the more benefits you will experience. Enjoy!

Tips:
1. Give it time. Meditation often takes practice. If you're expecting to do it 'perfectly,' you may actually create more stress for yourself than you relieve, and you won't want to stick with it.
2. Start with shorter sessions—like five minutes—and work your way up to longer sessions—like 30. With practice, this type of meditation becomes easier and more effective.
3. If the experience is frustrating for you and you don't really want to continue, you may find more success with other types of meditation.

Open Monitoring (OM) Meditation

While varied, OM practices share a number of core features, including especially the initial use of FA training to calm the mind and reduce distractions. As FA advances, the well developed monitoring skill becomes the main point of transition into OM practice. One aims to remain only in the monitoring state, attentive moment by moment to anything that occurs in experience without focussing on any explicit object. To reach this state, the practitioner gradually reduces the focus on an explicit object in FA, and the monitoring faculty is correspondingly emphasised. Usually, there is also an increasing emphasis on cultivating a "reflexive" awareness that grants one greater access to the rich features of each experience, such as the degree of phenomenal intensity, the emotional tone, and the active cognition.

Although the enhancement of the monitoring awareness continues until no explicit focus is maintained, the monitoring itself does not create any new explicit focus. Thus, unlike FA, OM involves no strong distinction between selection and deselection. For example, the FA monitoring faculty detects a state's emotional tone as a background feature of the primary focus, but in OM the emotional tone is detected without it or any other object becoming an explicit or primary focus. It is as if emotional tone and such remain in the background, even though there is no contrasting cognitive foreground. In this way, the "effortful" selection or "grasping" of an object as primary focus is gradually replaced by the "effortless" sustaining of an awareness without explicit selection.

This distinction between the "effortful" and the "effortless" points to the contrast between skills employed during the state and traits developed as practice progresses. For example, initially the practitioner frequently "grasps" at objects in a way that requires

Meditation

the skill to deliberately disengage that focus, but eventually, a trait emerges such that one can sustain the "non-grasping" state, which has no explicit focus.

A central aim of OM practice is to gain a clear reflexive awareness of the usually implicit features of one's mental life. It is said that awareness of such features enables one to more readily transform cognitive and emotional habits. In particular, OM practice allegedly leads one to a more acute, but less emotionally reactive awareness of the autobiographical sense of identity that projects back into the past and forward into the future. Finally, heightened sensitivity to body and environment occurs with a decrease in the forms of reactivity that create mental distress.

In "open monitoring meditation" one begins to practise "awareness of thinking." All we must do to practise this form of meditation is to be aware of our thoughts and feelings and observe them without attachment. In many ways the meditator becomes a scientific observer of the workings of his or her own mind, and begins to have an increasing awareness of just what thoughts bring about changes in emotions: what makes them happy and what makes them sad.

For those who practise open monitoring meditation, there are two forms of thought. First, there is the "stream of consciousness" that we associate with the mind. This is the "voice in our head" that provides us with judgements, worries and self-criticisms. The second form of thought (or rather, "awareness") is the "awareness that is aware" of the voice in the mind. If you take a step back and allow yourself to be aware of your stream of consciousness, eventually, the chatter will subside and all that's left is a sense of stillness and peace. This is the essence of open monitoring mediation, or what some others may call, "Zen."

But how can you prove that this "sense of awareness" is any different from regular thinking? The short answer is: "You probably can't", but there IS evidence to show that the meditator's brain works very differently from the non-practitioner's brain. According to EEG scans, meditators who practise open monitoring meditation increased gamma-band oscillations in the brain. These are generally very faint for most people, but are quite pronounced in the meditators' brains. These gamma-band oscillations are associated with higher levels of attention, focus and working memory. My guess, however, is that it goes much further that that.

The practice of open monitoring meditation is quite simple

You can practise this meditation while doing any activity, even just walking down the street. As you walk down the street, feel your feet against your socks and shoes, and feel the pressure of the ground against your soles. Also, be aware of your breathing, and of every sight and sound. Don't judge what you see or hear, just be be aware of it. If you do judge, just be aware of the judgement, and refrain from judging that. When you do this, all thought is focused what you're doing right now, and whatever you think you have to do, whatever email you have to answer can wait until you're actually sitting in front of your computer with your inbox open.

The practice of bringing a meditative quality to every action you perform can do much to reduce anxiety and worry, since much of what you're worried about isn't actually happening right now. Also, it can be an easy habit to adopt because all it takes is a few meditative moments per day and sooner or later meditative focus becomes an element in everything you do.

Build Mental Armour with Meditation

Mindfulness meditation works wonders to boost stress resilience, say experts from the University of Pennsylvania who are using the practice with military personnel. "We teach them to focus on the present moment instead of catastrophising about the future," says Amishi Jha, PhD, an associate professor of psychology at the University of Pennsylvania. After 8 weeks of meditation training, Marines became less reactive to stressors—plus they were more alert and exhibited better memory.

For the rest of us: Take short-mindfulness breaks.

"Even I get too busy to meditate," says Jha. "Then I remember the Marines in the study calling my colleague while they were deployed to ask for mindfulness pointers, and I think, If they can do it in a war zone, I can do it in my office!" Try this technique Marines use anywhere: Sit upright, focus on your breath, and pay attention to a physical sensation, such as the feel of air in your nostrils. When your mind wanders, notice the disruption, then return your attention to that simple sensation. Jha herself now meditates 5 to 10 minutes at a time, several times a day.

Fruits of Yoga Nidra Meditation

Iraq Vets Learn Yoga Nidra

Richard Miller, PhD, of the Centre of Timeless Being in Sebastopol, California, has been working at the Walter Reed Army Hospital in Washington, DC, with war veterans who have post-traumatic stress disorder (PTSD). Miller teaches the soldiers a guided meditation practice, called yoga nidra, which encompasses physical, emotional, and mental relaxation; observation; and acceptance. The 18-session course spans 10 weeks and includes daily home practice with recorded guidance.

In a small pilot study with a handful of volunteers, Miller saw promising results. Five soldiers completed the course and the post-training evaluation. All showed dramatic decreases in stress. Miller points out that the results of the pilot study need to be interpreted with caution because there were so few participants. The results did make people take notice though, and he already has Department of Defense support to start a randomized controlled trial with 200 soldiers to see if the approach will pan out in a larger group.

Several of the soldiers from the pilot study told Miller that the skills were noticeably helpful. In one case, a soldier had to undergo an MRI for evaluation of clinical issues not related to the yoga nidra or PTSD. When he climbed into the machine he experienced a vivid flashback, which is a common symptom of PTSD. The soldier bolted from the room and felt totally defeated. However, after attending a yoga nidra session later in the day he decided to try again. This time he focused on his breath and did yoga nidra while in the scanner and was able to finish the test. He left feeling victorious.

> *"That is how they are using it,"*
> *"They are learning how to use it in the midst of their life."*
> ---*Miller says*.

A self-directed meditation practice is not advisable for anyone suffering from serious psychological distress, however. Goldin cautions that not everyone nor all conditions will benefit from meditation. He says he would be concerned about introducing meditation to someone in the midst of a depressive episode. Self-focused attention may enhance rumination, he says, and because the quality of such an individual's thoughts are so negative, more harm than good might come from such an experience.

Rather, he would prescribe asana at such a time because it will get a person off the couch and active—which is known to help break the cycle of depression and looping thoughts. Once someone has regained a healthier mood, then meditation might be the right thing. "It is super important to do more research to know what kind of problems benefit from which kind of practice."

The Magic in 'Yoga Sleep'

According to Aree Chaisatien's special report to The Nation, working on a semi-conscious level, yoga nidra can change your life.

Nidra, a Sanskrit word, means sleep. Yoga nidra, or yogic sleep, is not just a form of profound physical and mental relaxation but helps improve consciousness and awareness, says Wararuk Sunonethong, yoga instructor, health and wellness trainer and author of the book "Palung Hang Yoga Nidra" ("The Power of Yoga Nidra").

One hour of *Yoga Nidra* is believed to equal four hours of normal sleep, and is the secret of great yogis both today and in past.

"It is a science of conscious relaxation when the state of mind is between wakefulness and dreaming. It opens deep phases of the mind, which allows the evacuation of stress from the unconscious, and can change behaviour, personality and also develop relationships with those you love."

But yoga nidra is not just another trend, following in the footsteps of Hot Yoga, Ashtanga Yoga, Iyengar Yoga, Power Yoga, Kundalini Yoga, Anusara Yoga, Yin Yoga.

While it is little known among the yoga community, history indicates that it's been known to sages of the Himalayas for a long time. It is not a brand name, trademark, nor a proprietary style."

Yoga nidra is a technique experienced and developed by Swami Satyananda Saraswati, who died in 2009 at the age of 85. While he was still with his guru, Swami Sivananda, he was assigned to take care of children at a school. His duties involved watching over them at night but the swami usually fell into a slumber around 3 am. Before he woke, the children would rise and recite vedic chants.

At a subsequent festival, the children once again recited their vedic chants and Swami Satyananda Saraswati could not understand why they sounded so familiar. His guru, aware of the younger man's sleeping, explained he had heard the chants during his slumber and that one can remain conscious and receptive even while sleeping.

This was tested by Swami Satyananda Sarawati on many disciples. One stubborn lad refused to go to school so the swami chanted the Bhagavad Gita scripture while the youngster slept. After a week, the boy was able to recite the scripture. Swami Satyananda Sarawati continued this technique for two years, reading the Upanishads, the Bible, the Koran, English, Hindi and Sanskrit texts. When the boy grew up, he could speak 11 languages.

"In *Yoga Nidra*, you relax fully, awareness can grow, brainwaves are at delta and the mind is powerful, which is very useful. That's the power of yoga nidra," says Wararuk, 40, who works as customer relations manager at LM Investment Management, and has a two-year-old daughter. "And when you make a resolution, whether it's to heal yourself, change your lifestyle or achieve your ambitions, it can be achieved through yoga nidra if you practise it at least three times a week for one month."

The best time for practising yoga nidra is from 4 to 6am. The room should be dim but not too dark, because the mind will easily fall asleep and not too bright, because the mind will be too stimulated.

Before practising yoga nidra, which normally takes 60 to 90 minutes, Wararuk suggests preparing the body and mind by doing the nine basic *asana yoga* poses. These are *Pavanmuktasana* (wind relieving pose), *Shavasana* (corpse), *Bhujangasana* (cobra), *Salabhasana* (locust), *Paschimotanasana* (seated forward bend), *Sirsasana* (headstand), *Sarvangasana* (shoulder stand), *Halasana* (plough) and Matsyasana (fish).

The first step, and key to the practice, is setting a resolution (*Sankalpa* in Sanskrit), a short positive mental statement such as "I will be healthier and happier", "I will live abundantly and meaningfully" or "I will be better in every way every day."

"Always use positive words. Don't set a resolution like 'I will reduce my weight', as the word 'reduce' is negative," she explains.

The next step is rotation of awareness through the body followed by breathing awareness, creating opposite sensations and feelings and visualisation. The practice finishes with repeating your resolution.

"The technique is to record your own voice and act accordingly without thinking or analysing. For example, say, 'Now I feel relaxed. I am aware of my whole body. I am aware of my right hand. I am aware of my thumb', and so on. 'Now I am practising Yoga Nidra'.

"I set a resolution. 'I will live a good life. Now I am aware of breathing in. Now I am aware of breathing out. I feel the heaviness of my body. I feel the lightness of my body. I feel the coolness in my body. I feel the heat in my body. I feel happy. I feel sad.' Now imagine that I stand peacefully in a garden in the morning. After the visualisation, repeat your resolution three times and slowly return to external awareness."

Sounds like hypnosis? "As far as I know, in hypnosis, our brain, our thoughts and feeling are shut down and in unconscious state, while in *Yoga Nidra*, the brain is awake, in a conscious state," explains Wararuk. "The most important thing is not to fall asleep while practising."

Wararuk has practised *Yoga Nidra* for three years now and feels her resolutions have become reality. "My resolution was 'I will be successful in yoga and I will be a writer'. Now my book about yoga is in bookstores. I did that without having any connections with a publishing house," says Wararuk, adding that her next resolution is "to be a positive force for the world."

Instructions for doing Yoga Nidra are also available on YouTube.

5 Steps to Balance the Brain's Negativity Bias

Here is a short practice you can come back to again and again at work or at home as a way to prime your mind for good — experiencing The Now Effect in daily life.

The Practice:
1. Think of a moment of receiving in the last day or week. You may have received something physical, or maybe a meal, the beauty of the sun, a smile, support from a coworker or the help from a stranger. It could be something that you may normally consider mundane.
2. Revisit the memory like a movie in your mind, picturing where you are, who you are with and pausing the reel in the moment of receiving.
3. As you're recalling the memory, have awareness that you are receiving this, feeling into a sense of gratitude. Noticing how it feels in your body and allow it to get as big as it can get "Allow the glow to grow."
4. In your mind, picture who or what is giving you this gift and intentionally express thanks.
5. Be on the lookout for moments of gratitude throughout today.

Theologian, philosopher and mystic Meister Eckhart said "If the only prayer you said in your whole life was, 'thank you,' that would suffice." This practice will prime your mind for gratitude, which we know is connected to feeling well in life. The fact is, what we intentionally practise and repeat in life changes the architecture of our brains to make it more automatic. What would the days, weeks and months ahead look like in your life if you prasticed these 5 steps daily? Allow the answer that arises to light your path.

Four Steps to Oust Self-defeating Thoughts

What are the Four Steps?
Originally developed by Dr. Schwartz to help people with obsessive-compulsive disorder (OCD), the Four Steps is a powerful, yet easy-to-

follow method that teaches you how to enhance your awareness and focus your attention in the ways you want to, while simultaneously changing your brain in positive and healthy ways.

Together, Dr. Schwartz and Rebecca Gladding have spent the last few years revising and enhancing the Four Steps to ensure that they apply to all kinds of deceptive brain messages and situations in life, not just OCD. Here is a synopsis of each of the steps:

Step 1: Relabel. Identify the deceptive brain messages (i.e., the unhelpful thoughts, urges, desires and impulses) and the uncomfortable sensations; call them what they really are.

Step 2: Reframe. Change your perception of the importance of the deceptive brain messages; say why these thoughts, urges and impulses keep bothering you (it's not ME, it's just the BRAIN!).

Step 3: Refocus. Direct your attention towards an activity or mental process that is wholesome and productive — even while the false and deceptive urges, thoughts, impulses and sensations are still present and bothering you.

Step 4: Revalue. Clearly see the thoughts, urges and impulses for what they are: sensations caused by deceptive brain messages that are not true and that have little to no value.

How could you use the Four Steps if you check your e-mail every 5 minutes when you are at home on the weekend (and it is not necessary to check at all)?

Step 1: Relabel — Say what is happening, "Oh, I am having the urge to check email again."

Step 2: Reframe — Remind yourself why this is bothering you. Say, "I am having the urge to check e-mail again because it gives me a rush when there's something in the inbox...it feels good. Checking my messages also decreases my anxiety that I might be missing out on something." Remind yourself that you are not your brain and you do not have to respond to every impulse your brain generates.

Step 3: Refocus — *Go for a walk, call a friend, play a game.* Do something that will interest you and is fun. It's the weekend after all!

Step 4: Revalue — Recognise that this urge to check e-mail is nothing more than the feeling of a deceptive brain message. It is not something that needs to be taken seriously or paid attention to. In fact, giving into this urge just makes the underlying brain circuitry stronger. The more you check, the more frequent and intense the urges will become. So, dismiss this deceptive brain message and go do something healthy and productive instead.

The key to the Four Steps is 'practice'. You literally need to keep using the Four Steps over and over. By becoming more aware of what is happening and learning how to Refocus your attention in healthier and productive ways whenever a deceptive brain message strikes, you teach your brain new, beneficial responses. With time, you will learn how to place your attention where you want it to go, not where your brain is beckoning you to follow.

You Are Not Your Brain: Key Messages
Here is a summary of the key messages:
- *Deceptive brain messages* may be running and ruining your life or at least impinging on your happiness.
- *The brain reinforces* whatever internal messages we innocently focus upon repeatedly.
- *These faulty messages* become strongly entrained in the brain at a physical and survival level.
- **As these untrue messages** grow stronger through repetition, they solidify dysfunctional behaviours you use to relieve the uncomfortable feelings and sensations that are triggered.
- *Since these faulty messages* become the preferred pathway in the brain, you are literally compelled by the brain to repeat them again and again.
- *Although you may rightly feel* – in one sense – that you are at the mercy of your brain, the good news is that you are not your brain.
- *According to the authors, the brain and the mind are two distinct entities.* You don't have control over the arising of deceptive brain messages, but you can choose how to react to them.
- When deceptive brain messages arise, you can learn how to use your mind to veto them, refocus your attention in positive ways, and work around the untrue messages.
- Gradually, through using the 4-steps provided, you will physically rewire your brain. In so doing, the deceptive messages lose their force and are replaced with positive, life-affirming ones and positive behaviors.

What Are Deceptive Brain Messages?

So what are these deceptive brain messages? There are probably as many variations as there are people on the planet, but here are just

a few common ones:
- I'm not good enough.
- There's something wrong with me.
- I don't deserve to be happy.
- No one likes me.
- I have no control.
- I don't matter.
- My worth depends upon taking care of others.
- My value depends upon being perfect.
- My wishes or goals are unrealistic or unattainable.

As you might guess, deceptive brains message typically get implanted and reinforced in childhood. This may occur due to a dramatic or traumatic event or childhood, but it can even happen as a result of a casual comment or confusing situation. Children are very sensitive and receptive to the messages they receive from their caregivers and the other significant people in their environment.

The effectiveness of the 4-Step Solution has been scientifically validated. A research study on the effectiveness of the 4-Step Method was conducted with people with OCD (Obsessive-Compulsive Disorder). Brain scans demonstrated actual positive changes in the brains of people who had used the 4 steps over a 10-12 week period. These brain changes were equivalent to the changes that take place in people who take medications to treat OCD.

The 4-Step Solution

The 4-step self-treatment program presented by the authors helps you to refocus your attention in beneficial ways. It starts with identifying your deceptive brain messages and then applying the four steps outlined below:
- Step 1: **Relabel**
- Step 2: **Reframe**
- Step 3: **Refocus**
- Step 4: **Revalue**

These 4 steps are explained in detail so that you will be able to apply them successfully on your own. Simple, useful exercises are provided to help you identify your deceptive brain messages and integrate the 4-steps into your daily routine. Practical advice is offered from clients who have used the 4 Steps successfully to overcome debilitating emotions and habits.

The 'Now' Effect

Breaking Free

Here are 4 steps to increase your chances of breaking free from a

downward spiral and increase your chances of experiencing the Now Effect:
1. Intentionally be on the lookout for the mind snowballing or when you're in a low mood. This will prime your mind to pop out of it more often.
2. Bring awareness in that moment to how you are feeling. Name the feelings if possible.
3. Think about how your interpretation of the situation may be influenced by the mood you are in.
4. If you are feeling an uncomfortable emotion or pain, apply some self-compassion and do something pleasurable or kind for you that day. This will send the message internally that you care for yourself and allow for the discomfort to come and go quicker as it naturally would.

As you practise and repeat this with intention, like all things, it will start to become more automatic. In other words, rewiring a healthier and more mindful auto-pilot.

STOP stands for Stop, Take a breath, Observe your experience (Body, Emotions, and Thoughts) and then Proceed by asking yourself what's most important to pay attention to.

Everyone loves this practice because it is so accessible and practical. You can use it in so many aspects of life. If you're a frantic parent and find yourself overwhelmed you can practise STOP for one minute to regain composure; if you're at work and you find yourself continually pulled into distractions, you can practise STOP to get back in touch with your intention. Before eating a meal on auto-pilot, practise STOP and give yourself the chance to enjoy what is there. If you're just wanting to be grounded more throughout the day, many people put a reminder in their phones to practice STOP a few times a day and get back in touch with what matters.

The Wisdom in Golf Balls

> "It is not too uncommon for people to spend their whole life waiting to start living."
> —*ECKHART TOLLE*

A professor stood before a philosophy class holding an empty jar. As the students took their seats, she began filling the jar with golf balls. When they reached the top, she asked the students if the jar was full. They agreed that it was. The professor then took a bag of pebbles and poured them into the jar, and they made their way into the spaces between the golf balls.

Again she asked the students if the jar was full, and they agreed that it was.

But the professor had another trick up her sleeve. She brought out a bag of sand and proceeded to pour the grains into the jar, filling up more of the remaining space. Again the question came: "It's full now, correct?" The answer was a resounding "Yes."

The professor then took a sip of her coffee and dumped the rest into the jar, filling up spaces that no one thought were there.

> "So what does it mean?" the professor asked. A witty student raised his own coffee mug and asked, "There's always room for coffee?"

The professor, along with the rest of the class, had a good laugh. Then she said, "Imagine that this jar represents the space in your life. The golf balls represent what's most important—family, children, health, friends, things that you're passionate about—the things that at the end of your life you would be glad you paid attention to.

> "The pebbles are essential but less important, such as your house, your car, maybe your job.
> "The sand is all of the small stuff in life that we're trying not to sweat.
> "The coffee, well, you already answered that one."

The professor continued, "There is room for all of this only if you put the golf balls in first. If you put the sand or pebbles in first, there won't be room for the golf balls. The way we pay attention to our lives works the same way. If you spend your attention or mental space sweating the small stuff in life, you won't have the capacity to pay attention to what is most important to you."

This is a classic story that speaks to becoming more mindful of what really matters. Why? Thoughts of what is most valuable fly into and out of our minds all the time, and we don't see the space between our awareness and these thoughts. This exercise provides a physical representation of thinking about what really matters and simultaneously makes us aware of the space in which we have the opportunity to choose a response. The practice of intentionally paying attention to what matters primes the mind to become more aware of what is meaningful.

The biggest question at this stage of the process is, what in life really matters to you? Is it your relationship to your partner, paying attention to your children, taking care of your body, sharpening your mind, being kind to yourself or others, making room for play, or living with greater ease?

Paying attention to the things that you value in life is fundamental to your happiness. We know that our minds have an inclination to follow the path of least resistance, so we need a compass to help us intentionally come back to our priorities.

Now Moment

Creating a way to be aware of our values can help us break out of autopilot and guide us back to what really matters.

1. Sit in a space to take care of the golf balls first—the things that really matter. What are your priorities in life? Let's bring some awareness to them, because at the end of the day, the rest is just sand. Make a list in your mind or write down what truly matters.
2. Sitting exercise: Take a few moments to relax, close your eyes, and practise "Breathing in, I am aware of what truly matters, breathing out, I let go of living on automatic."
3. Go find a jar and a box of golf balls or some nice stones. Label each golf ball or stone with something that really matters in your life. If you don't have a physical jar, you can draw a picture of a jar on a piece of paper along with golf balls or stones or perhaps just picture them in your mind. Actions speak louder than words, so check to see where in your life you're bringing action to your values. Maybe you're taking your partner out to dinner, responding to people and yourself with greater kindness and compassion, being less judgmental, playing games with your kids, getting back into exercise or yoga, making space for that round of eighteen holes, or spending time in meditation.
4. Put the jar in a prominent place somewhere in your house or office where you can't miss looking at it. Every time you intentionally look at the jar, your mind is more likely to incline toward what truly matters. As you do this, you prime your mind to respond to those values during the spaces of your daily life.

Meditation Technique to Open The Third Eye

There are several third eye opening meditation techniques, however one of the most powerful ones is a very simple one to implement.

Here are the steps for you to follow:
a. Close your eyes
b. Slow down your breathing, to a nice, slowly steady pace
c. Lower your chin down towards your chest, as if pulled by its weight

d. Just simply continue breathing slowly until you feel you are nicely relaxed
e. While your eyes are closed, look up with the inner eyes towards your third eye area. Simply focus your attention to that area and you will see that you are 'looking up', without having your eyes actually open
f. Keep breathing nice and slow
g. Relax your eyes while they are closed and they are looking upwards. Try to not force your eyes to 'look up', leave them relaxed
h. Keep at it for a couple of minutes at a time Incorporate this meditation type in your daily practice, preferably during the same time everyday, and in the same place, so your body and mind accept that place as your regular meditation place. This will ease you into a meditative state faster than otherwise you would. With practice, your third eye chakra will open, and eventually, little by little, you will notice small things that you might not have noticed before, your perception to details, and your 'sixth sense' will be increased. This meditation technique will help you quiet your mind from a busy, stressful day, and it will allow you to draw inner strength from yourself.

Discover the Power of your Pineal Gland

If you live to be ninety, you will have spent thirty years of your life in another dimension called 'sleep'. During sleep, your dreams seem very real to you but when you awaken, you realize they were just dreams. The same is true for your awake world. It is possible to awaken from that, too.

The first step in waking up from 'reality' is to recognize that it is an illusion created by your five senses. Your eyes tell you the earth is flat and the ground is stationary but the truth is - you are spinning through space at thousands of miles per hour. You may worry about your weight but the truth is - you are weightless and it is only gravity that keeps you from floating skyward.

The entire physical world that seems so 'real' isn't really there. It's just recycled atoms. There is no near or far, up or down, big or small, future or past. There is just infinite energy. You see the world with your brain, not with your eyes. Your eyes input light waves of energy. Your brain then interprets, configures and projects that input onto your mind's "internal" 3D movie screen as animated shapes and colors. It appears as though your 3D picture of the world is outside of you but the truth is, you are seeing the world with your brain as configured images. Your brain's 3D software allows you to manipulate, interact with and navigate through the world of energy. There is no physical world.

When you watch a movie, you get involved with the characters and the action on the screen. You may gasp, laugh or cry as the story unfolds. If you suddenly stop watching the movie and withdraw your attention from the screen, you snap out of the illusion that the movie created for you. The projector continues projecting images onto the screen but you know it is only light projected through film. It isn't real and yet it is there. You can watch the illusion on the screen or you can close your eyes and ears and withdraw from it.

By logging off your five sense reality, you are free to turn inwards. Through deep meditation and practice, you can open the door to infinity and transcend the illusion of physical separateness.

Dr. Dean Hamer, a molecular geneticist, claims he has identified the god gene in human DNA. The god gene is the gene that gives us the experience of bliss by releasing the "feel good" chemicals in our body - dopamine and serotonin. It is the DNA gene of our pineal gland.

What's the pineal gland? It's a small gland that resembles a pine cone and it's located directly behind our eyes right smack in the middle of our cranium.

Our powerful pineal gland is believed to be the seat of our soul and the gateway to the universe and to higher realms. Because its structure is remarkably similar to our eye balls, it's called the 'third eye' or the 'mind's eye'. It actually has a lens, cornea and retina. The ruling families revere it as the 'all-seeing eye' and have featured it on the US one dollar bill.

The pineal gland is bio-luminescent and is sensitive to light. Like a cell phone, it has a built-in wireless transmitter and is the connecting link between the physical and spiritual worlds and higher frequencies. By awakening our pineal gland, we can speed up our learning and memory abilities, enhance our intuition and creativity, trigger our psychic healing abilities and experience bliss.

The symbol of the pineal gland is the pine cone. It is so revered by the Vatican that a special Vatican court was built called the 'Court of the Pine Cone' where the world's largest pineal gland symbol is on display! The symbol is also found on the staff of the Pope and the Egyptian god Osiris. Why has this powerful gland at the center of our cranium been ignored and given so little mainstream attention? Because it is our power source and the ruling families know this.

Medical science refers to the pineal gland as "the atrophied third

Meditation

eye". By the age of 12, it has already calcified and hardened and by adulthood, it is dormant and atrophied from lack of use. Recent research reveals that fluoride which is a toxic additive to our water supply and toothpaste accumulates in the pineal gland where it wreaks havoc.

There is an ancient technique that has been passed down through the centuries for reactivating the pineal gland. The technique produces the same results that the Tibetan monks achieve through trance meditation. This exercise technique should not be attempted by anyone who does not feel ready to explore higher realms of consciousness beyond the five senses. To begin the exercise, you need to find the right vibrational tone. Hum the word love not in a low or high pitched voice but somewhere in between. When you find the right tone, it will feel right.

Sit comfortably with your back straight and your eyes closed and scan your body for any sign of tension. Take 3 long deep breaths through your nose and exhale all the tension through your mouth. Visualize your third eye opening to a loving universe where all that exists is bliss. Take another deep breath through your nose and hold it for a few seconds. Just before you exhale, purse your lips and place your tongue between your teeth. Press down gently on your tongue with your teeth. As you slowly exhale through your pursed lips, loudly hum the word love and vibrate the V sound until all of the air is expelled from your lungs.

Repeat this exercise four more times taking a few moments rest between each repetition. To awaken your pineal gland, you need to repeat this exercise again for two more days in a row at 24 hours apart. The entire exercise only has to be done once to be effective. Coupled with meditation exercises, it may take six weeks or more to experience your newly awakened abilities. Once you enter the door to infinity which is always open to you, will learn that you don't need a reason to be happy.

It is your fear of the unknown that prevents you from developing and exploring other senses which you already possess. By developing your intuitive sense, you will be able to feel, read and interpret energy using your 'gut feelings'.

POSITIVE THINKING

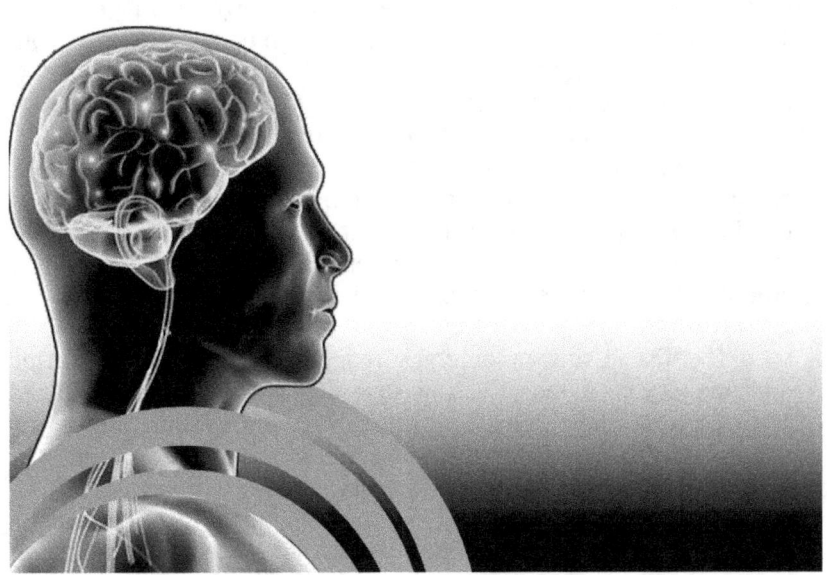

POSITIVE THINKING

Exercises to Stimulate and Retrain Your Brain

We've all heard that drugs and alcohol can kill brain cells. But when we find our hair dryer in the refrigerator and misplace our car keys for the fifth time in a week, what we really want to know is, "How do we make brain cells grow back?"

The truth is, it's not the brain cells you want to increase, it's the connections between them.

So how exactly do you increase the number of connections in your brain? Just like you work any other muscle: repetitive exercises. Here are a few to get your started:

Habla español? Learning a new language requires that you analyze new sounds, which not only improves auditory processing skills, but also memory. Most local libraries have foreign language CDs or videos that you can check out, or you can sign up for a class at your local community college.

Count on it. The Sudoku has taken the world by storm. You can't stand in line at look store without seeing a pocket-size booklet. The numbers (but not math) game can help increase your logic and reasoning skills, as well as memory. And because logic and reasoning are skills that can (to a certain extent) be taught, there are now strategy books for the game. Look for Sudoku booklets that offer gradient difficulties (easy, medium and difficult) so you can work your way up.

Lose the list. Using mnemonics (triggers to aid memory using visual imagery or sounds, such as rhyming) is a great way to boost your brain while developing a system to remember things when you just can't get to a piece of paper. Here's one example of a number system: 1=tree (think of the one trunk), 2=legs (think two legs), 3=stool (three legs), 4=truck (4 tires) and 5=glove (5 fingers). Link the items that you need to remember to your memory objects. If you're upstairs and realize you need to buy toilet paper, envision yourself wrapping a tree in toilet paper. While you're emptying your trash, you run out of bags, so you visualize yourself hopping around on two legs in the garbage bag. You just ate the last of the yogurt, so picture yourself pouring yogurt all over the stool. When you get to the grocery store, just remember your number system and what you linked to them.

Get in the game. Play board games like chess or Scrabble, or surf the

Web for free brain-boosting games, like those found at www.eons.com.

Trivia games can boost memory, jigsaw puzzles can help visual and spatial skills and Mah Jong can help executive function (the capacity to control and apply your mental skills). Although cliché, scientists are proving that when it comes to your brain, "use it or lose it" is an old adage worth heeding. Look for ways to stimulate your mind on a daily basis and you'll likely not only remember where you put your keys, but someday, you might be able to recall the names of your great-great-grandchildren.

How Positive Thinking Re-Wires Your Brain

Positive thinking really does change your brain. Not in some magical, kind of way, but in a real physical way.

Here are some actions you can take to change your own brain during the bad times.

Fear of failure.

Everyone fears doing something new because we don't wait to fail. The truth is, we can do most anything if we take action, stop negative thinking, and shift our perceptions of the truth about our abilities.

Action Steps: Force yourself to stop thinking about reasons you can't do something, even if you don't feel brave or capable. Every time a negative thought creeps in, retrain your brain to think a positive thought about your abilities instead. Then take small actions every day toward achieving your goal or desired change. Nike's slogan, "Just do it," has real validity.

Overthinking/Worrying

Have you ever found yourself trapped in obsessive over-thinking about a problem or in a state of anxiety or worry that lasts for days or even weeks? It drains your energy, affects your sleep, and spirals your mood and outlook on life. Focusing on your problem only strengthens the worry function in your brain.

Action Steps: When you find yourself in that cycle of worry or compulsive thinking, remember the **three R's** — *rename, re-frame, and redirect*. When the worry begins, mentally yell "Stop!" Rename the issue by reminding yourself that worry isn't real. Rename it as a compulsive reaction, not reality. Re-frame your thinking by focusing on positive or distracting thoughts, even if you still feel anxious. Force yourself to think different thoughts. Redirect your actions. Go do something uplifting, fun or mentally engaging. The key is following these steps repeatedly, every time you worry obsessively, to break the pattern and rewire your brain.

Mood Disorders/Phobias
Sometimes we might feel blue or out-of-sorts, and it's just a temporary fog that settles in and lifts after a few days. Some mood disorders, like depression or serious anxieties that morph into phobias, can be debilitating and unrelenting. Psychologists and therapists have used treatments based on neuroplasticity to get to the cognitive root of these disorders and put a patient's life back on track.

Action Steps: A serious mood disorder or phobia requires the help of a trained counselor. **Cognitive Behaviour Therapy (CBT)** is a type of treatment that helps people learn how to identify and change destructive thought patterns that have a negative influence on behaviour and feelings. If you suffer from severe anxiety or depression, you need someone skilled to help you get to the root of these thoughts and to show you how to change them.

How to Train Your Brain to Think Positive in 21 Days

If you can raise the level of positivity in your brain, your brain will perform at a significantly higher level. Your intelligence will rise, your creativity will rise and your energy levels will rise. Your brain at positive is 31% more productive than it is at negative, neutral or stress. You are 37% better at sales and doctors are 19% faster and more accurate at coming up with the correct diagnosis.

There are ways you can train your brain to be more positive. In just a two minute span of time done for 21 days in a row you can actually rewire your brain allowing your brain to actually work more optimistically, and more successfully. At the end of the 21 days your brain will start to retain a pattern, scanning the world not for the negative, but for the positive.

Here are the steps to start thinking more positive today:
1. Write down 3 new things that you are grateful for each day to start a habit of positive thoughts.
2. Keep a journal and write about one positive thing your experienced over the last 24 hours each day.
3. Exercise 2-6 times a week to teach your brain that your behaviour matters.
4. Meditate at least 4 times a week to get over cultural ADHD that we've been creating by trying to do multiple tasks at once allowing the brain to focus on the task at hand.
5. Commit to a random act of kindness (conscious act of kindness) in the form of one email a day praising or thanking someone in your social support network.

By doing these activities and training your brain, just like you train your body, you reverse the formula for happiness and success. When you reverse the formula for happiness and success you not only create ripples of positivity, but create a real revolution in your life.

MEMORY TRAINING

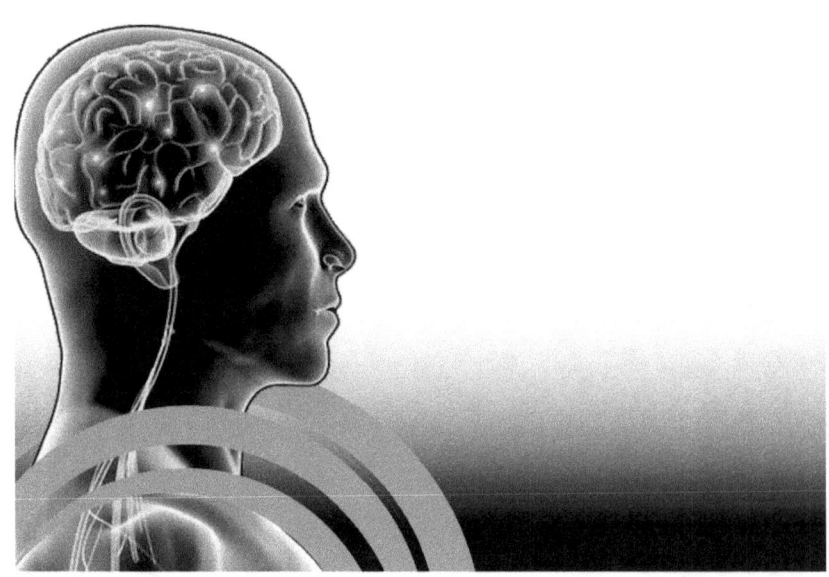

Memory Training

Five Simple Techniques to Improve Your Memory

Most of us might have complained about our memory one time or other. But some of you have been frequently complaining about your poor memory. When we generally talk about *poor memory, we are really talking about poor recollection*. Recollection is possible only if the content is retained in memory. This is possible only if we have recorded it into memory. That is, unless we have assimilated, we cannot recall at all. That is why William James and many others including mnemonists emphasise how we record things into our memory.

Now let us discuss *five simple techniques* to improve memory: Four of these techniques are used to improve assimilation and thus to have longer retention. The last one is a simple strategy for recollection.

Chunking

Perhaps, *Chunking* is the oldest method used in *memorisation*. In this method, the items to be memorised are divided into small and easily memorizable chunks or groups. This method works best when the order of the items is not important.

This method is found to be particularly well suited for memorising multi-digit numbers (eg., ID nos., telephone nos., etc.) and for *committing complicated spellings to memory*.

Example:
1. The number 472627607 may be memorized easily if it is grouped as 472, 627,607 or as 47, 26, 27,607.
   These chunks may then be learned by rote. Learning and retention are much facilitated if you further explore the nos. by finding some relationship among these different chunks. Finding the digital root will also be helpful. *The more explorations or relations you do, the better.*

2. Words like *mathematics* may be divided into mat+he+mat+ics, Together may be divided into to + get + her; Important may be divided into im + port + ant. This technique will make us learn much faster.
3. The list Apple, cucumber, paper, ink, cabbage, banana, grapes, beans, stapler, orange can be better learnt by rearranging and applying chunking as:

   Apple, banana, grapes, orange, cucumber, cabbage, beans, paper, ink, stapler -- 4 fruits, 3 vegetables and 3 stationary items.

If possible, organise the material as meaningfully as you can and think out relationships among each group. This not only improves learnability and retention, but also aids in faster and effortless recollection.

Psychologists doing research on *Human Memory* have found that the capacity of **Short Term Memory (STM)** for humans is 7+2, i.e., from the range 5 to 9 items. So you should take care to keep the chunks you create within this limit.

Rhyming

This is also one of the popular and oldest methods in memorisation. This technique makes use of the fact that we have a natural tendency to remember rhymes and rhythms. The following is a very popular example of application of this technique which almost all school students are familiar with.

"Thirty days haveth September
April, June and November
All the rest have thirty-one
February has twenty-eight alone
Except in leap year, then the time
When Feb's days are twenty-nine."

If possible, create rhymes like this and it will not only aid in improving your memory, but in improving your creativity as well.

Mediation/Bridging

In this method, a bridge is built in between the items given to be memorised. This technique is best suited for learning material involving word pairs or material that can be reduced to word pairs. An example often cited by memory experts is the learning of the capital of Poland. The capital of *Poland* is *Warsaw*. The World War II started with Germany's attack on Poland. Thus, it may be arranged as *Poland SAW War first*.

Here, the word pair to be connected together is Poland and Warsaw. The additional information of the World War II is used as a bridge or mediator in bringing these two words together.

Again, like other techniques, the mediation technique calls for the learner's active participation in the learning process. This is because one is to bring in the mediator or the bridge from relevant items one has learnt.

Bed-time Recital

In this technique, you do your recital or rote learning just before going to bed. The mind in the process of sleeping would then arrange the information in a systematic and effective way when you are sleeping. Psychologists have also found that if you sleep after thinking about your problems, there is a better chance that you arrive at a solution the next day.

Steps for Memory Improvement

1. Be in a relaxed mood.
2. Write down the things that you are supposed to remember in a piece of paper.
3. Read it aloud (if possible) once or twice and recite it two to three times.
4. Now go to sleep without worrying or thinking about anything.

You will surely retain the item longer and find it more easy to recall it when in need.

20 Memory Tricks You'll Never Forget

Try these expert-recommended strategies to help you remember.

Brain Freeze #1
- **Pay attention.** When you're introduced to someone, really listen to the person's name. Then, to get a better grasp, picture the spelling. Ask, "Is that Kathy with a K or a C?" Make a remark about the name to help lock it in ("Oh, Carpenter — that was my childhood best friend's last name"), and use the name a few times during the conversation and when you say goodbye.
- **Visualize the name.** For hard-to-remember monikers (Bentavegna, Wobbekind), make the name meaningful. For Bentavegna, maybe you think of a bent weather vane. Picture it. Then look at the person, choose an outstanding feature (bushy eyebrows, green eyes) and tie the name to the face. If Mr. Bentavegna has a big nose, picture a bent weather vane instead of his nose. The sillier the image, the better.

- **Create memorable associations.** Picture Joe Everett standing atop Mount Everest. If you want to remember that Erin Curtis is the CEO of an architectural firm, imagine her curtsying in front of a large building, suggests Gini Graham Scott, PhD, author of 30 Days to a More Powerful Memory.
- **Cheat a little.** Supplement these tips with some more concrete actions. When you get a business card, after the meeting, jot down a few notes on the back of the card ("red glasses, lives in Springfield, went to my alma mater") to help you out when you need a reminder.

Brain Freeze #2
- **Give a play-by-play.** Pay attention to what you're doing as you place your glasses on the end table. Remind yourself, "I'm putting my keys in my coat pocket," so you have a clear memory of doing it, says Scott.
- **Make it a habit.** Put a small basket on a side table. Train yourself to put your keys, glasses, cell phone or any other object you frequently use (or misplace) in the basket — every time.

Brain Freeze #3
- **Start a ritual.** To remind yourself of a chore (write a thank-you note, go to the dry cleaner), give yourself an unusual physical reminder. You expect to see your bills on your desk, so leaving them there won't necessarily remind you to pay them. But place a shoe or a piece of fruit on the stack of bills, and later, when you spot the out-of-place object, you'll remember to take care of them, says Carol Vorderman, author of Super Brain: 101 Easy Ways to a More Agile Mind.
- **Sing it.** To remember a small group of items (a grocery list, phone number, list of names, to-do list), adapt it to a well-known song, says Vorderman. Try "peanut butter, milk and eggs" to the tune of "Twinkle, Twinkle, Little Star," "Happy Birthday" or even nursery rhymes.
- **Try mnemonic devices.** Many of us learned "VIBGYOR" to remember the colours of the rainbow, or "Every Good Boy Deserves Favours" to learn musical notes. Make up your own device to memorize names (Suzanne's kids are Adam, Patrick and Elizabeth, or "APE"), lists (milk, eggs, tomatoes, soda, or "METS") or computer commands (to shut down your PC, hit Control+Alt+Delete, or "CAD").
- **Use your body.** When you have no pen or paper and are making a mental grocery or to-do list, remember it according to major body parts, says Scott. Start at your feet and work your way up.

So if you have to buy glue, cat food, broccoli, chicken, grapes and toothpaste, you might picture your foot stuck in glue, a cat on your knee looking for food, a stalk of broccoli sticking out of your pants pocket, a chicken pecking at your belly button, a bunch of grapes hanging from your chest and a toothbrush in your mouth.

- **Go Roman.** With the Roman room technique, you associate your grocery, to-do or party-invite list with the rooms of your house or the layout of your office, garden or route to work. Again, the zanier the association, the more likely you'll remember it, says Scott. Imagine apples hanging from the chandelier in your foyer, spilled cereal all over the living room couch, shampoo bubbles overflowing in the kitchen sink and cheese on your bedspread.

Brain Freeze #4

- **Shape your numbers.** Assign a shape to each number: 0 looks like a ball or ring; 1 is a pen; 2 is a swan; 3 looks like handcuffs; 4 is a sailboat; 5, a pregnant woman; 6, a pipe; 7, a boomerang; 8, a snowman; and 9, a tennis racket. To remember your ATM PIN (4298, say), imagine yourself on a sailboat (4), when a swan (2) tries to attack you. You hit it with a tennis racket (9), and it turns into a snowman (8). Try forgetting that image!
- **Rhyme it.** Think of words that rhyme with the numbers 1 through 9 (knee for 3, wine for 9, etc.). Then create a story using the rhyming words: A nun (1) in heaven (7) banged her knee (3), and it became sore (4).

Brain Freeze #5

- **Practise your ABCs.** Say you just can't remember the name of that movie. Recite the alphabet (aloud or in your head). When you get to the letter R, it should trigger the name that's escaping you: Ratatouille. This trick works when taking tests too.

Brain Freeze #6

- **Read it, type it, say it, hear it.** To memorize a speech, toast or test material, read your notes, then type them into the computer. Next, read them aloud and tape-record them. Listen to the recording several times. As you work on memorizing, remember to turn off the TV, unplug your iPod and shut down your computer; you'll retain more.
- **Use colour.** Give your notes some colour with bolded headings and bulleted sections (it's easier to remember a red bullet than running text).
- **Make a map.** Imagine an intersection and mentally place a word, fact or number on each street corner.

Retrain Your Stressed-out Brain

Richard Davidson has done research on what he calls "emotional styles" — which are really brain styles.

One brain style tracks how readily we become upset: where we are on the spectrum from a hair-trigger amygdala - people who easily become upset, frustrated or angered — versus people who are unflappable.

A second style looks at how quickly we recover from our distress. Some people recover quickly once they get upset, while others are very slow. At the extreme of slowness to recover are people who continually ruminate or worry about things - in effect, who suffer from ongoing low-grade amygdala hijacks. Chronic worry keeps the amygdala primed, so you remain in a distress state as long as you ruminate. Given the many realistic stresses we face, those first two styles - being unflappable and capable of quick recovery - are the most effective in navigating the troubles of the world of work.

The third style assesses a person's depth of feeling. Some people experience their feelings quite intensely, some people quite shallowly. Those who have stronger feelings may be better able to authentically communicate them more powerfully — to move people.

There's another piece of suggestive data about the left-right ratio. Barbara Fredrickson at the University of North Carolina finds that people who flourish in life — who have rich relationships, rewarding work, who feel that their life is meaningful — have at least three positive emotional events for every negative one. A similar positive-to-negative ratio in emotions has also been documented in top teams, where it's five-to-one; the ratio for flourishing seems to operate at the collective level too.

When we're pitched into an amygdala hijack, whether intense or low level but ongoing, we're in sympathetic nervous system arousal. As a chronic condition that's not a good state. While we're hijacked, the alarm circuits trigger the fight-flight-or-freeze response that pumps stress hormones into the body with a range of negative results, such as lowering the effectiveness of our immune response. The opposite state, parasympathetic arousal, occurs when we're relaxed. Biologically and neurologically this is the mode of restoration and recovery, and it is associated with left prefrontal arousal.

If you want to cultivate greater strength of activity in the left prefrontal areas that generate positive emotions, you can try a few strategies. For starters, take regular time off from a hectic, hassled routine to rest and restore. Schedule time to "do nothing":

walk your dog, take a long shower, whatever allows you to let go of leaning forward into the next thing in your on-the-go state.

There are many kinds of meditation, each using a different mental strategy: concentration, mindfulness, and visualization, to name a few. Each meditation method has specific impacts on our mental states. For example, visualization activates centres in the spatial visual cortex, while concentration involves the attention circuitry in the prefrontal cortex but not the visual area. A new scientific field, "contemplative neuroscience," has begun mapping exactly how meditation A versus meditation B engages the brain, which brain centres it activates, and what the specific benefits might be.

Herbert Benson at Harvard has shown that the relaxation response (20 minutes of focusing on a positive meaningful word) turns on genes involved in the reduction of stress.

Seven Days To A New More Positive You!

Here are five tips to get underway:

1. Carry a small pad and write down every negative thought you have. Anytime you have a negative thought - say to yourself, 'No! Stop!' or 'Cancel!' In the beginning you'll be amazed at how many you have each day.
2. Replace negative thoughts with a new positive ones. Write down the new positive thought after the negative one.
3. Look for patterns. Review your notes and categorize your negative thoughts. Are you more negative in a certain area of your life vs. others such as relationships, career, money, self-esteem etc? Or, have you allowed yourself to become chronically negative in every area? Don't worry - you can retrain your brain!
4. Create positive affirmations to override these patterns. Repeat the affirmation to yourself numerous times after becoming aware of your own feedback loops. Make sure you use the present tense when you come up with your affirmations.
5. If you must spend time with negative thinkers don't try to change them. Just listen politely - but do not accept what they say. Mentally tell yourself that you choose to reject this type of thinking. When you stop responding to other people's negativity and just remain quiet, but respectful they eventually start to hear the hollowness of their own words and change - at least around you anyway.

Rewire Your Brain for Happiness

Shawn Achor refutes conventional wisdom that teaches us that success, equates to happiness. In fact, he shows that recent discoveries have shown that this formula is completely backward. Instead, happiness is actually what fuels success. When we are positive our brains are more creative, resilient and productive at work. For example, according to the studies in Achor's book, *The Happiness Advantage*, optimistic salespeople outsell negative sales people by 56%. Happy employees are proven to take significantly less sick days than their negative peers. Positive managers increase customer satisfaction by 42%.

A few points he makes, worth considering:

"It's not the reality that shapes us but the lens through which your brain views the world that shapes your reality. If we change the lens not only can we our happiness. We can change every business and educational outcome at the same time."

"90% of your long term happiness is predicted not by the external world, but by the way your brain processes the world. And if we change it, if we change our formula for happiness and success, we can change the way we can then affect reality."

"The traditional model, "If I work harder, I'll be more successful. If I'm more successful, then, I will be happier is broken for two reasons:

1. Every time your brain has a success you just change the goalpost of what success looks like. If happiness is on the opposite side of success, your brain never gets there.
2. Our brains work in the opposite order. Your brain at positive performs significantly better than at negative-neutral stress... If we can find a way to become positive in the present our brains work more successfully.

You can train your brain to be more positive. In 2 minutes span of time done for 21 days in a row you can actually rewire your brain. Write 3 new things of what you're grateful for 21 days straight. At the end of that, your brain starts to retain a pattern of scanning the world for the positive and not the negative.

Eight Tips for "Rewiring" Your Brain Naturally

You can change your lifestyle to boost your brain health by making the following changes:
1. **Take omega-3 fats.** The omega -3 fatty acids eicosapentaenoic acid (EPA) and docosahexaenoic acid (DHA) keep the dopamine levels in your brain high, increase neuronal growth in the frontal cortex of your brain, and increase cerebral circulation.

Krill oil made from a species of krill [Euphausia superba] is an excellent source of omega-3, and may even be superior to fish oil.

2. **Exercise.** Exercise may encourage your brain to work at optimum capacity by causing nerve cells to multiply, strengthening their interconnections and protecting them from damage.
3. **Sleep well.** It's during sleep that your mental energy is restored, and a lack of sleep may cause your brain to stop producing new cells.
4. **Eat healthy.** Like the rest of your body, your brain depends on healthy foods to function. While protein is the main source of fuel for your brain, vitamins and minerals from fresh veggies are also important, as is limiting sugar.
5. **Get out into the sun.** This will help you maintain optimal vitamin D levels. Scientists are now beginning to realize vitamin D is involved in maintaining the health of your brain, as they've recently discovered vitamin D receptors in the brain, spinal cord, and central nervous system.

    There's even evidence indicating vitamin D improves your brain's detoxification process. For children and pregnant women, getting enough vitamin D is especially crucial, as it may play a major role in protecting infants' brains from autism.
6. **Turn off your TV.** Allowing children under the age of 3 to watch television can impair their linguistic and social development, and it can affect brain chemistry as well.
7. **Protect your brain from cellphones.** Recent studies have found that cell phone users are 240 percent more prone to brain tumors, and a study back in 2004 found that your risk of acoustic neuroma (a tumor on your auditory nerve) was nearly four times greater on the side of your head where your phone was most frequently held.
8. **Avoid foods that contain artificial sweeteners and additives.** Substances such as aspartame (Nutrasweet), artificial colour and MSG, which are common in processed foods, can damage your brain. For instance, consuming a lot of aspartame may inhibit the ability of enzymes in your brain to function normally, and high doses of the sweetener may lead to neurodegeneration.

And there you have it. Simple, succinct and smart strategies to encourage your brain to function at its best, and continue to grow and make new connections, whether you're 19 or 90.

Brain Strengthening Exercises

Walking Increases Nutrients to the Brain

According to the *Franklin Institute, going for a stroll will help boost your memory, concentration and recall abilities by increasing oxygen and glucose to the brain tissue*. Walking does not exert your body's muscles as much as more strenuous physical activities such as running, so it takes up less energy, oxygen and glucose. Walking also increases your breathing rate and heart rate, which increases blood flow to your brain. This strengthens the brain cells and enhances the removal of wastes and toxins for improved performance on mental tests.

An exercise from Brain Games at *Lumosity.com* can be done while you're waiting at the doctor's office. It helps improve visual memory, attention, concentration and recall ability. Choose a page of a magazine that has a photo with several different objects in it, such as a photo of a room filled with furniture and décor. Focus on the photo for about one minute, memorising as much detail as possible. Close the magazine and list as much detail as possible about the photo. This list can be written down or just recited mentally. Keep count of how many things you can recall with detail, such as 'the sofa is sage green and has four square gingham patterned cushions with three buttons each.' Look at the photo again and check to see how much detail you were able to recall. Try the exercise again with a different photo and less time to memorise the details.

Number and List Recall Exercise

This exercise helps *strengthen your brain's ability to focus, concentrate and pay attention to audio cues*. Have someone read a list of random numbers to you slowly and recite them back. Begin with two numbers and add a number in each line until you reach eight numbers. Repeat the exercise but this time say the numbers backwards. For example, after your friend slowly reads the fifth line of numbers: 2,4,8,9, 0,15 you recite them backwards from memory: 15,0,9,8,4,2. Try this regularly and see how many numbers you can recall correctly.

George Rebok of the John Hopkins Bloomberg School of Public Health also recommends *learning lists to improve memory*. He suggests making lists of coupled objects with picture associations and practising by recalling them. For example, to remember a clock and a pie, picture the pie with the hands of a clock on it. Do this for 20 or more pairs of objects and try to recall them.

Rewire Your Brain

According to the *Canadian Institute of Neuroscience,* the brain can become stagnant when it does not learn new things. Unlike the muscles of the body that can only be exerted physically to a limited point, the brain can learn and rewire itself constantly and without reaching a threshold. Children forge new brain connections and pathways because everything they learn is new to them, but as adults we tend to stick to routines. Keep your brain limber by surprising it with new things to adapt to. For example, use your non-dominant hand to brush your teeth or to use the mouse on your laptop. Also try this mental exercise to stimulate new neuron connections: Recite the days of the week and the months of the year backwards, timing yourself until you can do it as fast as reciting them forwards.

Positive Intelligence

Engaging in one brief positive exercise every day for as little as three weeks can have a lasting impact, research suggests.
Choose one of five activities that correlate with positive change:
- Jot down three things you are grateful for.
- Write a positive message to someone in your social support network.
- Meditate at your desk for two minutes.
- Exercise for ten minutes.
- Take two minutes to describe in a journal the most meaningful experience of the past 24 hours.

How Jon Gabriel Lost Over 103kg! (without dieting, drugs or surgery) and so can you...

Jon Gabriel has a Bachelor of Science in Economics from the Wharton School at the University of Pennsylvania. While there, he also pursued extensive coursework in biochemistry and performed research for the internationally recognized biochemist Dr. Jose Rabinowitz.

In 1990 Jon started gaining weight for no apparent reason. He tried every diet and programme he could to lose weight but in the end, he just kept gaining. The more he dieted, the more he gained.

The situation became critical in mid 2001 when he became morbidly obese and reached a weight of over 186 kilos. On September 11, 2001 he was scheduled to fly from Newark to San Francisco and it was only by a fluke of fate that he was not on the United Airlines flight 93 that was hijacked by terrorists. This event, as well as some equally life changing events that occurred in the weeks following 9/11 affected him deeply. It was this wake-up call that made him realise life was a precious opportunity not to be wasted.

He decided to start 'living the life of his dreams'. He also decided to apply all of his research skills and scientific background toward understanding and eliminating the real reasons he was fat. The result is arguably one of the most remarkable physical transformations of all time. Jon lost over 103 kilos without dieting and without surgery. Amazingly, his body shows almost no signs of ever being overweight at all – a fact that has astounded many professionals in the medical community.

Using the approach that has worked so well for him, he has now made it his life's mission to assist others in achieving tremendous success, not only in weight loss, but in every aspect of life.

Jon Gabriel's Six Simple Tips For Managing Stress For Weight Loss

1. **Breathe deeply and regularly**
   Doing so can actually decrease the tone of your sympathetic nervous system and increase the tone of your parasympathetic nervous system, which is the portion of your nervous system that promotes relaxation and good digestion.
2. **Spend some quiet time every day in prayer, meditation, or a purposeful relaxation session**
   All three have been scientifically proven to facilitate a relaxation response in your body that can decrease blood pressure, decrease pulse rate, and improve blood circulation. Meditation and relaxation sessions can be greatly enhanced by listening to any number of audio CDs that are designed to facilitate optimal relaxation and mental clarity.
3. **Practise visualisation**
   Almost all great athletes practise some form of visualization. As author Wayne Dyer says, "you'll see it when you believe it." Spend some time each day visualizing your ideal body and going about your day in a balanced and emotionally poised manner. You can include visualization in your prayer/meditation/relaxation session.
4. **Make sure that you are getting the nutrients that you need for a healthy nervous system**

Your nutritional status can make all the difference between being able to handle a certain amount of stress without breaking down versus quickly suffering health problems when faced with stress. While it's important to your overall health that you eat a well balanced and nutrient-dense diet, for emotional health specifically, it is important to ensure adequate intake of B vitamins, Vitamin D, and two long chain omega-3 fatty acids, DHA and EPA.

5. **Be honest about your feelings**

There's a reason why 'know thyself' is a wise proverb/saying in virtually every culture of our world. Striving to know yourself and what you are truly feeling on a daily basis is absolutely essential to preventing unpleasant but genuine emotions from becoming chronic states. Anger, frustration, and anxiousness can all help to fuel personal growth and character development if you are honest with yourself and seek to discover their root causes.

One of the best methods to increase your awareness of what you are truly feeling is journal writing. The rules are simple: no censorship, no possibility of another set of eyes being able to read your thoughts, just pure flow of thoughts from your mind and heart onto a piece of paper or your computer screen. Regular journal writing in this manner can be extremely beneficial to your emotional health.

6. Move your body

It's a well established fact that regular exercise is one of the best habits you can adopt that will help you avoid depression and stay emotionally balanced. It doesn't matter what kind of exercise you do. What's important is to be active and use your joints and muscles on a regular basis.

PHYSICAL TRAINING

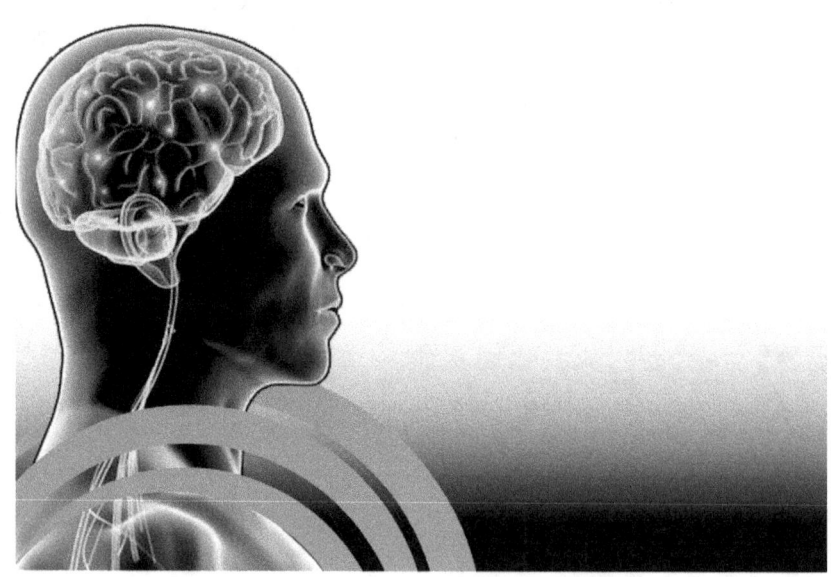

Physical Training

The Power of Stretching

Stretching Exercise
Stand with your feet shoulder, width apart.
   Knees slightly bent.
   Raise your arms straight up and grab your right wrist with left hand.
   Lean over to your left, gently pulling on the right wrist, until you feel a good stretch on your right side.
   Then, lean over from your waist and turn toward the left, still pulling on your right wrist - you should feel a fantastic stretch along the right side of your upper body into your hip.
   Hold for 15 seconds.
   Then come back to the start position and do the same thing going the other way. And then repeat two more times on each side.
   You can do this stretch every day and you should, if it is the only one you are doing.
   Try this stretch right now — you will sense a huge difference in how you feel.

Stretching Effectively and Enjoyably

Jacques Gautier is a self-taught expert on stretching who used the technique to cure himself of numerous ailments. If you follow *Gautier's guidelines*, stretching should be easy, enjoyable, safe and effective. Here are his keys to effective stretching:

- **Safety first!** If you have had injuries, surgeries or have health concerns, consult with your health care provider about how to modify the stretches.
- **Move slowly in and out of the stretches** — this helps prevent injury and allows to body to relax.
- **Pay attention to your body** — it will tell you how far to go. You should stretch to a point of gentle tension, but not pain.

- **Relax into the stretches** — Muscles elongate naturally as they relax. If you notice some tension or "holding" in the muscles during a stretch, let it go. You may find that as you relax into the stretch, you find yourself stretching even further.
- **Breathe slowly and deeply and pay attention to your breathing** — This helps keep you to relax, stay aware of your body and helps keep you from being caught up in thoughts.
- **Hold each stretch for about 30 seconds** — It has been found that holding a stretch for 25-35 seconds gives optimal results. Rather than count the seconds, you can time your breathing to find out how many slow, deep breaths you take in 30 seconds. Then you can time your stretches by counting your breath.
- **What is important is for the muscle to experience movement and be stretched** — not how far you go! If you are following stretches outlined in a book, for example, simply move in the direction of the stretch - you don't have to move into any certain position to get the benefit of the stretch.
- **Jacques' advice in his classes was to modify the stretches to suit our own needs** — If you are using specific stretches described in a book or program, you can modify the stretches to suit your body and for comfort.
- **Don't bounce!** You can injure yourself this way.
- **Stretching should be pleasurable!** If you are not enjoying the stretching, you may be trying too hard or straining to achieve a certain result. Stretching is not a competition, is simply an activity which benefits the body no matter what position you get into or how far you go.

The First Few Days are Always the Most Difficult — Don't Let That Stop You!

When you first start stretching there may be some discomfort as you begin to stretch muscles that haven't been used for awhile, but it should not be painful. Starting any new routine is usually awkward and uncomfortable at first. It can seem discouraging when we start to move and realize just how stiff or limited our bodies have become. But don't let that stop you — if you start to stretch regularly, it will get better!

Jacques stated that the first few days are the hardest and then it gets easier. That was certainly true for the people in his classes. It was amazing how quickly everyone became more flexible with this relaxed approach!

As we age, our muscles tighten and we have less range of motion in our joints. Simple activities that we once took for granted, like cutting our toenails, picking things up from the floor or zipping a dress, can all become difficult. A regular stretching program can help lengthen your muscles and make these daily activities easier and more enjoyable.

Stretching has so many benefits, including increased flexibility, improved circulation, decreased pain, more energy, and a greater sense of well-being.

Jacques has taught thousands in Canada and Europe over the years, and many have reported these kinds of benefits as well as recovery from conditions such as arthritis, headaches, fatigue, depression, back/neck/shoulder pain and even fibromyalgia.

What Jacques found from his experience with himself as well as people he taught was that stretching, done properly, is anti-inflammatory. He discussed this with many health care professionals in Canada. They agreed that this made sense and confirmed it in their work with their own patients.

There has even been research showing that stretching can relieve heel pain in those suffering from plantar fasciitis (an inflammation in the tissues in the sole of the foot).

Inflammation is the body's response to injury, so if stretching is done improperly it could actually cause inflammation. And of course, inflammation causes pain. If the result of stretching is pain, chances are you've stressed the tissues and caused inflammation. According to Jacques, the key is the slow, deep breathing and holding the stretches for about 30 seconds.

If you aren't stretching already, this should inspire you to start. Even stopping from time to time during the day to "stretch out the kinks" is beneficial. Following the stretching guidelines above should help you to develop an enjoyable and effective stretching routine.

How To Fit Exercise Into The Busiest Schedule

- **Make a commitment to exercise.** Write it down on your calendar, in 20-minute, 30-minute, or even 5-minute increments, but make sure you have some scheduled every day. "You can accumulate exercise minutes," experts say, "not do it in one big chunk."
- **Exercise during your lunch hour.** Bring your lunch to work, eat it at your desk, then use the rest of your lunch hour to go for a power walk.
- **Stretch at your desk.** While sitting at your desk, stretch your arms, shoulders, legs and back.
- Do jumping jacks for one to five minutes. You can do these in your office, at home, in the park, just about anywhere. When

Physical Training

you get tired of *jumping jacks*, try pretending to *jump rope, running in place,* or *shadow boxing.*
- **Exercise at your desk.** Punch your arms over your head for 30 seconds, then tap your feet on the floor quickly for 30 seconds, and repeat. Or, as long as your desk is sturdy, try desk push-ups by standing, putting your hands on the desk, then walking backward. Now you're ready to start your push-ups!
- **Do lunges as you walk.** If you find yourself in an empty hallway, take advantage of it and do lunges as you go. You can also do these outside on a sidewalk.
- **Instead of getting together with friends to see a movie, why not get together and play a game of soccer, tennis, or touch football?** Or share your DVD workout doing it together... having fun.
- **Bike, walk or jog to work.** Not an option? Try getting off the bus a stop earlier, or parking in the faraway parking lot, and walking the rest of the way. You can also bike, walk or jog to run some of your errands.
- **Exercise as a social activity.** Getting together with friends tonight? Do something active like playing tennis or racquetball. Want more family time this weekend? Take the kids for a bike ride.
- **Use the stairs instead of an escalator or elevator.** The extra steps add up. If you're really feeling motivated, try taking the steps two at a time.
- **Do your daily chores**. Housework and gardening count as exercise, especially, if you put on some music and do them at a semi-fast pace.
- **Walk more.** Whenever you have an opportunity to walk somewhere — whether it's to your favorite lunch spot, to do some brainstorming, or to get to your colleague's desk (instead of e-mailing) — do it!
- **Exercise during your commuting.** It can be done, and though it will yield subtle results, any exercise is better than none at all. While sitting in your car driving, try squeezing the muscles in your buttocks or stomach, holding the contraction for 10 seconds, then repeating 10 to 15 times. If you're at a stoplight, you can also try squeezing your triceps against the seatback, holding it for 10 seconds, then releasing.
- **Don't just sit and watch TV, exercise and watch TV.** If you're going to watch a television program or movie, use the time to jog in place, do jumping jacks, stretch or use a treadmill or elliptical machine, if you have one.

- **Lift "weights" while you cook dinner.** Take a can of food and do 12 bicep curls on each arm, or lift a bag of potatoes over your head to work your shoulders.
- **Get up earlier.** OK, this one involves changing your schedule just a bit. But if you get up 30 minutes or even one hour earlier, you'll have time to exercise.

Retro-walking: The Great Leap Backward

If your fitness regime isn't progressing very fast, you may be going the wrong way about it — literally.

Ever felt your fitness regime was heading into reverse gear? Yes, we've all been there — but now comes a new workout phenomenon whose purpose is precisely that. Retro walking is big, and growing: what it involves is running (or walking) backwards, and increasing numbers of enthusiasts say it is giving their exercise programme a whole new perspective. Indeed, so popular is this bizarre activity that events such as the New York Road Runners Backwards Mile are now being staged. This year's was held in Hudson River Park and was run, appropriately, on April 1. Meanwhile, backwards fun runs around Europe are attracting huge numbers of entrants.

Such is the growth of this sport that records are being set and broken at a far faster rate than those of forward-moving counterparts. Last year, Arthur Magni reached the finishing line of the New York event first, breaking the tape with his back in a time of six minutes 28 seconds while Timothy Badyna, known as Backwards Bud, back-pedalled his way through a full 26.2-mile marathon in under four hours. Why, you may ask? Proponents claim the technique is kinder to knee and hip joints, with less of the pounding associated with regular jogging and, inspiringly, burns a fifth more calories. "Your balance increases. Your hearing increases. Your peripheral vision increases," Badyna says. One wonders whether neck strain from twisting to see where you are going is common, but Badyna insists that while being blindsided is a downside, as long as you run somewhere safe, you can cut down the chances of unforeseen obstacles in your way.

Remarkably, scientists are beginning to discover there is some truth in the claims of retro-runners. A study conducted at South Africa's Stellenbosch University, published in the International Journal of Sports Medicine last year, found that backward training improved cardio-respiratory fitness while helping to streamline the physique of a group of novice runners. Researchers in the university's department of medical physiology looked at the effects of a six-week, thrice-weekly backward running programme on female

Physical Training

students compared with a group who stuck to their regular activity schedule. At the end of the study, the retro-runners were found to have significant decreases in oxygen consumption, meaning they had become aerobically fitter, and had lost an average 2.5% of their body fat. "Our results provide evidence that backward locomotion can improve cardio-respiratory fitness and possibly lead to positive body composition changes in young women," was the researchers' verdict.

Retro-running dates back to the 1970s, when a small group of physiotherapists began recommending it to injured athletes and footballers. There is less movement of the hips running this way which means impact on the joints decreases, making it an ideal substitute for rehabilitation from knee and back problems. "It's a reasonable way to incorporate another means of exercise to lessen the stress on any given part of the body," says Professor Barry Bates, a biomechanics researcher at the University of Oregon who has carried out extensive studies on the activity. His findings indicate that retro runners need move at only 80% of the speed of forward runners to gain the same physiological and fitness benefits.

Getting started requires some forward thinking. Aside from the fact that you are going to attract some bemused glances should you step backwards out of your front door and proceed to retro-run down the local high street, there is the significant drawback of a lack of hindsight. Professor Jon Wang, an orthopaedic surgeon at the University of Arizona and an adviser to Runner's World magazine, recommends newcomers to start somewhere safe such as a track or familiar road where you will avoid potholes, road signs and other hazards. He says backwards running works well as part of a cool-down at the end of a gym session. "Easing into a gentle backwards run lets you gradually decrease your heart rate, and it stretches your calf, quadricep and hamstring muscles, which have all been working hard during forward running," Wang says.

He confirms Badyna's hunch that it will also "improve your balance and coordination" and suggests progressing to running backwards towards the end of a regular jog. "Go slowly, taking small steps at first, and stay in control," he says. "Let the ball of the foot contact first, then allow the heel to touch just briefly. If this feels OK, repeat the one-minute segments two or three times, jogging forwards slowly in-between." After a few weeks he promises you will feel less anxious about collisions and can begin to step up your retro running to five or six minutes in total. "At this point, you can try taking longer steps and, if you want to stretch your legs more, try running backwards on a slightly downhill slope," he says.

Even sceptical experts concede that, while backwards shouldn't fully replace forwards, it can have a place in a workout programme. For some sports, it is an essential element of training. Champion boxer Gene Tunney ran four to eight miles a day backwards and Muhammad Ali incorporated it into his regime.

"Professional footballers, rugby players and referees as well as top track and field athletes all use it routinely," says Dr Nick Linthorne, a biomechanics researcher at Brunel University in London. "It does make sense for other people, especially the injured, to include a little backwards running or walking as the landing is smoother." But the real attraction for the masses, he says, is the novelty factor. Like striptease workouts and karaoke spinning, retro running will appeal to those prone to gym boredom. "If the prospect of running backwards inspires someone who wouldn't otherwise exercise to get out, then that can only be a good thing".

Retro-walking: One step backwards, two steps forward!

Everybody walks. Some stride, some march and some prefer to just saunter about without having a care in the world. Many of us love walking. In fact, the reason why you are here is enough proof of your appreciation for this natural and almost effortless exercise.

When we walk for health, there is a whole lot of creativity we all bring to it; from trying different kinds of shoes to choosing scenic spots to creating multiple playlists on our music players that suit our pacing or acoustic preference depending on our mood and what not! And all this just so our beloved exercise doesn't get boring.

For ages now, we have known and experienced the numerous benefits of walking. You have possibly conducted all kinds of experiments to make sure your walking routine is a new adventure each day and by now are hopeless. Don't be disappointed, smile, for there still remains a path untrodden and this is what it looks like! Even though the demonstration is on a special treadmill, you can walk 'backwards' for stretches just as you do in your favourite walking area.

Like what you see? No? Looks funny? But it won't feel as funny after we tell you what it does. What you see up there is called "Retro walking" and is said to triple, that's right, TRIPLE the benefits you receive from conventional walking.

Also known as backward walking, retro pedaling, retro locomotion etc; retro walking gained immense popularity in the year 2006 when the 'New York Road Runners' club held an event called 'Backwards Mile' where the participants had to jog backwards. Fitness freaks have once again begun celebrating this sport and trumpeting its

Physical Training

health benefits. More than anything, it's a blessing for your heart. Studies have found that when an athlete walks forward at a given pace, it enables his heart rate to rise to 106 bpm but when walking backward at the same pace his heart rate soars up to 156 bpm. The practice is quite a rage in many parts of Europe, Japan and China, as more and more people are beginning to discover its benefits for rehabilitation, muscle building, sports performance, or simply to improve balance and intuitive skills. In fact, Europe holds retro races ranging from sprints to 20+ mile marathons!

Benefits of Retro-walling

1. It Improves cardiovascular functions :
Backward walking can be extremely strenuous because of its difficulty but it definitely treats the body better that its forward walking twin. It puts greater strain on your cardiovascular system thus producing higher heart rate. A 100 steps backward walking is equivalent to 1,000 steps of conventional walking; which means that you can strengthen your heart and at the same time burn calories quicker than forward walking. That extra level of difficulty will summon your extra reserve of energy burning extra calories in return.

2. It's easy on the leg muscles and joints:
Retro walking strengthens the heart, lungs, muscles, joints, hips, legs and trunk, with minimal stress on any given part of the body. Over time, our leg muscles get used to walking only forward that works out the hamstrings and glutes but retro walking employs and exercises all the unused and by now, weak muscles such as the quadriceps and calves. Retro walking or exercising is also an ideal way to repair joint pain and knee injuries as it is gentler on the knees. There is lesser displacement of the body backward because you punch in a lesser percentage of your body weight; as a result the range of motion of the knee joint is reduced and they experience less trauma and the walker; less discomfort. It is highly recommended for elderly people and those with arthritis-related problems for it is can be an excellent slow paced, low impact workout that is absolutely gentle on the knees.

3. It exercises your body and mind:
When we walk backwards, we obviously cannot see what is happening behind our back so with regular practice our senses automatically build a defense mechanism against potential dangers. This gradually improves balance, peripheral vision and hearing skills. Retro walking is more of a neurobic activity; a physical activity that

unofficially invites the brain's enthusiastic participation. Neurobic activities create a nexus of brand new neural connections in your brain that help you stay mentally sharp, polish your memory and dodge the unwelcome and debilitating guests of later life such as the Alzheimer's.

Yes, we know we hit the right chord and we know you already are in love with this brand new tune. So before you rewind and play there are a few things you would have to bear in mind:

Take particular care while including this new regime into your walking routine. No matter how excited you are it is always best to begin slow. You can gradually gallop at a pelt once your senses get acclimatized to the newly acquired skills. Ensure your safety by practising it in a tripping-free, obstacle-free, pothole-free zone.

If you chose the treadmill then start even slower, a mile per hour should work just fine and be ever ready to hit the emergency stop. As you grow pro, you can increase the speed or inclination. DO NOT PERFORM THESE STUNTS IF YOU HAVE BALANCE OR CO-ORDINATION DIFFICULTIES. Also, try not holding on to the handrails. It completely disarrays your body posture and nullifies the wonderful plusses you would otherwise benefit from.

Another safe option is to have a friend-cum henchman who can walk (forward) or jog (forward) beside you and keep a watch on your behalf.

But if luck doesn't favour, keep looking over your shoulder intermittently to see if someone is in your way.

Physical Training

The Qigong Walk

The *Qigong Walk*, also called *walking kung*, is the main exercise of *Guolin Qigong*, and is the exercise that has helped thousands of people all over the world recover from *serious illnesses, notably cancer*. It was devised by Madam Guolin after studying Qigong notes left behind by her grandfather. It helped her recover from her own cancer that her doctors had given up hope of curing, and soon she began to teach this in the parks and many other cancer patients improved after practising it. She became a national celebrity in China and was invited to teach her Qigong all across the nation. Over the last 30 years her method (initially called New Qigong Therapy, and later Guolin Qigong in her honour) has spread all over the world.

It is difficult to learn correctly even the simplest standing Qigong exercise from written instructions. Learning the walking exercise this way will be more difficult. However, for those who do not have access to an instructor, you can have fun trying out these instructions.

The Basic Qigong Walk

There are many variations of the *Qigong Walk*, each with certain benefits for different organ systems. They are all modifications of the basic walk (also called 'natural walk'), which is itself actually an extension of the basic *Qigong stance*.

There are *five parts of the walk* that are different from our usual walk, and these changes ensure that the mind is always aware of all the actions (movements and breathing) during the walk, and qi flow is enhanced.

1. THE FOOTSTEP

When we walk, most of us do so almost in a flat-footed manner, with the front part of the foot only minimally inclined upwards as we take each step. Some are actually flat-footed while others drag their feet.

In the Qigong walk, we deliberately step on our heel, with the foot inclined about 30 degrees upwards as we take each step. Doing so is particularly good for qi flow in the kidney meridian channels, which is essential for general health.

Note that the legs are always relaxed and slightly bent at the knees. If you straighten and stiffen your legs, and do the Qigong step, you will be walking Nazi-style.

2. THE ARM SWING

In our usual walk, we swing the opposite arm forward as we take each step. This swing is automatic. Nobody walks normally without moving the arms. In the Qigong Walk, the arms are swung to the front of the body instead, with the hands coming near the lower main energy centre (Dan Tien) which is situated about three fingerbreadths below the navel (and about the same distance internally). On the backswing, the hands come beside the buttocks but not as far back as in the usual walk.

There are differences in the hand position for those with health problems. For healthy people, the palms face the body, whereas they face the ground or upwards for different diseases. For some diseases, the fingers point downwards.

3. MODIFIED BREATHING

When we walk, our breathing is so spontaneous that we hardly think about it. In the Qigong Walk, the breathing is made mindful by modifying the inhalation. We inhale twice (two sniffs) and then exhale as usual. It is possible to do so only with conscious-breathing. Breathing is through the nose, with the tongue always touching the upper palate.

The breathing is coordinated with the footstep, and since the latter is coordinated with the arm-swing, all three components are therefore consciously coordinated.

In the basic walk, the inhalation is simultaneous with the foot that takes the first step. Males start with the left foot, and females with the right. As explained previously, there are differences in the Yin and Yang (female and male) qi.

4. SIDEWAYS BODY SWING

In our usual walk, we actually swing the body very slightly to balance it as we lift each leg alternately to step forward. This is necessary since the centre of gravity is shifted as we lift each leg. In the Qigong Walk, the swing is exaggerated, and becomes obvious if the walk is done slowly.

5. HEAD TURNING

In the basic *Qigong Walk*, we turn the head about 60 degrees sideways every 2,4,6 or 8 steps (usually 4). This is coordinated with the feet, with the head always turning towards the side of the foot that is in front. This will facilitate the incorporation of modifications when the variations of the Qigong Walk are learned later.

During the *Qigong Walk*, look into the distant horizon and not at your feet. Initially, walk at whatever pace is comfortable for you. Different paces are recommended for different diseases.

The proper starting stance is unique but will not be described here. It will certainly be taught if you learn from an instructor.

Physical Training

This basic *Qigong Walk* is an excellent exercise for everyone to increase *qi* quickly. Twenty minutes of walking with inhalation on one foot, followed by another 20 minutes with inhalation on the other foot (a short standing exercise with arm movements is done in between) is the minimum exercise recommended. Another 20 minutes of stationary or other walking exercises will complete the required 1 hour of Qigong daily that is necessary to maintain optimum health.

Those with serious illnesses and cancers have to do up to 4 hours a day to reverse their diseases. This is usually split into morning and evening sessions, with plenty of rest in between each exercise. If they are too weak, they start with whatever they can cope with and increase the duration gradually. Those who are bed-ridden or immobile can start with the stationary exercises first (standing, sitting or even lying down).

It is not difficult to do the various Qigong Walks for longer durations because you do not get tired if you walk correctly, and you do not get bored if you walk among the fresh air, trees and interesting sceneries found in the parks and lake gardens. You will feel refreshed and charged-up with health-giving internal energy after each session.

It is truly amazing that just modifying the components of our usual walk has made it possible to reverse serious and terminal diseases. In Malaysia alone, every Sunday morning, many terminal-cancer survivors and several hundred non-terminal-cancer survivors do the Qigong Walk in the various parks all over the country. And there are many more cancer patients diligently practising in the hope of defeating the disease. Every week scores of cancer patients are joining these groups after hearing about what Qigong can do for them.

However, you should not wait until you get cancer to start practising Qigong. Prevention is better than cure, and you will gain health, vitality, rejuvenation and longevity in the process.

Qigong walking instructions are available on YouTube too!

Increase Your Muscle Strength by Just Imagining!

In a fascinating experiment, researchers at the *Cleveland Clinic Foundation* discovered that a muscle can be strengthened just by thinking about exercising it.

For 12 weeks (five minutes a day, five days per week) a team of 30 healthy young adults imagined either using the muscle of their little finger or of their elbow flexor. Dr. Vinoth Ranganathan and his team asked the participants to think as strongly as they could about moving the muscle being tested, to make the imaginary movement as real as they could.

Compared to a control group - that did no imaginary exercises and showed no strength gains - the little-finger group increased their pinky muscle strength by 35 percent. The other group increased elbow strength by 13.4%.

What's more, brain scans taken after the study showed greater and more focused activity in the prefrontal cortex than before. The researchers said strength gains were due to improvements in the brain's ability to signal muscle.

Pay attention to your breathing. Is it slow and deep, or quick and shallow? Is your belly expanding and contracting, or is your chest doing all the work?

Topics

Engage Your Brain
It is important to challenge your brain to learn new and novel tasks, especially processes that you've never done before. Examples include square-dancing, chess, tai chi, yoga, or sculpture. Working with modeling clay or playdough is an especially good way for children to grow new connections. It helps develop agility and hand-brain coordination, (like controlling the computer mouse with your opposite hand).

Travel Stimulates Your Brain
Travel is another good way to stimulate your brain. It worked for our ancestors, the early Homo sapiens. Their nomadic lifestyle provided a tremendous stimulation for their brains that led to the development of superior tools and survival skills. In comparison, the now-extinct Neanderthal was a species that for thousands of years apparently did not venture too far from their homes. (Maybe they were simply content with their lives - in contrast to the seldom-satisfied sapien.)

Early humans gained a crucial evolutionary edge from the flexibility and innovation required by their strategic lifestyle, which also led to a more diverse diet that allowed their brains to rapidly evolve.

Neurobic Exercises
Try to include one or more of your senses in an everyday task:
- Get dressed with your eyes closed
- Wash your hair with your eyes closed

Physical Training

- Share a meal and use only visual cues to communicate. No talking.
- Combine two senses:
- Listen to music and smell flowers
- Listen to the rain and tap your fingers
- Watch clouds and play with modeling clay at the same time

Break Routines:
- Go to work on a new route
- Eat with your opposite hand
- Shop at new grocery store

Reading and Housie

Consider your brain a muscle, and find opportunities to flex it. "Read, read, read," says Dr. Amir Soas of Case Western Reserve University Medical School in Cleveland. Do crossword puzzles. Play Scrabble. Start a new hobby or learn to speak a foreign language. "Anything that stimulates the brain to think." Also, watch less television, because "your brain goes into neutral," he said.

Challenging the brain early in life is crucial to building up more "cognitive reserve" to counter brain-damaging disease, according to Dr. David Bennett of Chicago's Rush University. And, reading-habits prior to age 18 are a key predictor of later cognitive function.

A cognitive psychologist in England found that when elderly people regularly played housie, it helped minimize their memory loss and bolster their hand-eye coordination. Housie seemed to help players of all ages remain mentally sharp.

Easy Ways to Take Charge of Your Lifestyle

1. Eat a Healthy Diet, With Lots of Antioxidants. Antioxidants can be vitamins, minerals or enzymes, and they exist in foods (fruits, vegetables, nuts and other whole foods) and certain supplements.
2. Exercise Regularly. Exercise at a level that's comfortable for you, and do it regularly, rather than overdoing it by exercising too often or too strenuously.

   An excellent addition to any exercise routine, simple as it may sound, is stretching. A few well-performed stretches can do wonders for your body and your mind.
3. Relax and Find Ways to Relieve Stress. Trying to fit too many tasks into a day, or filling your time with too many stressful activities, will wear you down, no matter how many fruits

and vegetables you eat. Organize your life so you have time to appreciate little enjoyments, spend time with family and friends who make you feel good, and take time for yourself when you need it.

'Sunshine' Vitamin Vital for Health

Recent studies have rechristened Vitamin D from a mere 'sunshine' vitamin to a hormone with significant bearing on bones, heart, kidneys, among other organs. Efforts are now being made to understand the extent of its deficiency in the population and fight it.

Some experts believe Vitamin D deficiency is a pan-Indian phenomenon affecting people from all age-groups and sections of society, reasons for which range from lifestyle, atmospheric pollution, skin pigmentation, clothing to duration and time of exposure to sunlight daily. Endocrinologist Dr Sudhindra Kulkarni, who consults with Fortis Hospital, Mulund, said Vitamin D has been proved to play the role of regulators of cell growth. "Almost all tissues and cells in the body have receptors for it and need it," he said.

Dr Vipla Puri, consultant (radioimmunoassay), department of Lab-Medicine at PD Hinduja Hospital, said there is epidemiologic evidence now to show Vitamin D is required for more than strong bones. "It plays a role in preventing chronic diseases involving the immune and cardiovascular system later in life," she said. "More recently it has become a general health indicator because of its associations with major conditions like cancer. Doctors too are becoming more aware and asking for this test," she said.

Head of the orthopaedic department at Parel's KEM Hospital Dr Pradeep Bhonsale said Vitamin D deficiency in adults was astonishingly high and more cases are coming to fore given increased awareness. "Over 50% of patients we treat in our hospital have this deficiency. This can also shunt a child's growth and give rise to bone deformities," he said. He added Vitamin D deficiency was responsible for unexplained pain in the back and joint pain in children as well as adults.

While global studies have established the importance of Vitamin D as a health parameter, there is little consensus in India on how much is too much or too little for an individual. Pediatrician Dr Deepak Ugra said concentrated Vitamin D supplements provide much less than the requirement of 400 IU/ day. *"Calcium tonics available in the market have only about 100ml of Vitamin D components,"* he said. The American Academy of Pediatrics recently updated its

Vitamin D guidelines, recommending infants children and teens should take at least 400 IU per day in supplement form.

Kulkarni said the time of exposure to sunlight is also a subject of debate. "Some studies say 20 minutes is fine while others say it has to be over 45 minutes. On the other hand, exposure to too much sunlight has also been linked to skin cancer so one has to exercise caution

Super-Brain Yoga

How would you like to synchronise both hemispheres in your brain with one quick and simple exercise?

This simple exercise has been called *Super-Brain Yoga*. It's easy, and can be done for 5 minutes in the morning, to supercharge your brain.

The effect of this exercise is that both your right and left hemispheres are activated. At the same time, the hemispheres sync so that your mind is acting in unison. You will notice mental clarity and focus after only a short period of practice.

Here are the simple steps to completing the *Super-Brain Yoga* exercise.

1. Stand up straight with your hands to your side and feet shoulder — width apart.
2. Take your left hand and with your thumb and index finger grab your right earlobe.
3. Now take your right hand, in the same way grab your left earlobe.
4. Your arms should now be crossed in front of your chest.
5. Now you are going to perform a leg squat by bending at the knees.
6. As you squat down with your hands still crossed, grasping your earlobes, inhale.
7. As you stand back up, exhale.
8. Repeat this breathing pattern, and continue to do squats for about five minutes.

"Super-Brain Yoga and its benefits are available on YouTube."

The Five Tibetan Rites: Exercises for Healing, Rejuvenation and Longevity

In 1985, a book called *The Ancient Secret of the Fountain of Youth* written by *Peter Kelder* was published, which for the first time fully described an exercise programme for "youthing" as opposed to ageing.

Potential Benefits of the Five Rites: looking much younger; sleeping soundly; waking up feeling refreshed and energetic; release from serious medical problems including difficulties with spines; relief from problems with joints; release from pain; better memory; arthritis relief; weight loss; improved vision; youthing instead of ageing; greatly improved physical strength, endurance and vigour; improved emotional and mental health; enhanced sense of well-being and harmony; and very high overall energy.

How the Five Rites Work

Medical professionals explain the benefits based on their personal perspective. However, the majority share the view that the rites represent a system of exercise that affects the body, emotions and mind. The Tibetans claim that these exercises activate and stimulate the seven key chakras that in turn stimulate all the glands of the endocrine system. The endocrine system is responsible for the body's overall functioning and aging process. This means that the Five Rites will affect the functioning of all your organs and systems, including the physical and energetic systems and that includes the aging process. The man who brought these Five Rights out of Tibet stated that "performing the Five Rites stimulates the circulation of essential life energy throughout the body."

Chakras

Chakra is an *Indian Sanskrit word* that translates to mean *"Wheel of Spinning Energy"*. *Chakras* are spinning wheels or vortexes of energy of different color that perform many functions connecting our energy fields, bodies and the Cosmic Energy Field. *Chakras* are powerful electrical and magnetic fields. Chakras govern the endocrine system that in turn regulates all of the body's functions including the ageing process. Energy flows from the Universal Energy Field through the chakras into the energy systems within our bodies, including the Meridian System.

Our bodies contain seven major chakras or energy centers and *122 minor chakras*. The major *chakras* are located at the base of the spine (*Root Chakra*), at the navel (*Sacral Chakra*), in the solar plexus (*Solar Plexus Chakra*), within your heart (*Heart Chakra*), within the throat (*Throat Chakra*), at the centre of your forehead (*Brow or Third Eye Chakra*), and at the top of your head (*Crown Chakra*). These chakras are linked together with all other energy systems in the body and various layers of the auras.

The Speed of the *chakra* spin is a key to vibrant health. The other keys to vibrant health that relates to the chakra is ensuring they are clear of negative energy and that they are perfectly shaped and not distorted.

The Five Rites speed up the spinning of the chakras, coordinate their spin so they are in complete harmony, distribute pure prana energy to the endocrine system, and in turn to all organs and processes in the body. This is one of the major requirements for vibrant health, rejuvenation and youthfulness.

The Five Rites Exercise Programme

This programme is often described as a modified yoga programme. Simply put, yoga is a science that unites the body, mind and spirit. Today this is often called Mind/ Body Healing. Yoga was brought to Tibet from India in the 11th or 12th century and Tibetan monks over time developed and modified these exercises and developed an effective programme of exercises that western society now calls the "Five Tibetan Rites". The rugged mountainous conditions these monks live in may well account for their particular emphasis on vigour. Many of the yoga exercises and practices being taught in the western world today are very new. The "Five Tibetan Rites" are exactly what the ancient Tibetans developed over many centuries of time. Therefore it's very important to do the "Five Tibetan Rites" exactly as they are presented without altering the form or sequence to achieve some of the benefits accrued to these "Rites".

Beginning the Five Rites Exercise Programme

1. For the first week, and only if your are relatively healthy and fit, do each exercise, three times.
2. If you are inactive, overweight, or have health problems begin these exercises doing one of the first three, each day, and only if you feel totally comfortable doing this. Later I will describe exercises you can do to help yourself strengthen so you can begin to do the "Five Rites". If you have any concerns whatsoever, please consult with your physician. Individuals on serious medications should consult their physicians.
3. If you are overweight, do not do Rites #4 and #5 until you have developed some strength and endurance. Do the substitutes

for #4 and #5 until you yourself feel ready to begin doing #4 and #5 of the "Five Rites".
4. Do only what you feel comfortable doing. That may be only one of each exercise for the first week. Build up to two of each exercise the second week, three of each exercise the third week, etc. or at a faster pace only if your body does not hurt when you do these exercises.
5. *21 is the maximum of each exercise you should ever do.* If you want to enhance your programme, do the exercises at a faster pace, but do not so more than 21 of each exercise each day. Doing more than 21 repetitions of each exercise in any day will affect your chakras negatively and can create imbalances in your body.
6. The "Five Rites" may stimulate detoxification and often creates many unpleasant physical symptoms. This is why it's recommended to increase the number of each exercise gradually on a weekly basis.
7. If you have not exercised for some time, prepare to begin your "Five Rites" exercise program by walking daily, for a half hour each day if possible. Another alternative in preparation for the Five Rites is a stretching programme with a gradual increase in the types of stretching exercises and the duration of this programme.
8. A sugar free and low fat diet is an important support when integrating the "Five Rites" exercise programme into your life. Also check for Digestive Food Sensitivities and eliminate all foods you do not digest easily.
9. Do the Five Rites exercises every day. The maximum you should skip is one day each week. If the exercises are done less than six days each week, the results will be greatly reduced.
10. If on certain days your time is limited, do 3 repetitions of each exercise. This takes less than five minutes.
11. For maximum benefit, do the exercises before breakfast in the morning, if at all possible. If this is not possible do them anytime during the day.

"Five Tibetan Rites" Exercise Programme

SPECIAL CAUTION: Spinning and stretching through the following exercises can aggravate certain health conditions such as any type of heart problem, multiple sclerosis, Parkinsons's Disease, severe arthritis of the spine, uncontrolled high blood pressure, a hyperthyroid condition, or vertigo. Problems may also be caused if you are taking drugs that cause dizziness. Please consult your physician prior to beginning these exercises if you have any difficult health issues, or if you have any other concerns.

The Five Tibetan Rites

Rite #1
Stand erect with arms outstretched horizontal to the floor, palms facing down. Your arms should be in line with your shoulders. Spin around clockwise until you become slightly dizzy. Gradually, increase the number of spins from 1 spin to 21 spins.

Breathing: Inhale and exhale deeply as you do the spins.

Rite #2
Lie flat on the floor, face up. Fully extend your arms along your sides and place the palms of your hands against the floor, keeping the fingers close together. Then raise your head off the floor tucking your chin into your chest. As you do this, lift your legs, knees straight, into a vertical position. If possible, extend the legs over the body towards your head. Do not let the knees bend. Then slowly lower the legs and head to the floor, always keeping the knees straight. Allow the muscles to relax, and repeat.

Breathing: *Breathe in deeply as you lift your head and legs and exhale as you lower your head and legs.*

Rite #3
Kneel on the floor with the body erect. The hands should be placed on the backs of your thigh muscles. Incline the head and neck forward, tucking your chin in against your chest. Then throw the head and neck backward, arching the spine. Your toes should be curled under through this exercise. As you arch, you will brace your arms and hands against the thighs for support. After the arching, return your body to an erect position and begin the rite all over again.

Breathing: *Inhale as you arch the spine and exhale as you return to an erect position.*

Rite #4
Sit down on the floor with your legs straight out in front of you and your feet about 12" apart. With the trunk of the body erect, place the palms of your hands on the floor alongside your buttocks. Then tuck the chin forward against the chest. Now drop the head backward as far as it will go. At the same time, raise your body so that the knees bend while the arms remain straight. Then tense every muscle in

your body. Finally, let the muscles relax as you return to your original sitting position. Rest before repeating this Rite.
Breathing: *Breathe in as you rise up, hold your breath as you tense the muscles, and breathe out fully as you come down.*

Rite #5
Lie down with your face down to the floor. You will be supported by the hands palms down against the floor and the toes in the flexed position. Throughout this rite, the hands and feet should be kept straight. Start with your arms perpendicular to the Floor, and the spine arched, so that the body Is in a sagging position. Now throw the head back as far as possible. The, bending at the hips, bring the body up into an inverted "V". At the same time, bring the chin forward, Tucking it against the chest.
Breathing: *Breathe in deeply as you raise the body, and exhale fully as you lower the body.*

Exercises In Preparation For Doing the Five Tibetan Rites

The following group of exercises has been developed as a preparation for doing the Five Rites, or as an alternative when you are unable to do any of the Five Rites. Doing these exercises will help you strengthen and become more flexible to be able to do the Five Rites as they have been described above.

Do these alternative exercises in the sequence from one to five and when possible, substitute the Five Rite exercise into this alternative program until you have fully integrated the Five Rites.

As with the **Five Rites**, begin by doing two or three of each exercise daily, until you are able to do 10 each day. Once you are able to do ten of these alternatives, you should be ready to begin doing the Five Rite exercises themselves.

Alternative (for Rite#1) Exercise #1
Stand with your feet about 12 inches apart. Extend your arms palms down until your arms are level with your shoulders. Swing your arms to the right, letting your slapping your left hand against your right shoulder, with your right hand slapping against the small of your back. Then swing your arms in the opposite direction, having your right hand slap against your left shoulder and the back of your left hand slap against the small of your back. As you swing back and forth allow your torso and legs to follow the movement. Allow your heels to lift from the floor but do not allow either foot to completely leave the floor. As you swing right turn your head right, and turn your head left as you swing to the left.

Breathing: *Breathe in rhythm to your swinging movement.*

Alternative (for Rite #2) Exercise #2
Lie down on the floor and elevate your head and shoulders propping up on your elbows keeping your forearms flat on the floor, palms facing down. Keeping your legs straight, hold them off the floor for 20 or 30 seconds.
Breathing: *Inhale as you raise your legs, breathe in and out normally, while holding your legs up, and exhale as you lower your legs.*

Alternative (for Rite #3) Exercise #3
Stand with your back to the wall and your feet 12 – 18 inches apart. Without moving your feet bend forward from the hips so that your buttocks rest against the wall. Slide downward, bending your knees as you go. Keep sliding down until your thighs are horizontal, as if you were sitting in a chair. Hold this position for 15 seconds and then slide back up.
Breathing: *Begin to exhale as you slide down to the chair position and inhale when slide back up.*

Alternative (for Rite #4) Exercise #4
Lie flat on your back, your arms straight, palms down, feet flat, and knees bent. Press your pelvis up a few inches off the floor and hold it for 10 seconds. Release and lower your pelvis to its original position.
Breathing: *Inhale as you lift your pelvis and exhale as you lower your pelvis.*

Alternative (for Rite #5) Exercise #5
Begin in the table position. Curl your toes under and bend your hips raising your buttocks so that your body forms an inverted "V". Your knees will lift up off the floor, your legs will be straight, and your outstretched arms will be in a straight line with your back. Hold this position for 15 seconds.
Breathing: *Inhale as you raise your buttocks, breathe slowly and deeply while holding the position, and exhale as you return to the table position.*

Warm-up Exercises
The following group of exercises has been developed to open, relax, release tension, to strengthen various parts of the body, and to provide toning to different parts of your body.

If you are overweight, in poor physical condition, or experiencing serious illness, this group of exercises is an excellent to help you begin your journey towards physical fitness. I suggest you do these warm-up exercises prior to the Five Rites if you are overweight or have not exercised for a long time.

Begin this group of exercises by doing at least two of each exercise and then gradually increase the repetition until you are able to do **ten** of each warm-up exercise.

Warm-Up Exercise #1

Stand upright, tilt your head sideways towards your left shoulder and hold it for five seconds, then tilt your head towards your chest and hold it for five seconds. Then tilt your head towards your left shoulder and hold it for five seconds, and lastly, tilt your head backward and hold it for five seconds. Return your head to a normal position.

Breathing: *Exhale as you move your head around, and inhale as you return to the upright position.*

Warm-Up Exercise #2

Stand upright, slowly rotate your shoulders in a forward circular motion five times, then reverse the movement and rotate your shoulders in a backward circular motion for five times.

Breathing: *Breathe normally but deeply as you do this exercise.*

Warm-Up Exercise #3

Stand upright with your arms help up, your elbows bent, and your hands together in front of your chest, with your fingertips touching and palms apart. Press inward on your fingers until their inside surfaces are almost touching. Your palms should not be touching. Release and press your fingers again.

Breathing: *Breathe normally.*

Warm-Up Exercise #4

In a relaxed standing position, hold your arms in front of you. Clasp your right hand around your left wrist, with your thumb against the inside of the wrist. Squeeze gently but firmly for five times. Repeat the procedure with the left hand squeezing the right wrist.

Breathing: *Breathe normally.*

Warm-Up Exercise #5

Recline on the floor, resting the upper part of your body on your upper arms. Flex your knees and rhythmically bang them up and down against the floor in rapid succession. Your heels should remain on the floor throughout this exercise. Do this exercise for 20 – 30 seconds.

Breathing: *Breathe normally through this exercise.*

Warm-Up Exercise #6

Get down on the floor on your hands and knees with your hands positioned under your shoulders and your knees under your hips. Bring your chin up and rotate your hips so the tailbone moves up, arching your back down. Then tuck your chin into your chest and rotate your back so that your pelvis moves down, arching your back down.

Breathing: *Inhale as you move your tailbone up and exhale as you move your tailbone down.*

Conclusion: The daily practice of the exercises is an essential element of vibrant health. It's a proven fact that people who lose weight can only maintain their weight loss if they incorporate a daily exercise programme into their everyday lives.

These exercises will stretch muscles you haven't felt in years so approach this program gently and begin with one or two repetitions each day, increasing each exercise by one repetition every week. After you are able to do ten repetitions of the Alternate Exercise program, you should be able to begin to do the Five Rites.

And add a half hour of a brisk walk on a daily basis. Not only will it contribute to your physical health, it will give you the opportunity to enjoy all of nature around you. You will feel younger than you have felt in years.

Zone Exercises

Prescribed by Paul Chek, Holistic Health Practitioner

Dealing with stress is becoming an everyday part of modern living, with its information overload, long commutes and deadlines, let alone finding time for family and yourself. It's no wonder most people cringe at the thought of trying to squeeze exercise into their busy schedules. Yet there are simple movements that you can do that actually increase your energy and vitality take only minutes a day and don't require a trip to the gym.

Table 1: Zones, Muscles, Related Functions and Issues

Zone	Muscles	Related Functions	Related Issues
Zone 1	Pelvis, legs and feet	Adrenals and fight/flight response; Bones and skeletal structure	Financial stress
Zone 2	Lower abdominals, lumbar region, legs and feet	Sexual functions; Elimination; Water regulation	Stress over relationships and sex
Zone 3	Upper abdominals and middle back	Digestion; Assimilation; Musculoskeletal system	Personal power and self will; Digestive issues
Zone 4	Upper back and chest	Electromagnetic field generator; Blood pressure; Immune system	Stress over relationships and love
Zone 5	Lower neck, shoulder, arm and hand	Metabolism; Calcium regulation	Communication
Zone 6	Upper neck, face and head	Sleep/wake cycles; Hormonal and physiological regulation	Mental congestion, lack of mental clarity or creativity

How to Perform Zone Exercises

Look at Table 1 and determine which areas are key issues for you and which Zone these correspond to. You may have musculoskeletal problems, such as pain, repeated injury or weakness in a particular area. Issues within one or more systems of your body may be a priority to you, such as high blood pressure, poor digestion, difficulty sleeping, or hormonal fluctuations around menopause or menstruation. Alternatively, you may strongly identify with factors in the Related Issues column, such as feeling that financial stress is a major pressure in your life at present. Prioritize your top three or four issues, whether within your body or seemly from an external source; many people find that these fall into just one or two Zones.

There are several exercises demonstrated for each of the six zones. Try each of the exercises and choose the one that you feel is most effective. If you have more time you can do more than one Zone Exercise because they don't cause fatigue—they energize.

Zone Exercises can be done any time. If you feel tired or sluggish, perform a Zone Exercise and your energy levels will likely increase. Performed before or after eating, Zone Exercises can improve digestion. This is a good time to determine how much effort to use with Zone Exercises. If you are working too hard, your digestion will feel compromised. If you are exercising at the correct level for a Zone Exercise, your digestion will feel improved.

When performing Zone Exercises, always remember that the faster you move your body, the slower Chi energy moves and the slower you move your body, the faster Chi energy moves. If you experiment with your Zone Exercises, you will soon experience this interesting phenomenon.

For anyone trying to cut down on sugar, caffeine or any other addictive substance, you may find Zone Exercises provide energy to compensate for the fake, or empty energy often provided by addictive substances.

Zone Exercises can help you unwind. By performing Zone Exercises, you bring more Chi into your body. If you have a hard time falling asleep or sleeping through the night, practise your Zone Exercises just before going to bed. Chi is intelligent—it knows when to speed up specific cells and body systems and when to slow them down!

Zone 1

Qigong Toe-touch
- Stand with feet together and slide hands down legs, bending your knees.
- Place hands directly over toes, fingers aligned with toes.
- Inhale, raise hips up and roll slightly back onto heels until you feel a gentle hamstring stretch.
- Exhale and drop down again, rolling slightly forward toward the balls of feet. Slowly move your head and hips in a circle during the exercise. Repeat ten times.

Breathing Squats
- Take a comfortable stance, wide enough to squat down between your legs. Place your arms at your sides or in front.
- Inhale through your nose, then lower yourself down as you exhale through your nose. If you need to exhale through your mouth, keep a little tension in your lips. Go as low as comfortable, pause, then inhale and return to standing.
- Repeat at the pace you naturally breathe, up to 100 times.

Superman
- Start face down on the floor.
- Lift left arm and right leg so that they are at about the same height. Your arm should be 45-degrees from your head with thumb pointed up.
- Hold this position for as long as you can with good form (up to 10 seconds) and switch sides. Do five each side.

Zone 2

Leg Tuck
- Lie on your back with your knees bent.
- Inhale, then draw legs into chest as you exhale (you may open the legs to pull them in closer).
- Inhale again as you return legs to the floor. Repeat ten times slowly.

Front-to-Back Pelvic Rock
- Stand with soft knees, or sit upright on a Swiss ball.
- Inhale, imagining that you have headlights on your butt and shine them up to the ceiling.
- Keep your trunk still as you move your pelvis.
- Exhale and roll your pelvis back underneath you, so the headlights shine down. Repeat ten times.

Zone 3

Piston Breathing
- Stand in a relaxed posture, inhale deeply, allowing your belly to expand.
- Exhale forcefully through your nose. (If you cannot breathe through your nose, exhale through your mouth while pursing your lips like a trumpet player).
- Inhale again slowly and repeat up to 100 exhalation pulses.

Energy Push
- Stand with arms raised straight out in front of you.
- Inhale and bring hands back in towards your body.
- Exhale and push your arms straight out with the intent of projecting energy from your core out of your arms and hands.
- Repeat, pushing to the centre, front left, front right and back left and back right.
- As you push to the sides and back, keep your feet planted and turn your body towards the direction you are pushing.
- For the back position, only go as far as you comfortably can. Do not over-rotate your spine.
- Do up to 20 pushes in each direction.

Zone 4

Prone Cobra
- Lie face down with your arms at your sides.
- As you inhale, pick your chest off the floor while simultaneously squeezing shoulder blades together and rotating arms out so that palms face away from body with thumbs pointing up to the ceiling.

Physical Training

- Keep your head and neck in neutral alignment, and toes on the floor.
- You should feel the muscles between your shoulder blades doing the work. If you feel stress in your low back, squeeze your butt cheeks together prior to lifting your body.
- Hold until you need to breathe out, and exhale as you lower your torso to the floor. Repeat 10-20 times.

The Fish
- Lie back, resting on your arms. Inhale, pick your chest up as high as you can. Hold for 10 seconds then relax and repeat 10 times.
- If this in uncomfortable for you, stand with good posture, inhale and open your arms wide as if flying like a bird with your palms up. Exhale and bring arms back across your body.

Zone 5

Thoracic Mobilisation
- Hold arms straight out to the side and stay relaxed.
- Inhale, turn your right arm up and left arm down and look down the left arm.
- * When you naturally want to exhale, turn your head to the other side and reverse arm positions. Repeat 10 times each side.

Shoulder Clocks
- Stand or lie on your side with your knees bent.
- Visualize that your shoulder is in the middle of a clock. Elevate shoulder toward ear (12 o'clock), then roll shoulder either forward (1, 2, 3 o'clock) or backward (11, 10, 9 o'clock) around the clock. Inhale as you move through the back half of the clock (7 - 12 o'clock) and exhale as you move through the front half of the clock (1 through 6 o'clock).
- Keep your head looking forward and arm relaxed. Do 10 circles in each direction and repeat on the other arm.

Zone 6

Alternate Nostril Breathing
- Plug one nostril with a finger or your thumb.
- Breathe in through your open nostril—your chest should rise in the last third of your breath only. Breathe out through your nostril, keeping the other one plugged.
- Try to breathe in and out for the same amount of time; i.e. five seconds in and five seconds out.

- Alternate nostrils with each complete breath or with each inhalation. Repeat 10 times each side.

Cross Crawl
- Raise your arms up. Pick up your left leg and bring your right elbow to the left knee as you exhale.
- Alternate sides 10-20 times.

12 Steps to Higher Consciousness Healing

1. Identify the uncomfortable emotion you feel (anger, sadness, or fear) and define your problem clearly;
2. Measure the intensity of your emotional pain on a scale of 0 to 10. Note the number;
3. Sit or lie down and relax a little;
4. See or sense your higher consciousness in a way that suits you, feeling the beams of unconditional love that its presence surrounds you with;
5. Ask your higher consciousness to please give you a healing symbol to overcome your suffering. The best symbols have bright colours and beautiful shapes;
6. Thank your higher consciousness for the symbol;
7. See your personal symbol in your heart region. When you breathe out, radiate the positive vibrations of love, comfort and happiness of your symbol throughout your body. Let these qualities form a bubble of light around your body, the diameter of your outstretched arms. See the colour and brightness of the symbol that you received;
8. Wish yourself to be happy and see your higher consciousness sending you love;
9. Direct healing light to the part of your body where you feel pain;
10. If others are involved in your problem, while you breathe out, see them enveloped in another bubble of love, comfort and happiness. Wish them happiness. If someone has hurt you, imagine that they would regret what they have done if they were deeply happy;
11. Practise this for two minutes twice a day for two weeks;
12. At the end of two weeks, measure the intensity of your emotional pain on a scale of 0 to 10. Compare this with your beginning emotional state. (See # 2 above)

Physical Training

Eight Keys to Life Hardiness and Resilience

Helen Keller once wrote: "Character cannot be developed in ease and quiet. Only through experience of trial and suffering can the soul be strengthened, vision cleared, ambition inspired and success achieved." As we navigate through challenging times towards a better future, it's useful to visit some tried and true ideas regarding life hardiness and resiliency. This is not meant to be an exhaustive list, but rather a reminder of some essential ideas we sometimes set aside as we tend to the hectic details of daily life. If you find these instructions, share them with those whom you care about who are in need. The power in good will reverberate.

1. The power of perspective

Life is not always easy. We all know that. How we choose the way we think, feel, and act in relation to life's challenges can often make the difference between hope versus despair, optimism versus frustration, and victory versus defeat. With every challenging situation we encounter, ask questions such as "What is the lesson here?", "How can I learn from this experience?", "What is most important now?", and "If I think outside the box, what are some better answers?" The higher the quality of questions we ask, the better the quality of answers we will receive. Ask constructive questions based on learning and priorities, and we can gain the proper perspective to help us tackle the situation at hand.

2. Don't focus on the mud

We should learn from the past, but not be stuck in it. Sometimes life circumstances and personal setbacks can haunt and prevent us from seeing our true potential and recognizing new opportunities. What has already happened we cannot change, but what is yet to happen we can shape and influence. At times the first step is simply to break from the past and declare that it is you, not your history, who's in charge. Ask empowering questions such as "What matters to me now?", "How can I make a difference in this situation?", and "What's the next step for my best interest and well-being?" Every moment we're alive we can make new choices that help us move on and step toward a better future. If we pay attention to only mud on the ground after a storm, we won't notice that the sky above us has already cleared. Goethe reminds us: "Nothing is worth more than this day." Don't focus on the mud. Make better choices today and move on.

For more information on how to eliminate your negative emotions and develop a positive attitude.

3. All you have to do is ask...the right individuals

In life we sometimes may feel like we're walking alone, but we don't have to be as long as we're honest with ourselves, and ask for help when needed. You can find strength and support through a "board of advisors" you create. These are your "go-to" people when you're in need of sound advice, a new perspective, a certain expertise, or simply an empathetic ear. Members of the board can include individuals you know whose opinions you respect and character you trust. Your personal B.O.A. can also include your role models from past and present, historical or fictional. Ask, for example: "What would (role model A) say about my situation?", or "What would (role model B) do if she were in my shoes?" Asking for help is not the same as complaining. Habitual complainers dwell on what's wrong. Successful people assume responsibility for finding the support they need to solve the problem.

4. Thrive on your strengths while exploring new potentials

We each have certain dispositions in which we naturally excel. Some of us are great with people, others are handy with tools, yet others thrive on information. A mismatch between what you're naturally good at and your work in life is wasted potential. There are a myriad of assessment tools available that can help you determine your natural strengths, as well as your areas of greatest potential.

5. Keep the fun and enjoyment

Van Wilder from the movie of the same name said: "You shouldn't take life too seriously. You'll never get out alive." No matter how difficult the circumstances, resolve to keep the fun and enjoyment in your life. Make a point to take a "mini-vacation" everyday; be it walking in the park, exercising, hugging a loved one, or taking a nice, hot bath. The more challenging and stressful life is, the more important it is to take good care of yourself so you can relax your body, ease your mind, and rejuvenate your spirit. After recharging your batteries, you may see the same situation in a different, more positive light.

6. Keep your options open

There are many paths to opportunity, success, and happiness. We can begin by asking ourselves what true success and happiness means and looks like to us, and let our answers show the way. When one path seems to be at a dead end, look another way and see what new openings may be waiting just around the corner. Options can come from consulting the aforementioned board of advisors, thinking outside the box, daring to dream, doing something different, or simply letting go of a habit or condition that has clearly outlived its usefulness. We're never stuck unless we have blinders on. Keep your options open.

7. Keep the faith

There are many ways to keep your faith alive: Faith in yourself, faith in your place in this world, and faith in answers the Universe has in store for you. Go to places and engage in activities that give you the greatest feeling of inner peace. When you give yourself this gift on a regular basis, what psychologists call the Higher Self emerges, as insights, inspiration, and a sense of deep knowing spring forth from the depth of your soul.

The following quote by Anne Frank is just one example: "The best remedy for those who are afraid, lonely, or unhappy is to go outside, somewhere where they can be quiet, alone with the heavens, nature, and God. Because only then does one feel that all is as it should be and that God wishes to see people happy, amidst the simple beauty of nature."

As you immerse yourself in peace, ask: "What if what I'm going through is a blessing in disguise? What greater meaning exists for me now?" Put forth these and any other constructive questions that come straight from your heart. Don't try to figure out the answers during these moments, but rather "empty your mind" and let the solutions come to you. The answers may come at that moment or later: sometimes when the time is right; sometimes when you least expect them. All you have to do is hold the questions and pay attention.

Keep the faith. Find your peace within, and the answers will come!

8. Resolve to never, ever give up

I once heard a courageous person say that there are no losers in life, except for those who give up on themselves. If you're still alive and breathing, your purpose in this life time is not yet fulfilled. The great adventure is in discovering what that purpose is, and to live it until your last breath. If you're reading this book, you're probably being pulled by an inner calling to do more. That calling is your adventure waiting to happen. What are you waiting for? And what are you willing to do now?

A Simple Switch in Your Brain Can Make You Happier

Can you learn to be a happier person by repeatedly visualising two tiny parts of your brain and imagining yourself tweaking them?

Colorado teacher and musician Neil Slade says you can.

Slade has developed brain exercises, described on NeilSlade.com, aimed at lifting your spirits and calming your fears. The website has become something of an underground sensation, attracting an average of 750,000 hits a month through word of mouth alone.

Slade suggests visualizing part of the primitive brain called the amygdala, commonly described as the seat of emotional experience. The two amygdalae, each about the size and shape of an almond, are located on either side of the head, between the eye and ear, about an inch in. Studies have shown the amygdalae have a part to play in everything from memory storage to anxiety.

Slade recommends locating your amygdalae in your thoughts, and visualising a switch on each one, with the click-back position turning on the fear feelings, and the click-forward position turning on feelings of pleasure. Picture yourself purposefully clicking the switch forward.

Another way to stimulate lighter and happier feelings is to visualise yourself tickling each amygdala with a feather.

When University of Toronto psychologist Adam Anderson heard about the exercises, he laughed. The assistant professor is also the Canada Research Chair in cognitive neuroscience, and his research focuses on what the amygdalae contribute to human emotion. Anderson believes they are one of the elements of our feelings, but human emotions result from a delicate balance of the functions of different brain parts.

"I'm not saying it can't work, but it's a really silly idea that you actually have to picture your amygdala," he says. "You could teach people to visualise their left elbows and it might be just as effective.

"It's a form of relaxation and, if it works, more power to the people who do it. But as a scientist, I see it as maybe a form of meditation or a distraction from what's bothering you."

Slade thinks there is more to it than that. He believes visualising the amygdalae can create physiological changes in the brain.

"You can directly elevate your mood through behavioural change such as laughter or physical exercise, or you can elevate it through mental stimulation like these amygdala exercises."

Marie-Louise Oosthuysen de Guitierrez, a Mexico City teacher who is studying brain research in education, says Slade's exercises work for her. "Visualising clicking forward stimulates the prefrontal cortex," she says. "It helps me to control intense emotions if I feel upset or angry. I immediately feel calmer."

Janice Dorn, a psychiatrist and brain anatomist who has studied the brain for 41 years, believes Slade's exercises stimulate the connections between the primitive, or limbic part of the brain and the more evolved prefrontal cortex in order to develop habits of happier thought and feeling.

Many people could learn to be happy by regularly repeating thought and visualization practices.

It's a matter of reprogramming your brain to have a tendency towards happiness instead of emotional pain, and most people can learn to do it.

She says choosing happiness over emotional suffering requires first consciously rejecting negative thinking.

She recommends quieting the mind and putting a larger perspective or a positive spin on your circumstances, imagining this moment 10 years in the future. Ask yourself how you can learn something useful from the experience.

"Look for a way to turn any part of it into a positive experience: that's how the prefrontal cortex operates," Dorn says. "The amygdala is always talking to the prefrontal cortex. So tell it about joy instead of telling it that you are a frightened, unhappy person who deserves to suffer."

She suggests another exercise: Try to visualize your amygdalae lit up and shining beautifully. At that moment, take yourself to a time when you were as happy as you have ever been. Send the joy you feel to your prefrontal cortex so you can remember it.

"The more you practise these things, the more you can voluntarily increase the activity of the front cortical processing system. The more you do it, the better you get at it, and the better you feel."

Those with serious mental illness or addiction problems should seek professional help, she adds. Instinct and emotions were once thought to originate in the limbic part of the brain, the first part to develop in humans.

The prefrontal cortex, the more evolved part of the brain , was believed to control higher functions such as judgment and permanent memory.

But Anderson says no one knows for sure where feelings originate. Still, much like cognitive therapy, he believes people can use their thinking to change the way they feel and this is how Dorn's or Slade's suggestions could work.

"Studies show that thinking supported by the prefrontal cortex can increase or decrease limbic responses," Anderson observes. "You can reframe an event to make it look sunnier or feel better to you.

"There is new evidence from studies measuring brain activity that the prefrontal cortex can be called upon to turn up or down the activity in the ... limbic regions such as the amygdala and hypothalamus. That is, having thoughts about how to make yourself feel better or worse actually changes the responses in primitive neural circuits, resulting in a genuine change in how emotions are created."

There are two amygdalae in your brain, one inside the left hemisphere of your brain and one inside the right hemisphere, about one inch inside from the temples midway between your eyes and ears. Point there with your fingers, now. Your brain is in fact divided exactly in half, into two separate although connected right and left halves called hemispheres. Each brain hemisphere gets its own amygdala switch which controls and gives accurate feedback as to how well and how well your brain is working.

These other structures are other internal structures, the brain's "limbic system" (the "mammal brain"), of which the amygdala is part. Additionally, the amygdala is a gateway/switch that turns on the most advanced part of your brain: the frontal lobes.

AMYGDALA CLICKED BACKWARD:
A. Your brain is working poorly and "Life stinks!". Brain energy moves into your brain stem and the small primitive core of your brain- your "reptile brain".
B. Being clicked backward means you are only using a fraction of your potential brain power.
C. When your amygdala is clicked backwards you are primarily computing primitive reptile brain thoughts and behaviors: self-defense and counter attack; fight or flight; basic survival.
D. Being clicked backwards automatically results in negative emotions.

To get things working better (an understatement), and to turn on limitless amounts of creativity, intelligence, and pleasure, you need to click your amygdala forward and turn on "the other 90%" of your brain.

AMYGDALA CLICKED FORWARD:
A. This opens the neuro-pathways in your brain to allow energy to effortlessly flow into the rest of your brain and your magnificent frontal lobes.
B. Your frontal lobes are the entire front 1/3 part of your brain. Hold your forehead. Everything under your entire hand is frontal lobes.

Physical Training

C. Your frontal lobes compute "CICIL": Cooperation-Imagination-Creativity-Intuition-Logic.
D. Clicking forward automatically results in positive "Life is FUN!" emotions. When you control your amygdala and click it forward into your frontal lobes, true Brain Magic happens.

MEMORISE the paragraphs above. Test yourself by writing down the key ideas on a separate piece of paper- Backward, A, B, C, D; Forward, A, B, C, D.

The brain's advanced electrochemical circuits are controlled with THOUGHT. To click your amygdala forward you don't need any machines, gadgets, pills, nor do you need to sign up for expensive retreats or courses.

Clicking your amygdala forward is like wiggling your finger. Only it happens inside your brain instead of on the end of your arm. Do this: wiggle your right index finger. Easy, isn't it? Okay, wiggle your left big toe. Easy too? Now, locate your amygdala. You click it forward using your frontal lobes- IMAGINE that your amygdala is like a click toggle switch- Now "click" the switch forward towards your forehead. There! You did it. It's a thought process that changes how you think, and how your brain works. Click it again. Smile!

Proper amygdala forward clicking is indicated by all kinds of indicators, primarily positive emotional feedback: You feel good, a good feeling that lasts. Studies done by brain and behavior researcher T.D. Lingo at the Dormant Brain Research and Development Laboratory form 1957 to 1987 showed dramatic and measurable increases in intelligence and creativity by mastering control of this key part of the brain. This included substantial and measurable increases on the Getzels-Jackson Creativity Index and the Stanford Binet I.Q. as well as greatly enhanced and enduring emotions of well being and pleasure. Additionally, many persons report highly increased sensitivity to paranormal abilities once they learn how to keep their amygdala clicked forward.

A very helpful visualisation is to imagine you have a feather, and that you are tickling the front part of each amygdala. Tickle the front part of your right amygdala and the front part of your left amygdala. Or left then right, or both together (it doesn't matter). Whoooosh! Ha ha ha! Click! That's it!

"Tickling" your amygdala (via abstract imagination) AUTOMATICALLY causes it to click forward, at least momentarily. This thought process will quickly and automatically begin to activate your frontal lobes connections turning on the most advanced part of your brain. Massive creativity, cooperative energy, intuition, logic will quickly follow provided you keep it up. Imaging an amygdala tickle is the fastest way that you can start clicking forward that we've found. It works from the very first minute you try.

Keep tickling until you get the desired results and long lasting positive emotional feedback. The effects are progressive and accumulative.

Clicking forward is VERY simple. That's why you use a feather and not a sledgehammer. It is as easy as clicking on a light switch. Click! Imagine your amygdala is a toggle click switch, and click it forward. Click! By clicking on your imagination, you instantly send electro-chemical brain energy to flow forward through your amygdala into your infinite potential frontal lobes. These simple IMAGES of tickling or clicking your amygdala forward turns the ignition key and starts the frontal lobe's engine. It primes the pump. It's the match that lights the fireworks fuse.

Most people feel a slight sensation when they first click: a tingling in the forehead; a giggly light feeling; a cessation of internal noise; an automatic smile. A few see lights and hear sounds. Some feel a wave of euphoria. Others sense sudden calm. First time clicking in a quiet secluded environment helps. Eventually it can be done anywhere, anytime, any place.

Because this is a simple process, don't be mislead into thinking it isn't powerful and that it won't help bring you the big results you're looking for. You start the most powerful automobile or jet airplane engines with the click of a single "on" switch. And it only takes a simple click to get your brain started running at its most efficient level.

- Clicking your amygdala forward begins Cooperative intelligence.
- Clicking your amygdala forward jump starts your Imagination.
- Clicking your amygdala forward begins new Creative thinking.
- Clicking your amygdala forward connects you to higher Intuition.
- Clicking your amygdala forward adds on common sense and Logic.

All you have to do is click forward to access these natural advanced frontal lobes skills and watch them begin to grow. Cooperation means working together. Imagination means spontaneous unrestricted thought. Creativity means finding a new way. Intuition means knowing deep down inside. Logic means seeing how the pieces link together. (I think you've probably got the idea now.) Once you've gained basic control of your amygdala click switch, your CICIL skills grow and expand. You call upon an infinite variety of abilities your brain creates to achieve your life goals and purpose.

You have a daily choice: Do you want to keep clicking backward into primitive and miserable reptile self-defense/counterattack thoughts and behaviours, or do you want to control your own amygdala, and click forward into wonderful and effortless frontal lobes advanced whole Brain Magic?

What shall it be?

The concepts here are a summarisation of exceedingly complex workings of the human brain. However, by understanding these few basic ideas, you gain superior PRACTICAL perspective and control over your brain. Voila!! Congratulations!

Techniques

Before being able to click your amygdala you must first be able to locate it and this is very easy.

Method #1

"Well, like the brain man said, it's as easy as clicking on a light switch. Of course, you've got to FIND the clicker first. Here's a good simple way to demonstrate it actually exists (as opposed to just reading about it and imagining it via your frontal lobes)."

"Your NOSE is connected DIRECTLY to your amygdala, attached by way of olfactory nerves."

P.S. There is no need to actually participate in step one as we all have the ability to recall a time when we smelled something which we disliked. Just recall, imagine, and be self-aware.

"Very Easy Amygdala Click Demonstration

STEP 1 (Don't do this part too much, it will give you a bad headache.) Go outside and find your neighbor's smelly garbage can. Put your nose right in the bottom of it. GO ON, DON'T JUST SIT THERE!~ Rub your nose around in the lid. ! (You may optionally find something else to smell equally repulsive.) Note the rather unpleasant convulsions your body is experiencing. DON'T COME BACK HERE AND READ ANY MORE TILL YOU DO IT! GO ON....................

Congratulations! YOUR AMYGDALA JUST CLICKED BACKWARDS. (Now go wash your face).

STEP 2 Go get something that smells really good, TO YOU. It might be a rose, or popcorn, or your wife.

Okay, now smell this nice thing..... When you smell this "thing" subtle waves of pleasure permeate your head. It travels from your ears down your neck into your fingers and you drool with delight. Congratulations! Your amygdala has just clicked forward, and you did it ON PURPOSE all by yourself. (This is important, it wasn't an accident.)

STEP 3 See the difference between a frontwards click and a backwards click?

Wait a minute, you say...."This is so obvious!!" OF COURSE IT IS! You've been walking around with this switch in your brain since the day before you were born!

Once you learn a few techniques for DIRECTLY clicking forward, any time, any place YOU WILL BE AMAAAAZED at how your life changes! You will be in CONTROL of your own positive emotions and about a million other fantastic things. You ain't seen nothing yet......(Many more and advanced lessons in The Frontal Lobes Supercharge and other brain books.)"

Method #2

"A very helpful visualization is to imagine you have a feather, and that you are tickling the front part of each amygdala. Tickle the front part of your right amygdala and the front part of your left amygdala. Or left then right, or both together (it doesn't matter). Whoooosh! Ha ha ha! Click! That's it!"

"Keep tickling until you get the desired results and long lasting positive emotional feedback. The effects are progressive and accumulative."

"Desired results" include "a tingling in the forehead; a giggly light feeling; a cessation of internal noise; an automatic smile. A few see lights and hear sounds. Some feel a wave of euphoria."

Method #3

Visualise light switches in your brain were your amygdalae are and imagine them clicking forward.

"Now, locate your amygdala. You click it forward using your frontal lobes- IMAGINE that your amygdala is like a click toggle switch- Now "click" the switch forward towards your forehead. There! You did it."

"Imagine your amygdala is a toggle click switch, and click it forward. Click! By clicking on your imagination, you instantly send electro-chemical brain energy to flow forward through your amygdala into your infinite potential frontal lobes. These simple IMAGES of tickling or clicking your amygdala forward turns the ignition key and starts the frontal lobes engine. It primes the pump. It's the match the lights the fireworks fuse."

Tips

Try method one before two or three. Clicking in a quiet secluded environment helps during the beginning. Be self-aware (emotionally) and concentrate on the sensations within your body.

MANAGE YOUR EMOTIONS

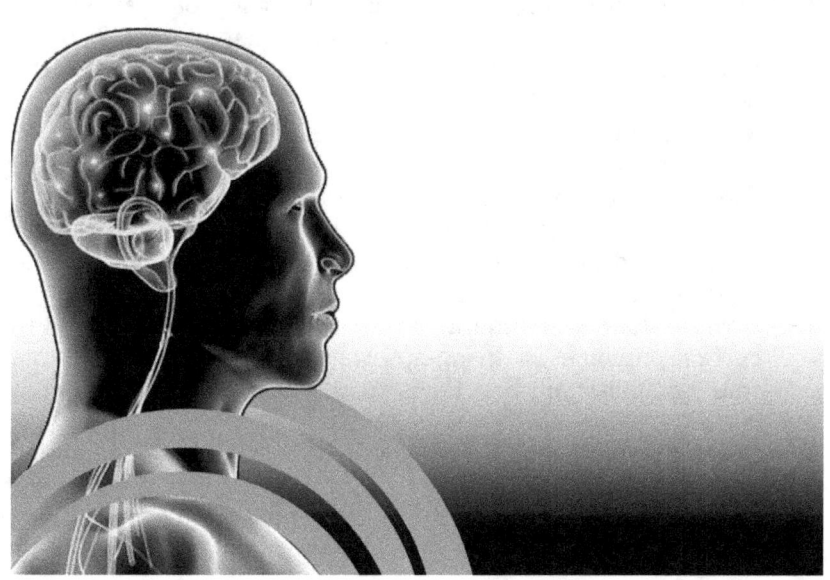

Manage Your Emotions

25 Suggestions for Living a Contented Life by Managing Your Emotions

Below are some suggestions for coping with intense emotions.

1. **Practise mindfulness.** Mindfulness helps reduce anxiety and stress for everyone. Consider a way to practice mindfulness everyday that is easy to remember. Maybe mindfully brush your teeth or mindfully drink your coffee. Consider using a bracelet or a sticky note to remind yourself.
2. **Play:** If possible, find a way to laugh today. Be silly. Giggle. Dance, watch a comedy, run in the park, buy a balloon, dabble with paints, gather friends for games or play games designed for one player. Just for a few minutes. Enjoy a simple pleasure and focus completely on the activity – not on your concerns.
3. **Practise gratitude:** Each evening go through your day and list three things you are grateful for. Be specific. Then focus on those three experiences or interactions or things. Savour the positive
4. **Nurture relationships:** Friends will likely always make you angry or upset, but having friendships is one of the keys to contentment. When you spend time with friends, focus on what you like, what energizes you. Review the positive experiences in your mind to equal out the natural inclination to go over and over painful experiences.
5. **Give up your attachment to outcome:** Being too attached to certain outcomes or living a certain way or having a certain solution limits you and leads to suffering. Be open to what comes.
6. **Learn something new:** You don't have to choose something difficult. Learn a little about another culture or learn a new word or two. Read a magazine about a hobby you know nothing about or read about life in a different country. Cook a new

dish, play a new game, or explore an area of town that is new to you. See the world anew, with the eyes of a child.
7. **Let go of urgency:** Sometimes we feel urgent about everyday tasks, persuading someone to agree with us, achieving goals, getting the gift that we want or getting our way about an issue. We create desperation and pain when very few tasks or experiences are truly urgent, and acting as if situations are emergencies only gets in our way and creates anxiety and suffering. Be mindful, let go of urgency when it isn't really urgent. Slow down, breathe, take small steps.
8. **Stay focussed on what is in your control:** Attempting to control other people or events creates anxiety, anger, feelings of helplessness and turmoil. For example, you can't control how someone else treats you, but you can often choose how much time you spend with them or work on how you react to the way they treat you. You can't control that someone you love chose to spend the weekend with other friends, but you can control how you spend your weekend.
9. **Accept Imperfection:** Life is messy and imperfect. Striving for perfection that doesn't exist crushes joy and contentment.
10. **Stop comparing to others who have it better:** Comparing is a way of evaluating and judging ourselves and others. Most often we compare ourselves to a characteristic of someone else who we see as superior to us. It's also a way of competing. See yourself as part of a community where each person's success benefits us all. Practice saying, "Good for them, good for us all."
11. **Get out of the box of pre-defined holiday celebrations:** Having a big family get together with lots of activities is just one way to celebrate and not necessarily the preferred way for everyone. Walking mindfully along the ocean with yourself, watching old movies with friends, meditating and recuperating from all the activity of the year, and focusing on a spiritual journey are just some of the alternatives.
12. **Make a point of noticing what works:** Did you get to your job without a problem? Did you enjoy your dinner with a friend? Did you use a skill when you needed it? Did someone help you with a task? It is easy to overlook what goes right!

Cheerfulness: A psychosynthesis technique

Exercise For Evoking Cheerfulness
1. **Relax all muscular and nervous tensions:** Breathe slowly and rhythmically, express cheerfulness by smiling (It will help to

assume this expression before a mirror, or visualise yourself doing so).
2. **Reflect on cheerfulness, conscious of its value and usefulness**, especially in our agitated modern world. Appreciate and desire it.
3. **Evoke cheerfulness directly by pronouncing the word several times.**
4. **Imagine yourself in circumstances likely to worry or irritate you:** for instance, in the presence of unfriendly people, having to solve a difficult problem, obliged to do various things rapidly or finding yourself in danger, and yet keeping cheerful.
5. **Plan to remain cheerful all day, to be a living example of cheerfulness**, to radiate cheerfulness. This exercise can be done (with appropriate modifications) not only for cheerfulness but other qualities as well: courage, joy, patience, will and so on.

This exercise is based on the *Exercise for Evoking Serenity* published in the book Psychosynthesis: A Manual of Principles and Techniques by Roberto Assagioli (N.Y.: Hobbs, Dorman, 1965; paperback-Viking Press, 1971).

Eight Health Benefits of Laughter

Is there anything better than a contagious giggle that you absolutely can't control? (OK, maybe not so good in school or church.) Laughter works wonderfully well in the moment, but it also has some surprising long-term health benefits. In the book, A Better Brain at Any Age: The Holistic Way to Improve Your Memory, Reduce Stress, and Sharpen Your Wits (Conari Press, 2009), author Sondra Kornblatt explores how laughter can truly make you feel better. She writes that the new field of gelotology is exploring the benefits of laughter. It was brought to the public's awareness in Norman Cousins' memoir, *Anatomy of an Illness*. Cousins found that comedies, like those of the Marx Brothers, helped him feel better and get some pain-free sleep. That's because laughter helps the pituitary gland release its own pain-suppressing opiates.

What can laughter do?:

Lower blood pressure
- Increase vascular blood flow and oxygenation of the blood.
- Give a workout to the diaphragm and abdominal, respiratory, facial leg, and back muscles.
- Reduce certain stress hormones, such as cortisol and adrenaline.

- Increase the response of tumour- and disease-killing cells, such as Gamma-interferon and T-cells
- Defend against respiratory infections-even reducing the frequency of colds-by immunoglobulon in saliva.
- Increase memory and learning; in a study at John Hopkins University Medical School, humour during instruction led to increased test scores, improve alertness, creativity, and memory. Humour and creativity work in similar ways, says humour Guru William Fry, M.D., of Stanford University — by creating relationships between two disconnected items, you engage the whole brain.

Humour works quickly
- Less than a half-second after exposure to something funny, and electrical wave moves through the higher brain functions of the cerebral cortex.
- The left hemisphere analyzes the words and structures of the joke; the right hemisphere "gets" the joke; the visual sensory area of the occipital lobe creates images; the limbic (emotional) system makes you happier; and the motor sections make you smile or laugh. So let's laugh.
- What makes you laugh? Tell us your favourite funny movie, or how about a good joke?

Seven Laughter Exercises

1. **Find out what's funny.** Something's funny when you snort milk out of your nose-but what makes you laugh? Absurd humour replaces the familiar with the unexpected. Wile E. Coyote chases Road Runner after being smashed by a piano. Superior humour-like lawyer jokes-rearrange life's hierarchies. In dark humour, you laugh at what scares you.
2. **Laughter without a joke.** Laughter may also be about relationships, says Robert Provine, professor at the University of Maryland. In fact, you may be "tuned" for laughter from family and culture. It helps you cope with life-or a rude in-law-by relieving mental and physical tensions.
3. **Immerse yourself in humour.** Check out comedy books, movies, and tapes at the library or stores.
4. **Trigger laughter.** Our mirror neurons trigger humour by hearing others laugh. Just like yawning, but more fun. Ha. Start smiling when you listen to laugh sounds from the Bachorowski Lab. Ha ha. Or buy a laughter CD-60 minutes of chuckles. Ha Ha Ha. great background noise for a party.

5. **Read the comics in your newspaper or online.** From the traditional to the old-Baby Blues, Betty, or Bizarro, they're a daily dose of humour.
6. **Try laughter meditation, consisting of stretching laughing and silence.** It can transform your energy and mood.
7. **Join a laughter club or a laughter yoga class.** Participants playfully imitate breathing and sounds of laughter, until simulated laughter turns into the real thing. They receive healing, company, humour, and the physical sensation of deep laughs.

Emotions and Your Health

All healing is really about emotional healing. It's literally an "inside job." That's why I call it healing from the inside out.

Repressed emotions can cause a disease. How this disease manifests in each of us is completely individualised. Releasing emotions can heal disease. Even cancer. Even diseases that Western medicine deems incurable.

Anger, fear and sadness: These are three primary emotions that may be the causes of a disease. They are normal and natural feelings, and we all experience them as natural aspects of our wonderful humanness. But when these feelings remain internalised without avenues for expression and release, they can create a vibrational state in our body-mind that disrupts our natural homeostatic balance.

This imbalance can express itself in body-mind symptoms. I use the term body-mind because these symptoms can express themselves in physical symptoms or as emotional symptoms or both. When symptoms become loud enough, *we may have a label for them in Western medicine—a disease.*

Repressed Emotions

Where do repressed emotions come from? This depends on your worldview.

First, they may come from experiences that we've had in this lifetime that were traumatic. Most often, in early childhood, this occurs after we lose the wonderful state of being unselfconscious and become aware and attuned and sensitive to the experiences around us. We may have experiences that are painful emotionally, and one natural response may be to protect ourselves and internalise these emotions.

Often it is easier, given the paradigm of Western medicine, to first consider the physical body, symptoms, or "dis"-ease. Focussing on the physical body can be a starting point for healing and transformation on many levels. Yet unless we address emotional roots and links, we cannot heal completely on any level.

In Chinese medicine, the lung is the repository for grief, the liver for rage, and the kidney for fear. In Ayurveda, the *vata dosha* may yield arthritis and worry; the *pitta*, ulcers and rage. It may be helpful to consider these connections when reflecting upon your own health concerns.

There are many, many ways to enable healing. I will briefly summarise some of these.

Some tools and techniques are "passive"; others are "active." Passive approaches are those that are done to you, such as *acupuncture* and *massage*. Active ones are those that you can do yourself, completely on your own, such as *pranayama*, or breathing exercises. Active techniques can be truly empowering, but passive ones are useful too! Sometimes it is helpful to have an experience to shift one's body-mind state without having to put forth a lot of effort.

Breath and Food

Breath is the fuel and life force for our body-mind. Western science has well documented the relationship between respiration and physical and emotional health. Interestingly, this is an inherent tenet of global healing traditions. Qi and prana are considered life force in traditional Chinese medicine and Ayurveda, respectively. Without breath, we do not exist.

Compromised breathing can cause illness; optimised breathing can enable healing. Learning natural breathing as well as specialised breathing techniques can affect our body-mind, our emotional state, and can be a conduit to emotional healing.

Food is medicine for our body-mind. All foods have effects on our emotional states. These effects are unique to each of us. Hippocrates, considered the father of Western medicine, wrote of these concepts. He believed that "food should by thy medicine and thy medicine food," and also taught that it is "more important to know the patient that has the disease than to know what disease the patient has".

Lead A Happier, Healthier Life by Managing Your Fears

Soothing Movie Music
1. Think of a situation where you feel fear.
2. Dissociate: See yourself in the situation like you would a movie with you in it.

3. Imagine running the memory from the END of the fearful situation, BACKWARDS to the START. Do this very fast in less than 1 second!
4. Think of some music that makes you feel the opposite of fear. For example, soothing classical music makes you feel relaxed. Perhaps, certain rock or dance music makes you feel energised/courageous, etc.
5. Now hear the music, nice and loud, inside your mind whilst looking at yourself going through the situation from START to END.
6. Break the state. Now think of the situation you choose in Step1 and notice how your fearful feelings have diminished.
7. What will you see or hear just before you want this new feeling to set in?

Visualising Healing

Gail Denton details eight different visualisations that you or your helper can guide you through to enhance neurological healing. These are all best done in a relaxed or trance-like state, where the conscious mind is less likely to interfere with the healing results. She recommends resting the mind both before and after doing each visualisation, and repeating them on a daily basis. The names that follow for the exercises are Gail Denton's.

a. **Deblocking.** Simply invite your brain to remember, and make available to you, "what you know visually, kinesthetically, auditorilly, by smell and taste and by intuition."
b. **Orienteering.** Imagine that there is a question that some place in your brain needs an answer to (Point A), and that the answer lies in another place (Point B) which is somehow blocked off from Point A. Invite a friendly team of your brain cells to find a new route from A to B, which may be more or less direct. Once you have imagined that happening, thank your team.
c. **Phone Company.** Visualise the two hemispheres of your brain connected by a telephone system. The communication is done by an old fashioned human-operated switchboard like those you can see in very old movies. When the lines are down, telephone service people work on the lines on each side of the divide, repairing connections so that messages get through. Take a few minutes each day to imagine this repairing happening.
d. **Office Manager.** Imagine an old style office manager in a room filled with filing cabinets, boxes, of papers, computers and other reference materials. This office manager runs your brain. Introduce yourself to the office manager and ask her/him to

help you find specific information that you need. Watch the manager going about this job, and ask her/him to draw and provide you with a map to the office to help you find things faster.

e. **Hall of Answers.** Imagine yourself seated in a large, comfortable chair in a big room with large double doors. When you are ready, walk to the doors and open them. They lead to a long hallway with many doors and walls full of drawers. The drawers are organized both alphabetically and in order of dates. Every door or drawer is labeled. Ask a question and search for the drawer or door with that label on it. Imagine opening the drawer or door and finding the answers.

f. **Cross-crawl.** Gail Denton recommends practising real life cross-crawling movements (where your left hand touches your right knee and then your right hand touches your left knee, repeatedly, for example) to reconnect the two sides of the brain and train them in complex coordination. When you are lacking the physical energy to do such exercises, she suggests imagining going through the exercises step by step in your mind, feeling each movement is occurring fully and perfectly.

g. **Progressive Muscle Relaxation.** Scan through the body from the toes to the head, checking each place is fully relaxed, feels good and is serving you well.

h. **I'm OK Today.** Affirm that your body is healing and attracts energy which your body will use to heal your brain. Affirm that everything you are doing is contributing to this healing, both active exercises and resting, and that you will do what it takes to heal. Affirm that you are OK now, and that what you can do today is enough for today. Let go of any old beliefs and doubts that no longer serve you. Feel that you are lovable and attract loving support.

i. **Inner Smile.** This *Chi Kung* exercise is usually done sitting on a chair. Sit on the edge of the chair with your feet flat on the floor. Your back needs to be straight but relaxed; an effect which you'll get by imagining that your head is suspended by a cord from the crown up to the ceiling. Close your eyes and gently press your tongue against the top of your mouth. Clasp your hands together gently. Remember a time that you can feel comfortable recalling, when you felt caring or loving. Perhaps a time when you were caring for a plant, or an animal, or for a child. Imagine that you can see this time, and the gentle smile of caring it brings, as a picture about three feet in front of your eyes. Allow your forehead to relax, and draw the energy of caring into the place between your eyes. Experience it as a limitless source of caring energy flowing to this place, and from there flooding through your body as a smile.

Allow the smiling energy to flow across your face, relaxing it. Smile into the neck and throat, through the thyroid and parathyroid glands, which control your metabolic rate and keep your bone tissue balanced. Smile down to the thymus gland in the upper central chest area; the gland which co-ordinates your immune system. From there spread the smile back to the heart, allowing it to relax and blossom in a shining red light, transforming hastiness and irritation to joy and love. Flow the smile out on each side to the lungs, filling them with white light, transforming sadness and grief into the ability to discriminate what's right for you, and enhancing their ability to take in energy from the air. On the right, flow the smile down through the liver, filling it with leaf green light, enhancing its hundreds of cleaning and organising functions, and transforming resentment and anger into an assertive kindness to yourself and others. On the left flow the smile through the pancreas, which assists in digestion and regulation of blood sugar. The far left is the position of the spleen which forms and stores blood cells, and here rigidity and stuck thinking are transformed to openness. Fill the pancreas and spleen with yellow light. On each side the smile now flows to the back at waist level, flooding through the kidneys which filter the blood, and the adrenal glands atop them which give your body the energy burst of adrenalin. As these glands relax, fill the kidneys with dark blue light, and feel fear transformed into a gentleness. Finally, flow the smiling energy down through the urinary bladder, and through the sexual organs, including the glands (ovaries or testes) which balance the cycles of your life. Conclude by flowing the smile to a place just below the navel and a couple of centimetres in from the front. Feel the energy spiral into this centre, called Dan Tien in China, as a storage for the day. As you flow this smile, check for the "feeling" that each organ is smiling back. Take the time it needs to allow this to happen.

Draw the smile again into the place between your eyes. This second time, flow the smile down your nose and mouth into the digestive tract; swallowing as you do, and imagining that the saliva you swallow is also full of smiling energy. Smile through the stomach, just below the ribs, and through the intestines. Having flowed the smile down through the whole digestive system, draw the energy back to the Dan Tien centre below the navel. The third time, draw the smile into the centre between your eyes (actually called "upper Dan Tien") and circle your eyes nine times clockwise (as if watching a speeded up clock face right in front of your eyes) and nine times counter-clockwise. Draw the smile back through the brain itself, smiling deep into the brain tissue, where the glands which co-ordinate your entire hormonal system reside. Flow the smile down the spinal column, and through the neurons (nerve cells) out to every part of the body. Feel as your brain and neurological system respond to the healing energy that you have been generating throughout your body. As you continue to draw the smile into your body from an infinite source of love and healing, imagine the smile flowing out from your body into the air around you, and across the entire room. The smile, remaining infinite, flows out beyond the room across the whole area, across the whole country, into the oceans and across the continents, until the entire planet is filled with the smile. As the smile continues to expand, just check back in your body in the room. Check if there is anywhere in your body where there was an excess of energy (perhaps an area where there was some tension -just an indication of energy not flowing on easily yet) and draw the energy back to lower Dan Tien, feeling it spiral in there as a store for the day.

Milton Erickson categorised eleven methods of dealing with pain. These categories, which overlap somewhat, are:

1. Directly suggesting that pain disappear.
2. Indirectly suggesting that pain disappear (as Erickson does in *Bandler and Grinder's original 1975 study of his work saying*, for example on page 37 of that book "You know Joe, a plant is a wonderful thing, and it is so nice, so pleasing just to be able to think about a plant as if it were a man. Would such a plant have nice feelings, a sense of comfort".")
3. Creating amnesia for past experience of the pain.
4. Creating numbness or analgesia in the painful area of the body. In traditional hypnosis this is done by teaching the person to create numbness in their hand and then "transferring" this numbness to the affected body part.
5. Creating a more total anesthesia by having the person imagine they are somewhere far from the pain.
6. Altering sensations of pain into sensations of itching, warmth, coolness, or other less disturbing sensations.
7. Displacing the pain to a more manageable area of the body (eg moving abdominal pain to a hand.
8. Dissociation, e.g. by having the person imagine that they are across the room observing themselves.
9. Reinterpreting the pain as a feeling of heaviness, pulsation or movement.

10. Distorting time perception so that a prolonged period of pain seems to go by much faster.
11. Suggesting that the pain will reduce itself very gradually; so gradually that the person cannot even monitor whether or not this is happening.

Train Your Brain to Be Happier

Harvard's Dr. Ben-Shahar's advice, "The question should not be whether you are happy but what you can do to become happier".

We are now going to explore the four key concepts of Dr. Ben-Shahar's statement — 1) "you", 2) "can", 3) "do", and 4) "happier" — from a neuropsychological perspective.

1) Who is "you"? According to latest scientific understanding, what we experience as "mind", our awareness, emerges from the physical brain. So, if we want to refine our minds, we better start by understanding and training our brains. A very important reality to appreciate: each brain is unique, since it reflects our unique lifetime experiences. Scientists have already shown how even adult brains retain a significant ability to continually generate new neurons and literally rewire themselves. So, each of us is unique, with our own aspirations, emotional preferences, capacities, and each of us in continually in flux. A powerful concept to remind ourselves: "you" can become happier means that "you" are the only person who can take action and evaluate what works for "you". And "you" means the mind that emerges from your own, very personal, unique, and constantly evolving, brain. Which only "you" can train.

2) Why the use of "can"? Well, this reminds me a great quote by Spanish neuroscientist Santiago Ramon y Cajal, who said that "Every man can, if he so desires, become the sculptor of his own brain". Each of us has immense potential. However, in the same way that Michaelangelo's David didn't spontaneously appear out of the blue one day, becoming happier requires attention, intention, and actual practice.

Attention: Every second, you choose what to pay attention to. You can focus on the negative and thereby train your brain to focus on the negative. You can choose to watch TV five hours in a row, thereby training your brain to become a passive spectator of events. Or you can do the opposite. Attention works outwards and inwards: you can pay attention to your own meaningful emotions or try to ignore them. Many times we are not aware of the choices we are really making and their implications, which is why practices like mindfulness meditation can help.

Try this experiment on selective attention.

Intention and Mindset: Our frontal lobes equip us to: 1) Understand our environments, 2) Set goals and define strategies to accomplish our goals, 3) Execute those strategies well. Becoming happier is as worthy an endeavour as our education and professional careers, or our efforts to be fit and slim by exercising our bodies. Please use those frontal lobes to define the goals that can work for you.

Practice: We need to stress the importance of "rituals" to make it easy to practise new skills. Great idea. Let's talk more about that in the next point.

3) The critical word "do": You may have heard the expression "Cells that fire together wire together." Our brains are composed of billions of neurons, each of which can have thousand of connections to other neurons. Any thing you do in life is going to activate a specific constellation of neurons. Visualize one million neurons firing at the same time when you order your next cappuccino. Now, the more cappuccinos you order, the more those neurons will fire together, and therefore the more they will wire together (meaning that the connections between them become, literally, stronger), which then creates automatic-like behaviours. For example, try this experiment: Quick! say aloud the colour you see in every word in the picture on the right. DON'T simply read the word. Tough, isn't it? Well, that is because, during many years, you have trained your brain to read words. You can also choose to train your brain to say the colour with attention, intention and practice. This point has an enormous implication: whatever we do in life is, in practice, training our brains. How do you want to train your brain next?

4) The objective measure of "happier". Being "happy" is subjective. No scientist could look at you, read some instrument, and measure your happiness. But there are ways to measure, and train being "happier." For example, stress and anxiety are key obstacles to happiness. Appreciating the beauties of life often, and developing positive emotions, are key allies. Fascinating research is showing how emotional self-regulation happens, helping all of us identify those states as they happen (stress, anxiety, appreciation and positive emotions) and allow us to intervene and "regulate" our response as we wish. Some of the most promising applications are biofeedback programmes (that measure body variables giving you great visual feedback in realtime on your level of stress, as in the image), meditation,

and cognitive therapy. Take an extreme example: We probably all would agree that, if you happened to have visceral fear of spiders, suddenly facing a spider wouldn't be one of the happiest moments in your life. In a 2003 paper on the impact of cognitive therapy on people with extreme spider fear, scientists observed how the fear induced by viewing film clips depicting spiders was correlated with significant activation of specific brain areas, like the amygdala (the "fear centre of the brain") that, once activated, trigger specific body reactions (like the "fight or flight" physiological response). After the intervention was complete, however, viewing the same spider films did not provoke activation of those areas. Those individuals were able to "train their brains" and managed to reduce the brain response that typically triggers automatic stress responses. And we are talking about adults with extreme phobias.

BREATHING TECHNIQUES

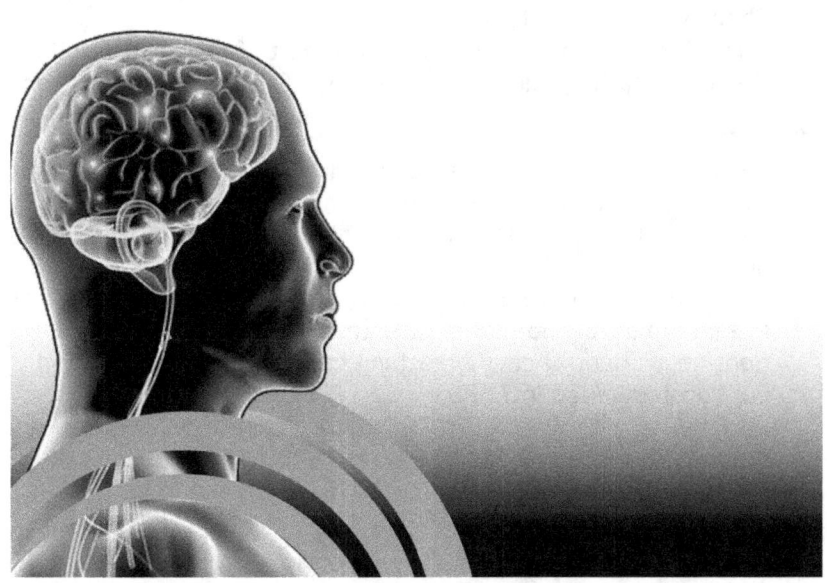

Breathing Techniques

Three Steps of Rhythmic Breathing (SRB)

The three steps of **3 SRB** involve the *technique, volume and rhythm of breathing*.

TECHNIQUE
- While breathing, both your chest and abdomen should rise and fall simultaneously.
- The chest will require more air because of the space created by the rib cage.
- The abdomen should not be blown up unnaturally during inhalation.
- To figure out if you are breathing correctly, get a friend to observe you or lie down before a mirror with two heavy books, one on the chest and the other on the abdomen.
- Check if both move together.
- Our habit of breathing from the lower part of the chest results in shallow breathing, depriving the body of much needed oxygen.

VOLUME
- When you breathe in, it is particularly important to note that the breath flows freely and fully from neck to navel. This simply means that the middle and lower abdomen should be filled to normal capacity.
- The volume of breath intake during 3 SRB should be the same as the intake during normal breathing.
- Continuous deep, heavy breathing can exhaust a person and is not recommended in 3 SRB.
- Initially, to establish the rhythm, your breath will be deeper, but once you are comfortable with 3 SRB and the volume of air that is to be drawn in, the breath will become normal.

RHYTHM
- ◌ To establish the correct rhythm of breathing, inhalation should take three seconds and exhalation two seconds.
- ◌ To keep to the pattern of rhythmic breathing, do not retain the breath between inhaling and exhaling.
- ◌ One complete breath takes five seconds or six pulse beats. The exact rhythm is to count 1-2-3, while inhaling and 5-6, while exhaling-4 is not counted.
- ◌ Unlike breathing exercises, in normal breathing rhythm, the duration of inhalation is longer than that of exhalation.

To master **3 SRB**, you must consciously work to complete *12 cycles of breath in a minute*. Inhale to the count of 3, exhale to the count of 2, and repeat the cycle 12 times in one minute. Initially, as you sit down to observe your breathing pattern, you will find that you probably breathe beyond 18 cycles per minute. This can be reduced to the mandatory 12 breaths a minute with the practice of 3 SRB.

Be, Breathe, Blossom

Instructions, Preparation

Sit facing east in a cross-legged posture, with your spine comfortably erect. Keep your hands upon your thighs, with your palms facing up. With your face slightly upturned, eyes closed, keep a mild focus between your eyebrows.

The Meditation

This meditation will happen in three stages:

Stage 1:

Inhale and exhale gently, slowly. With each inhalation, mentally say to yourself: "I am not the body." The inhalation should last the whole duration of that thought. With each exhalation, mentally say to yourself: "I am not even the mind." The exhalation should last for the whole duration of that thought. Repeat this for 7 to 11 minutes.

Stage 2:

Utter a long "A" sound (as the "a" in father). The sound should come from just below the navel. You need not utter it very loud, but loud enough to feel the vibration. Utter the long "A" sound 7 times, exhaling fully into each sound.

Stage 3:

Sit for 5 to 6 minutes with a slightly upturned face, and keep a mild focus between your eyebrows.

The total time of this practice is between 12 to 18 min. You can sit longer if you want.

Breathing Techniques

PLEASE NOTE
While you sit for the technique, do not pay attention to the activity of the mind or body. Whatever is happening in your body or your mind, just ignore it and simply sit there.

Do not take a break in between, as it will disturb the reorganisation of energies that happens during the practice.

Each time you do the *kriya*, you must do it for a minimum of 12 minutes, and twice a day for 48 days (considered as a full *mandala* or cycle), or once a day for 90 days. This is your commitment. This is your *Gurudakshina*. Anyone can practise this *kriya* and enjoy its benefits. Simply follow the instructions without making any changes. This is a simple but very potent *kriya*.

You can remind yourself that " I am not the body. I am not even the mind" anytime during the day.

Breathe Your Way to Super Health

Babies breathe abdominally, which has been associated with better health than chest breathing.

Breathing is the most overlooked, easiest and accessible tool we have to enhance our state of body-mind health. There is a direct link between breathing and health. Improper breathing can cause or aggravate all diseases and health issues. Learning to breathe correctly can have immediate and profound effects on mental, emotional, and physical states of imbalance or disease and allow our body-mind to be in an optimal state for healing.

The concept of breath as being tantamount to life is an essential tenet of global healing traditions worldwide. "Qi" and "prana" are considered life force in traditional Chinese medicine and Ayurveda, respectively.

Our first experiences with breathing were the most natural: Correct breathing is innate breathing. As infants, our breathing is natural, spontaneous, and unlabored. Infants breathe naturally with the belly. If you observe a baby breathing, you'll notice his or her belly enlarges on an inhalation.

As children, when we become self-aware and self-conscious, we may lose touch with this natural and spontaneous way of breathing. Many of us, having forgotten how to belly breathe as we did when we were infants, become habitual chest breathers, holding the belly in and breathing from our chests.

Society and culture also influence how we breathe. Men and women receive subtle cues about the necessity of a flat stomach, of standing tall, and leading with the chest, thus inhibiting our natural, innate form of abdominal breathing.

Emotional states also affect our breathing. Fear, anxiety, anger, and other stressful feelings can unconsciously activate chest breathing, inhibit abdominal breathing, and even cause us to hold our breath or stop breathing momentarily.

Abdominal breathing is simply letting the belly expand when we inhale, as opposed to inhaling with the chest. The chest may rise a little, but most of the breath comes from letting the belly out. By letting the belly expand when we inhale, we make room for the lungs to expand more fully. The intestines move out of the way, making room for the lungs.

Abdominal breathing is sometimes referred to as diaphragmatic breathing. We are not actually breathing with the diaphragm. The diaphragm is akin to a swinging door that moves downward to allow for more lung expansion when we let the belly out while inhaling.

The autonomic nervous system. In the Western medical worldview, the autonomic nervous system is the control center for bodily functions. This nervous system consists of the sympathetic and parasympathetic systems. These two work in opposition to one another, like a toggle switch. When the sympathetic nervous system is on, the parasympathetic system is off, and vice versa.

What the sympathetic system does. This is the "fight or flight" nervous system. It is a fabulous system and serves us well when we need to be physically active, run around the block, be vigilant in our thinking, or be mentally or physically focussed.

For example, it sends blood and nerve impulses to our muscles when we need to run. It increases heart rate, blood pressure, and respiratory rate—all necessary increases to help us run around that block. It inhibits digestion, relaxation, and sleep and can inhibit sexual function.

What the parasympathetic system does. The parasympathetic system allows for the activation of our "vegetative functions": digestion, sleep, relaxation, and certain aspects of sexual function. When it is on, blood pressure, heart rate, and respiratory rate are reduced. The body's natural restorative and self-healing mechanisms are engaged when the parasympathetic system is engaged.

Abdominal breathing and chest breathing have immediate effects on our health. How we initiate our breath has immediate effects on our health. If we start breathing with the chest, not with the abdomen, the sympathetic nervous system is engaged.

If we initiate our breath with the abdomen, abdominal breathing, the parasympathetic nervous system is engaged. These nervous system effects are instantaneous, given the nature of the physiologic mechanisms involved.

Stressful emotional states, often causing us to chest breathe at the expense of abdominal breathing, will toggle on the sympathetic nervous system, thus causing or aggravating any health issues we may have. Chest breathing will increase emotional states of fear, anxiety, and anger. And these emotional states, in turn, can cause us to chest breathe, with the consequent ill effects on health. Abdominal breathing can alleviate these health issues.

A little more about chest breathing: To breathe fully, chest breathing is always involved. One's chest will rise and expand as one's lungs fill more fully. This is especially useful if we are doing strenuous physical activity and happens naturally and spontaneously. It is important to be aware that one initiates the breath via one's abdomen, not the chest.

How chest breathing can cause or aggravate illness: Chest breathing alone can cause and aggravate illness. Because chest breathing engages the sympathetic nervous system, it can inhibit digestive function, cause or aggravate cardiovascular problems, and make sleep, rest, relaxation, and even sex problematic.

In fact, all health issues are exacerbated by chest breathing: for example, circulatory diseases such as high blood pressure and coronary artery disease, respiratory disorders such as asthma, gastrointestinal issues such as gastritis and ulcers, and life-challenging diagnoses such as cancer and other chronic conditions that Western medicine deems incurable.

Digestion is also impaired by chest breathing: Peristalsis is directly inhibited by chest breathing. Since food is our first medicine, we can appreciate the profound and systemic effects of it on our body-mind health.

Learning to breathe naturally can alleviate health problems: By learning or actually relearning how to breathe naturally, through intentional abdominal breathing we can learn to consciously control which nervous system is activated.

Abdominal breathing will toggle on the parasympathetic system: We can improve our sleep, digestion, and concentration; enhance relaxation; relieve uncomfortable emotional states; improve cardiovascular function—any health issues that we may have. This parasympathetic state enables the optimal and necessary conditions for healing disease because a state of complete rest and relaxation is necessary for recovery from any illness.

Abdominal Breathing

You can practice abdominal breathing anytime, anywhere, in any position—sitting, standing, or lying down. Easiest may be in bed, upon waking, or just before going to sleep. This can even help with sleep. Practice at other times during the day, while sitting, standing, walking.

Start by placing one hand on your chest and the other on you abdomen, below your belly button. First, gently observe your breath. Breathing through your nose, start to gently allow the belly to rise on the inhalation and to fall on the exhalation. Ideally, the belly will rise and fall, but chest movement will be minimal. Breathe slowly and gently. Notice any tension in the process, on the inhalation or on the exhalation. Letting the exhalation be a little longer than the inhalation can help in relieving tension.

Practical Suggestions

Don't worry that you are not breathing correctly. There is no right or wrong. Simply be aware that different methods and techniques have different effects on our body-mind. And notice how you are breathing. Notice how your breath may change with different states of emotions. Just start by being aware. If you find yourself feeling anxious, worried, fearful, or experiencing any other uncomfortable emotion, experiment with abdominal breathing.

Notice how you are breathing during various daily activities, and experiment with intentional belly breathing if you notice you are starting your breath with your chest. Take advantage of downtime: While waiting for a computer to turn on, while in the line at a store, while driving, on a bus or a subway, observe and experiment with your breathing. Belly breathing can make being stuck in traffic actually feel pleasant if you're someone who feels challenged in traffic jams.

Consider taking time during your day, even if just for a minute or two, to notice and practice belly breathing. Over time, with practice, you'll find yourself breathing this way more spontaneously. The final suggestion is to be gentle with yourself. Be easy. Do not judge yourself. Such thoughts will impact your breath, your physiology, and your physical, mental, and emotional well-being. And, you may be likely to hold your breath!

Deep Breathing for the more ambitious

Highlights of Deep Breathing:
- Deep breathing is a mind-body technique.
- The long term practicing of deep breathing exercises improves wellness.
- Slow breathing is the healthiest form of deep breathing.

Deep Breathing Exercises
A typical Slow Breathing Exercise might proceed as follows.

You will need an analog clock with a large sweeping second hand, and the numerals 1 through 12 clearly visible on it, along with a silent electronic kitchen timer. Set the timer to 5 minutes or to the desired length of your slow deep breathing exercise session.

- Sit quietly and comfortably in a quiet room.
- Keep your eyes open through out the entire slow breathing session.
- Focus your attention on your breathing, as well as on the sweeping second hand of the clock.
- Breathe slowly at 6 repetitions per minute. Each complete breath should last 10 seconds. Breathe in through your nose for 4 seconds. And, then breathe out through your mouth for 6 seconds. As the sweeping second hand passes each number silently repeat the number to yourself: 1, 2. ... 12.

During this exercise, you will be concentrating on your breathing, as well as on the sweeping second hand of the clock. If your mind drifts passively bringing it back to silently repeating the correct number on the clock. Your timer will keep you from worrying about the time. All you have to do is keep up the correct inhaling/exhaling breathing rhythm while you silently repeat the correct number. If your mind drifts, bring it back to concentrating on the clock.

It is very easy to determine how this slow breathing mind-body technique is affecting your heart. All you have to do is measure, or monitor, your pulse rate and blood pressure before, during, and immediately after your deep breathing sessions. However, the research indicates that long-term benefits come from the long-term practice of slow breathing exercises.

Deep Breathing Relaxation Exercise
Your deep breathing exercises can be changed up, in a number of different ways.

You can add variety to your diaphragmatic breathing exercises as well as elicit different effects on your body by altering the numbers of breaths per minute breathed, the relative duration of the inhalation; holding; and the exhalation phases of each breathe, by changing the force by which air is blown out of the lungs during the exhalation phase of each breathe, and finally by changing the duration of the entire deep breathing session.

Breaths per minute, respiration rate, or rate of breathing:
- Slow breathing
- 6 or 5 breaths/minute
- Slow breathing is the healthiest method of deep breathing.
- Spontaneous, or normal uncontrolled, breathing
- 15 breaths/minute
- Fast breathing
- 20 breaths or more/minute (such as, the Lamaze childbirth rapid panting method)

Relative duration of the inhalation, holding, versus the exhalation phases of breathing.
- 1:0:1
- 1:1:1
- 40:0:60
- 1:0:2

The force by which air is blown out of the lungs during the exhalation phase.
- NEVER ever try to use forceful breathing or exhalation techniques.

The duration of the exercise session.
- 10 to 20 minutes, twice a day, is the usual duration.

Some types of deep breathing exercises can be dangerous and harmful to your health.

Many forms of authentic Yoga breathing exercises and forms are not at all healthy for anyone to practice, and, thus, should be avoided by all beginners.

All Fast/Rapid breathing techniques should be avoided. Yogic rapid breathing rates can get extremely high and might result in hyperventilation. Also, the research indicates that rapid breathing negatively affects your heart.

"Heart rate, rate-pressure product ... increased significantly."
"Bellows-type rapid and deep breathing"

- Do not ever try to use forceful breathing or exhalation techniques, because it is not safe to force air out of your mouth, nose, or nostrils under a lot of pressure.
- Practising longer than 20 minutes is not recommended. Deep breathing for several hours at a time and other excessive durations might cause hallucinations and, thus, should never be done.

Health Benefits of Deep Breathing
Controlled breathing exercises can be used to promote wellness.
- Breathing, especially the exhalation phase, has a natural automatic relaxing effect.
  One physical mechanism of action for this relaxing effect is the accumulation of carbon dioxide in the blood.
- **Self-perceived reductions in levels of tension and anxiety.**
- **Slow breathing (6 or 5 breaths/minute**
  "Slow, rhythmic, and deep breathing"
  "There was a significant decrease in basal heart rate in slow breathing group after three months of practice of slow breathing exercise."
  "Produced a significant increase in respiratory pressures and respiratory endurance."
  "Heart rate, rate-pressure product and double product decreased."
  Slow breathing (6 breaths/minute) increases resting oxygen saturation and improves exercise tolerance.
- "Several studies ... showed that 15 minutes of daily breathing exercise lowered BP [Blood Pressure] within 8 weeks by 12.1/6.1 mmHg as compared to 7.6q3.4 mmHg in the control group."
  "Slow breathing at 6 breaths/minute increases baroreflex sensitivity and reduces sympathetic activity ... suggesting a potentially beneficial effect in hypertension. ... Slow breathing decreased systolic and diastolic pressures in hypertensive subjects ... Slow breathing reduces blood pressure and enhances baroreflex sensitivity in hypertensive patients."
  Baroreflex is the system in the body that regulates blood pressure by controlling heart rate, strength of heart contractions, and diameter of blood vessels.

Benefits of Mindful Breathing

Mindful breathing corrects the tendency we have to tense our body, especially around the abdominal muscles.

When depressed or anxious, the breath is shallow, our shoulders are slumped, and lungs are collapsed. We aren't getting enough oxygen rich blood to feed the brain. Deep breathing, along with some adjustments in our posture, allows the lungs to expand to their full capacity so the body and mind receive more oxygen.

The practice of breathing, alongside other activities that naturally circulate oxygen, such as exercise, singing, dancing or even laughing, has been shown to have tremendous healing effects on the mind and body. With daily practice, there are many physical and emotional benefits.

Studies show that deep breathing alleviates depression and anxiety, restoring balance to the biochemistry of the brain by raising levels of feel-good hormones oxytocin, dopamine and prolactin, and lowering levels of cortisol, the stress hormone.

In psychotherapy, deep breathing is one of the most important components in managing panic attacks and anxiety, and other emotional overwhelm conditions.

With deep breathing we may also expect to see improvements in mental clarity, focus and attention, as well as physical improvements in circulation, heart and blood pressure.

It has been shown to actually heal certain nerves. With practice, we can even create a drop in our overall breath rate, from the average of 16 to 18 breaths per minute to 10 to 12 breaths.

Perhaps more importantly, conscious breath work can unlock doors to self-healing, self-awareness, acceptance, self-discipline, and peace of mind — all of which we need to increase and protect our happiness, improve our relationships, and live life at its best.

Cultivate a Deep Breathing Practice

Look at three ways our breath invites us to be an active persson in creating a fulfilling life and consciously connected, healthy and wise self.

First, let's consider:

- **Why do we often ignore the invitations?**
    How is it we so casually turn down an invite to open up space for our life and being in the present moment?

    Perhaps one reason is that, unlike in Eastern cultures, we don't learn early on as children to use our breath, as a resource that connects us to our inner world, for solutions to life's everyday problems.

    For centuries, cultural institutions in the West to include modern science have emphatically taught us:
- **To mistrust our inner world of meanings as unreliable sources.**
- **To discount the value of our own thinking.**

- **To dismiss the significance of our feelings, and avoid the painful ones.**

As a byproduct of this toxic thinking, we more easily 'see' the value of staying busy to get things done than the value of staying connected to our breath. This also teaches us to relate to our self and one another, first and foremost, like human doings, and to think about our inner life in ways that scare us out of connecting.

Not surprisingly, therefore, our brain routes any invitations to breathe, vital as they are, to a 'junk folder' in cellular memory.

We've learnt to mistrust our human nature, to avoid and numb pain any painful emotions or signs of vulnerability, and instead to trust expert authorities, and wait for idols and superheroes to rescue us from our problems.

This type of thinking is the cause of much suffering, emotional and relationship issues, i.e., addictions, phobia, relationship problems. Even worse, it spawns quick-fix solutions that exacerbate the suffering.

In the words of Albert Einstein, an activist for social change, "We can't solve problems by using the same kind of thinking we used when we created them".

Make no mistake, we have a lot to be proud of in our Western culture. It is the toxic thinking that we need to consciously sift through, tossing out what does not serve personal health, growth or society, as a whole.

- In the beginning, there was breath.

    Breath is life itself. Yet, we rarely ponder or talk about this way.

    All other things being equal, what is the main difference between a live body and a freshly dead one? **Breath.**
- Ancient civilizations well understood breath as an energy equated to life itself.
- The Sanskrit word for breath, for example, is *prana* means 'life force.'
- The Greek word for *breath* is *psyche* which means "spirit" or "soul," for example.
- The Latin word is "spiritus."

Our breath is beautifully designed to partner with us, as a resource for our own healing that, essentially, helps us attune to, understand and regulate our emotions.

As an active partner, the breath supports us to optimise our health and well being in at least three of the following ways:

1. *The breath acts as an ambassador for life*

As the breath is always with us, like an ambassador, it represents our mind-and-body self as a voice for what we most need for breath to vibrantly flow through our body as a healing energy; and what may be blocking the flow.

The word, *ambassador* is defined, according to several sources, as:
- The highest ranking spokesperson
- An officially appointed representative
- A messenger on a special mission with specific duties
- An advocate who acts as interpreter and voice

As an ambassador, what does the breath advocate?

The quality of our breath tells us, at any time, where we are in relation to where we inwardly yearn to be. It reminds us that we are wired with inborn drives, a hardwired value system, that compels us to seek to matter, to meaningfully connect, to find value in our contributions in life.

From the first to the last, our breath invites us to know and understand our self and our life and others, more and more, by better understanding our nature, that:

- We are born scientists, curious and wired to learn throughout life.
- Wired for an inner-driven life of rich connections — purpose driven to empathically connect and meaningfully contribute.
- We are endowed with a capacity (a beautiful responsibility?) to manage the energies of our body (love-seeking *vs* fear-avoiding) to keep fear or anger at levels that enhance rather than diminish our performance potential.

Naturally, other parts of the body also tell us what we most need and what is blocking the inner flow inside.

It is the breath, however, that is uniquely situated in a pivotal position to be the spokesperson, representing our body and life, on a special mission dedicated to helping us know who we are and what we are capable of realising with the inner resources we have.

2. *The breath as a barometer*

As our emotions affect the quality of our breath, the breath is also a barometer. It provides a moment by moment account of how safe we feel in relation to life in and around us.

- The body never lies.

The question is, are we present to listen and understand what it's telling us? Like a biofeedback device, our breath reflects what is presently going on inside, i.e., our thoughts, feelings, yearnings, etc.

Perhaps more importantly, it voices how we feel about (perceive, interpret, etc.) what is going on inside. When we do not feel safe, for whatever reason, the part of the mind that runs the body, the subconscious mind, blocks communication between the mind and body.

When fear sets off the body's survival response, known as the sympathetic nervous system, like a dictator, the subconscious mind usurps most of the flow of oxygen and re-directs it to systems that prepare our body to 'fight or flee' for our survival.

- More often, the first sign that we feel anxious or depressed, for example, is that our breath becomes shallow.

Shallow breathing means the higher thinking part of the brain is not getting enough oxygen, and as a result, it's not fully functioning. In survival mode, our ability for creative or reflective thought is limited. This explains why when we lose our temper, for example, we say things we normally would not.

- The breath, in a sense, reflects our truest felt experience of life at any given moment.

It is also the case, however, that how safe we feel is more indicative of how we interpret a situation, than the situation itself.

The fear response is as a natural protective feature of our body. When this becomes a reactive pattern of behavior, however, it often means that limiting beliefs are unnecessarily activating our survival system, and putting us at risk of emotional, mental and physical harm.

We can partner with our breath at any moment to understand what's going on inside. If we make changes to our perceptions, our breath and body will respond accordingly.

Calming thoughts activate emotions of safety and love; worries about the future or ruminating on past mistakes activate emotions of fear.

3. *The breath as an action signal*

Our actions reflect our perceived sense of safety, and in turn this directly affects our breath. It also works the other way around as well, however.

A third way in which our breath supports us to optimize our well-being is as an action signal. As such, it lets us know when we need to take action to calm our mind and body so that our body's survival system does not activate.

A top concern of our mind and body is how secure we feel in relation to life around us. The brain is always in either 'learning mode' or 'protection mode,' and this roughly equates to emotions of love and fear, respectively. In fear mode, the breath acts like a wall to block learning; in learning mode, the breath acts like a bridge that connects the mind and body.

- To our body, love is a safe harbour and fear is a treacherous reef.

  Like a bogus treasure map, limiting beliefs and toxic thinking cause us to look for the treasure of safety and love in places where it cannot be found.

  Our breath is there to partner with us, as a vital resource that supports us to stay present in moments when we need to safely navigate through upsetting emotions without getting triggered. Mindful breathing keeps us in the present moment, when it counts the most, to make informed choices on life issues.

  To calm our mind and body, we need to be aware and engaged with our breath and body. Breath work enhances our ability to grow our awareness of inner thoughts and feelings, to regulate our emotions, and to make healthy disciplined choices.

  As thoughts and beliefs are perception filters that the mind of the body uses to determine how safe we are, a conscious regulation of breath allows us to directly control the energies of our mind and body, through conscious shifts in our thoughts, presence and feelings.

  A practice of mindful breathing allows us to calm our body and mind, consciously. When we do, in effect, we are letting our subconscious know that we do not need to be rescued, and that we can handle the situation.

- Wired to learn to relate, communicate and partner.

  A practice of mindful breathing can be an essential step to building awareness, getting to know our self, and living a rich inner life.

  Our mental, emotional and physical health are all about the quality of oxygen flow in the body.

  The wiring of our brain makes our body a sophisticated communication system. Emotions are the electrochemical molecules that the systems of the body use to communicate with one another. Emotions show up as changes in our breath.

  Our breath is the primary way our body gets our attention, and invites us to partner in three ways. The breath is a spokesperson for our life, advocating for our deepest yearnings. It is also a barometer that lets us know, in any moment, how we feel inside about what is going on around us. And finally it is an action signal that prompts to take action to close the gap between where we are in relation to where we want to be.

At every step of our growth and transformation, the flow of breath in our body is there to support us.

No one, regardless how wonderful, can do for us what is our task alone to complete.

Whatever the situation, mindful breathing helps us access more clarity in our thinking and the energy we need to successfully take action to deal with the daily challenges of life.

It is our choice to breathe in and connect to our life from the inside where a healing energy flows.

Three Essential Principles

By definition, principles are basic truths or standards that, when followed, form a foundation for producing optimal results. In mindful practices, principles can also be thought of as consciously set intentions.

So, what three principles, set as intentions, form a strong foundation in cultivating a practice of mindful breathing?

- **An inner focus**
- **A present focus**
- **An optimal mind and body state**

These three principles are at once:
1. Key tools that, with regular use, ensure mindful breath work becomes a successful lifelong practice.
2. Core intentions that, when consciously set, transform our life and relationships, by raising our level of consciousness.

The choice to cultivate a practice of mindful breathing is a lifestyle option. We always have a choice in what we include into our lifestyle. A discussion of these three principles follows below.

1. An Inner Focus

Mindful breathing is a tool we have at hand, perhaps the most effective way to turn our focus to what is going on inside of us, that is, to use our breath to connect to our thoughts, emotions, felt sensations, inner yearnings, aspirations, wants, past experiences and so on.

Why an inner focus? It's where we access the sources of power available to us, inside, which can be transformative resources, depending on how we relate to them. To the extent we become comfortable with looking inside, we grow our self-awareness and an inside-out orientation to life, which research links to promoting health and happiness.

This information consists of personal knowledge, or messages that our body sends to us, directly, to let us know how we're experiencing (interpreting) our life at any given moment.

Socrates posited that to "know thyself' was essential to living free in wisdom and truth, yet when we come across the words of Sir Francis Bacon, "knowledge is power," we rarely think of inner knowledge of self as having power.

Living mindfully aware of our inner world is knowledge that empowers our choices, perhaps like no other. It:

- Allows us to better understand our personal experience of life from the inside-out.
- Develops our awareness and a sense of being an active agent in our experiences of life.
- Gives us an understanding of our self that is prerequisite to a better understanding our life and others.
- Grows our wisdom, and adds clarity to the choices we make, and the actions we can take.

In fact, feelings of powerlessness are often the result of not being connected to what our body is telling us. Our inner world of sensations is a rich knowledge bank that is letting us know, for example, where we are in relation to where we want to be, and perhaps what we can do about it.

Each attempt to cope with stress or problems via our defenses (which usually involves instilling fear, shame or guilt in our self or others), however, can leave us feeling more, rather than less powerless. We may have already noticed that, the more we try to force change, the less successful we are.

This is because, when become overly anxious, even about making positive changes, our body and mind are at odds with one another. When this happens, we lose access to our frontal cortex, where most creative thinking or decisions takes place, and instead, by default, trigger old defense strategies instead. In contrast, we can use our breath to check the flow of life energy in us.

Essentially, using mindful breath work to grow our inner awareness is like finding a treasure chest that contains all the materials we need to create the life we aspire – and realizing it's been at hand all along.

Suddenly, there are no worries or fears about feeling painful emotions fear, shame or guilt. By setting an intention to see and feel our feelings as vital information, we can better

Breathing Techniques

handle them. We can befriend, and breathe into them. It's all feedback. *A vibrant, happy and healthy life, an inside job.*

2. A Present Focus

Mindful breath work is also a powerful way to connect to what is going on in the present moment.

Naturally, a present focus is related to an inner focus; whenever we focus inside, this automatically places us in the present. A present focus, however, also extends to being aware of what is going on around us, as well as the connections between what we observe in and around us.

Living mindfully with a present awareness supports us to:
- Recognise that learning about our self and world is an ongoing process, not a destination.
- Sharpen our sensory acuity of both the new and the familiar, to 'see' life, self, others more clearly, as if for the first time.
- Adopt curiosity and interest as healthful orientations that keep our brain alert to learn (versus a judgemental orientation that sparks fear).
- Energize us to action to adopt changes in the direction of living life with balance, wholeness and integrity.
- Accept change as a natural way in which we break free of rigid reactivity, defensive patterns, and the like.

In contrast, emotional overwhelm is often the result of raising our own anxiety by either ruminating on the past (tends to produce guilt-inducing thoughts), or worrying about the future (tends to produce anxiety-inducing thoughts).

Either way, it results in a huge waste of energy.

Mindless moments can also waste energy. We've probably all had moments when we performed some activity robotically, for example, laying our keys somewhere in the house and later not being able to find them. Mindless moments are ones in which life occurs without registering on our mind.

Naturally, the best antidote to mindless moments is a mindful practice of noticing new things in whatever situation you're in. Connecting to our breath in those moment grounds our connection to the moment, and to the power of our choices.

We always have a choice whether we respond as owners of the energy inside us (or feel controlled by it).

Noticing new things puts us in the here and now, and being engaged in the present produces an array of other benefits.

When we embrace our power to choose, we own the exercise of our choices, hopefully, seeing the power of our choices as a responsibility to make life in and around us more wonderful. Being present, curious and interested in the moment makes life exciting. This and more are the gifts of being alive in the moment.

Wondrously, nothing needs to be boring. By setting an intention to be in the present, we see the world with fresh eyes. We can see, hear, smell, feel or taste in the moment. We can observe, and not judge. We can whisper calming words to our self, such as "Now. Now. Now."

3. An Optimal State of Mind and Body

Mindful breathing is also a tool we can use to shift the energies inside us, as necessary, to create optimal emotional states. An optimal emotional state is, for our body, an optimal physiological state, a state in which life-enriching hormones nourish the cells of our body.

We have this inner capacity at hand to command these processes. It's not as easy as it sounds, however. It requires us to make choices in how we respond to life situations, at any given time, and to respond in new ways that may make us feel uncomfortable, especially at first.

Every aspect of our growth, however, consists of painfully stretching out of old comfortable places. We may be born with the equipment; however, the less we use or access our inner resources, the weaker they become.

It's not easy to learn to turn to these inner resources to soothe our mind and body. It takes conscious effort. Perhaps the toughest part is breaking free of the fear of letting go of old familiar patterns of dealing with what triggers us, linked to rigid beliefs about what 'should' happen in certain situations, and so on.

At first, it takes work, determined effort. Paradoxically, the more fun we have, however, the more we get comfortable, and learn to accept and to enjoy the process, the easier it becomes.

Where do we begin? Our thoughts.

Thoughts are energies that trigger emotional sources of energy that fire and wire neural patterns. Emotions shape our behaviors, and our choices, as they decide the overall direction of these energies inside. What think (perceive, believe, etc.) at any moment activates felt emotion-driven dynamic processes throughout our body that are either, in varying degrees, optimally healthful or detrimental to us, emotionally, physically and mentally.

If we ruminate on what we are not happy about in our life, for example, our mind automatically triggers fear-based emotions, such as anxiety and depression that, in turn, can keep our focus on what we lack. Unpleasant emotional states cause stress for the body, and prolonged stress leads to illness.

In contrast, we can use our breath to consciously calm our mind and body, to remain in the present moment, where we can make more informed and wise decisions—and self-directed changes.

We can choose to optimise our experience, or what we prefer to experience, in a given situation. We can make changes, for example, to consciously choose thoughts that energise positive physiological states, such as confidence or enthusiasm, compassion or gratitude.

By setting an intention to command our thoughts and create the optimal physiological states we want to produce throughout your body, we also prevent upsetting emotions from taking us out of the present moment. Our breath makes this process possible, and more easily achievable.

Amazingly, it becomes easier to remain connected empathically to our self and one another. We own the power to create the inner sense of safety and calm we need to express our compassionate nature, and to remain engaged in the moment, to allow our body and mind to work together, optimally, as they are wired to do. We can do so knowing we always have a choice at any given moment.

The Power of Your Intentions.

In sum, deep breathing is a life tool we have at hand to use, at any moment, to enhance the flow of energy between our mind and body.

Mindful breathing helps us regulate this life energy inside that, depending on the quality of our breathing, can make or break the inner sense of safety we need at any moment to allow our body and mind to optimally communicate, so they work together as a team.

The healthful effects of mindful breathing increase in proportion to the quality of our inner focus, our sense of presence in the moment, and our skill in maintaining an optimal emotional state.

Practicing presence means being aware of what is going on in and around us in the present moment, and having the ability, at the same time, to remain empathically connected to our experience in the present moment. This allows us to stay fully engaged, and in particular, to process any upsetting emotions as information or action signals – rather than allow them to activate our body's survival system.

Absent this connection to inner sources of nourishment, we human beings tend to get lost looking, perhaps in desperation, to find outside sources of this 'feel-good' in other persons, substances, food or activities, and so on.

We cannot fool our body for long, however. We are wired to seek to empathically 'connect' to something that gives us a deep and lasting sense of feeling safe enough to feel our love, our life and we, as a person, matters in life.

An addiction is perhaps a cry-for-help, a signal from our body (or subconscious mind) that it has lost control of its ability to regulate our body's energies via homeostasis, and that it's up to us to take the reins as captain of our life, mind and body and lead us out of shark infested waters, so to speak. Quick fix releases of the safety-and-love hormone, oxytocin, or the reward hormone, dopamine, will simply never work.

Neither will new wonder drugs to artificially stimulate the release of oxytocin or dopamine. Drugs are the best option for the industries, such as pharmaceutical, that stand to profit from them.

What a gift, it would be to welcome our breath instead, as a partner that supports us to remain calm and confident in our ability to take command of our emotional energies, and release these nourishing hormones naturally. We do so when we:

- Set an intention to access our breath regularly to connect to our experience of life from within. An inner focus helps us access the vital sources within that optimize our power to choose. A sense of choice and personal agency fulfills inner yearnings, thus, can spark the release of feel-good hormones.
- Set an intention to notice what is happening in present moments, to see and think of our self as a curious student of life, an observer, rather than a judge. A present awareness works together with an inner focus to help us replace the habit of rushing past the present moments of our life, a common experience in busy lives.
- Set an intention to reach for optimal emotional states, and accordingly, to refresh the energies of our mind and body, and to consciously release these healthful feel-good hormones. An optimal emotional state prevents upsetting emotions from grabbing us out of the present moment, and sending us to places of anxiety about the future, or guilt about the past.

  Perhaps, one of the most important skills we learn in life is how to manage (balance) the emotional energies of our body. It's also one of the most vital skills to teach to our children, as parents or teachers, or leaders in some capacity.

  Children need us, more than ever, to lead them to connect to their human nature and to the real sources of nourishment inside them that technology can never replace.

  A fulfilling life depends on cultivating this ability, and knowing we have the power to do so. We can lead the flow of energy within us in a direction that creates the optimal emotional state we need, in a given situation, to most support us to be at our best.

So, let your breath delight you, and turn most daily challenges into joyful, present moments of relative calm for your mind and body, as you grow confidence in nourishing your own growth, healing and transformation.

Fr. G. Narsilio's Effective and Inexpensive way of Controlling Diabetes

Years ago, I received the communication below which I share with my readers for whatever it may be worth:

In May 1988 I went to St. Isabel Hospital, Chennai for a hernia operation . To my surprise my blood sugar level was 411, very huge indeed. All my friends said the doctor would not operate . With tablets and insulin it was brought to normal and the operation was performed.

In 1990 I started thinking: if I had some strong emotion, some sad news, the lachrymal glands would be stimulated and tears would come abundantly. If I put a sweet in my mouth saliva is produced in plenty -- then if I could stimulate the insulin gland, insulin would produced and it would absorb the sugar in my system! I asked a nurse friend, where is the insulin gland? In the pancreas, she said, on the left side, below the lungs. Well, I started to vigorously shake my left side with the result that my blood sugar was brought under control without tablets. I took the last glynase tablet on 20th January, 1990. My last blood test in November 1992, Fasting 107, Post Prandial 131.

I now eat sugar, cakes and ice cream without any worry thanks to my therapy. Many of my friends here and abroad. Have benefited from this effective and inexpensive method.

I have written this article with the hope that it may have wide publicity and may be of help and relief to all those suffering from diabetes. ***Fr. G. Narsilio, SDB***
Chaplain
Government General Hospital
Madras-600 003

Method:
Put your left hand on the left side below the lung. Shake, massage vigorously right and left for 10 seconds. About 20 times a day. Insulin will flow from the gland and absorb the sugar in the blood. Time: when you eat cake, ice cream etc. and when you think of it. No limitation of time in the use of this therapy.

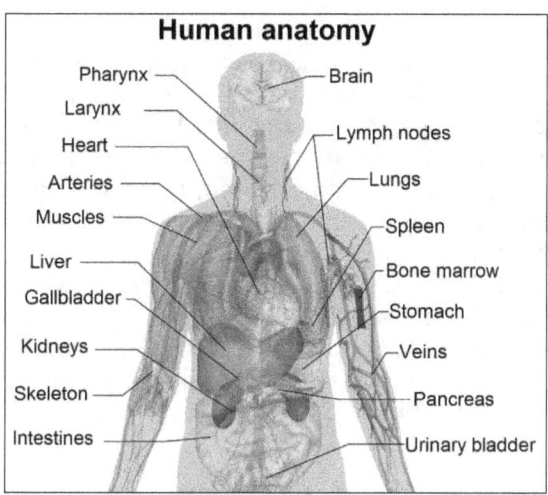

Develop a Leader's Mind

There are five essentials to optimising the health of your brain: *sleep, food, exercise, activity* and *positivity*.

1. Sleep
Sleep deprivation has been associated with events, such as the *Exxon Valdez Oil Spill*, the *Chernobyl Nuclear Disaster*, the *British Petroleum Oil Spill*, the *Union Carbide gas leak* and even the *Challenger Space Shuttle Crash*. More than 100,000 U.S. traffic accidents a year are attributed to *sleep deprivation*.

As a leader, it's vital to get enough sleep to function at your highest level. It is especially important for the prefrontal cortex, located in the front third of your brain, which is involved in CEO function: forethought, judgment, impulse control, organization, planning and learning from the mistakes you make. When there are problems with the prefrontal cortex, people have short attention spans. They get distracted; they're impulsive, disorganized and don't learn from their errors. It can cause some real trouble in their lives. These people tend to be brutally honest, which is usually not helpful and tends to drive away employees. (You should inhibit the first thought that comes into your head and think, Is this going to be helpful or hurtful in this situation?)

You can strengthen this part of your brain by getting good sleep. When *you don't get at least seven hours of sleep at night,* you have *low blood flow to the prefrontal cortex.* This leads to bad decision-making capability.

2. Exercise

Exercise benefits your brain in many ways—most essentially by increasing the blood flow and raising the *serotonin levels.*

The *emotional brain,* called the *limbic brain,* is involved with bonding, passion and motivation. When this area is unhealthy, you tend to get sad, negative, unmotivated, more socially isolated and less passionate. Exercise is amazing for this part of the brain, which relies on serotonin for proper function.

I recommend that you walk like you're late for 45 minutes, four times a week. Also lift weights twice a week because the amount of lean muscle mass on your body is associated with longevity and overall health. And you should do coordination exercises like tennis or dancing to keep your brain active in learning new skills.

3. Activity

Whenever you learn something new, your brain makes a new connection. So being a lifelong learner both physically and mentally is essential. Playing brain games can also be really helpful—try Words With Friends, Sudoku or crossword puzzles. There is also an online community at *TheAmenSolution.com* where they can test your brain and then give it fun exercises to optimise it.

As we age, too many of us allow our brains to become less active, which is why people have brain fog and memory problems. But you need to know: That fog is not normal. If you're having memory problems in your 40s, 50s, 60s—even your 80s—it's a sign that your brain is in trouble. But with a little forethought, you can slow or even reverse the aging process in your brain using the behaviors we've mentioned here. How cool is that?

4. Food

You have to avoid things that hurt your brain. It's not rocket science—actually it's some fairly sophisticated neuroscience. But one of the hardest things for people to avoid is the standard American diet. It's high calorie, low nutrition, filled with bad fat, lots of salt and sugar.

You probably know you should avoid this type of diet if you want to avoid being overweight. And two-thirds of us are; one-third are overweight enough to be classified as obese. It's a national crisis.

But diet isn't just about looking good. Eighteen studies now show that as your weight goes up, the size and function of your brain goes down. I always say, "That should scare the fat off anyone." **Obesity** is associated with *heart disease, diabetes, cancer, depression, Alzheimer's disease, cognitive dysfunctio*n and, now, a *smaller brain*.

Brain-healthy nutrition is critical. Food can make you focused, vibrant, happy and trim or unfocused, sluggish, sad and overweight. In general, I advise a diet high in antioxidants from fruits and vegetables and low in refined sugars. It should include high-fiber carbohydrates and a nominal amount of fat from sources like olive oil, walnuts and fish. In addition, at each meal and snack you should strive to consume lean protein, such as meat, cheese, eggs, soy or nuts.

And for your *brain's CEO*, the prefrontal cortex, the *protein in your diet helps to maintain a healthy blood sugar.* Low blood sugar, which occurs during fluctuations of a high-sugar, high-carbohydrate diet, contributes to low function in this area.

A large portion of your brain is made up of **DHA**, *a form of omega-3 fatty acids found in fish*. This fat helps your brain cells function properly, and it has been shown to promote a positive mood. **So indulge in fish weekly.**

There are a couple of areas of the brain that are particularly affected by your food choices, so let's take a look at those.

The brain's gear shifter, the *anterior cingulate gyrus*, is deep in the brain near the front. It helps you with flexibility and cooperation. It also helps you shift your attention, seize options, go with the flow and be creative. When there are problems in the ACG, it's usually due to low levels of a brain neurotransmitter called serotonin. People with low serotonin get stuck on thoughts; they worry, hold grudges and are rigid. They have to do things the same way, and they tend to focus on things that bother them. They are also argumentative and oppositional.

To fix this, or to help you be as flexible as you can, raise your serotonin level. *Eating smart carbohydrates will do this.* If you tend to be an over-focused person and you go on the Atkins Diet, which is high in protein-based fat, it makes you mean. You'll do much better augmenting your diet with sweet potatoes, vegetables, a little bit of fruit and some brown rice. Even some simple supplements can make a difference; if you tend to be a worrier, use St. John's wort. In some cases, pharmacologic support through antidepressants is needed, so consult your doctor if your symptoms are inhibiting your everyday life.

5. Positivity

It's important not to believe every stupid thought you have. I can't consistently eat well because I travel too much. I can't reduce stress because of my boss. My weight is in my genes. I can't start now because it's Friday. It's Saturday. Sunday, Monday, Tuesday, Wednesday, Thursday, etc. There's always an excuse to hurt yourself with poor choices. Getting rid of the little lies that make you sad, depressed and feeble-minded is crucial to staying well and staying motivated.

Here is a wonderful exercise to counter those negative thoughts that come into your mind automatically and ruin your day. Whenever you feel sad, mad, nervous or out of control, ask yourself what you're thinking, and then talk back to it, like you're a teenager talking back to your parents.

You need to get really good at talking back to the thoughts going on in your head because they're not protecting you; they're hurting you.

If you don't challenge and question that negativity, you believe it 100 percent and then act on it as if it's true. Instead, question, evaluate and then talk back. This technique has actually been found to be as effective as anti-depression medication for people with depression.

Again, your brain is the origin of your personality, character, intelligence and every decision you make. It rules your world. By making choices that create a healthy brain, you'll be happier, physically healthier, wealthier, wiser, and you'll make better decisions—all good traits for a great leader.

How to Influence Your Unconscious

This Betty Erickson's technique involves focusing on things you see, hear and feel in order to keep your conscious mind occupied so that it doesn't interfere with your unconscious mind as it works in the background to fulfill your goal for the session. Before fully describing the underlying principles of this technique, I'm going to list the steps involved to show how simple it is:

- Get in a comfortable position — Find a comfortable chair to sit in for the duration of the process. Then start breathing slowly, allowing yourself to become deeply relaxed.
- Determine the length of time for the session - 20 minutes is pretty standard, but you could go longer or shorter (15 or 30 minutes, for example).
- State your purpose for the session — Speaking out loud or inside your head, verbally state your goal. For example: "I'm

entering a special state of mind for 15 minutes for the purpose of allowing my unconscious mind to assist me in becoming very self confident (fill in the blank however you like)."

Then saying how you want to feel at the end of the session. I usually reinforce my goal by also including it in this sentence. "When I awake in 15 minutes, I will feel joyous, full of positive energy and very self-confident," for example. Or you might want to feel deeply relaxed at the end if bedtime is approaching. I usually only include three goals for my post-trance state, because I want to keep my mind focused on my main mission, but you could try including more.

Here's another example of how your statement of purpose might sound: "I'm entering a special state of mind for 20 minutes for the purpose of allowing my unconscious mind to assist me in becoming completely free of the need to smoke cigarettes. When I awake in 20 minutes, I will feel peaceful, committed to improving my health and completely free of the need to smoke cigarettes."

Experiment with different goals for your sessions. You might need assistance in becoming free of a particular obsessive/compulsive habit. For weight control, you could become committed to eating appropriate amounts of healthy food every day (adjust the language to your needs or liking).

Try simply feeling joyous if you're feeling down. Use the technique each morning with the intent of becoming very focused on working hard at your job today, and see how productive you become. As a professional writer, I always use it to become very focused on writing excellent stories on days when I have major assignments due, putting myself in the zone where all the right words speedily fall into place.

If I were using this technique to quit smoking or lose weight, I would employ it every day for reinforcement. Because so many people who quit smoking gain weight, you could consolidate goals into a single session: "I'm entering a special state of mind for 20 minutes for the purpose of allowing my unconscious mind to assist me in becoming completely free of the need to smoke cigarettes. When I awake in 20 minutes, I will feel balanced, committed to eating appropriate amounts of healthy food and completely free of the need to smoke cigarettes."

Immediately after you've made your statement of process, you're ready to begin the induction process.

- ☾ The Process – Looking in front of you, notice three things (one at a time) that you see. Go slowly, pausing for a short while on each. Look at small things, such as a spot on the wall, door knob, candle flame, crystal on the table, etc. Some people like to name the items as they look at them.

As you stare, focus all of your attention on the object's appearance and try to keep your mind as free of random thoughts as possible. Imagine any thoughts popping like bubbles if they float into your consciousness. (NOTE: It's okay if you can't completely still your mind of random thoughts. The process will still work. Just do the best you can.)

Now turn your attention to your auditory channel and notice, one by one, three things that you hear. You might notice the sound of a clock ticking, fan blowing, creak of a settling building, cars passing by outside, or birds chirping.

If it seems perfectly quiet in your particularly environment, notice the sounds of your breathing and swallowing, or create a sound by gently tapping your foot or clicking your teeth. Focus all of your attention on each sound for a short while. If it was just a momentary noise, replay it in your head a few times.

Next shift your attention to your physical being, and notice three sensations that you feel. Again, go slowly from one to the next. Try to use sensations that normally are outside of your awareness, such as the weight of your eyeglasses or the skin sensations created by a watch, piece of jewelry, article of clothing, hair on your forehead or neck, the soles of your shoes, your lips touching, etc. Even focus on an itch if you feel one.

Repeat the process with two different objects, two different sounds and two different feelings.

Repeat the cycle once again using one different object, one different sound and one different feeling.

At this point, you've completed the "external" portion of the process. Now it's time to begin the "internal" part by closing your eyes.

Imagine one small thing you see. Use whatever pops into your head (a leaf, diamond, toothbrush, etc.) and focus all of your attention on it for a short while.

Then imagine one thing you hear. It could be a part of a song or the sound of a lawnmower, whistle, running water, etc. Though this is technically the "internal" part of the process, feel free to use an actual environmental one if it comes to the forefront of your attention. It's better to incorporate such a noise than be distracted by it.

Next, imagine one thing you feel. You could think of the feelings created by the sun on your nose, wet sand under your toes, a kiss on the lips, dental floss between your gums, a razor shaving your face or legs, etc. Try your best to focus all of your attention on these sensations as if they were actually happening. Again, if an actual physical sensation comes to your attention, feel free to use that.

Repeat the process with two different images, two different sounds, and two different feelings.

Repeat the cycle once again using three different images, three different sounds, and three different feelings.

Then you're done. Open your eyes and go about your day. You'll often find that your body's internal clock works so well that you're done exactly at the end of the allotted amount of time. But even if you're a little over or under your desired period, it doesn't matter.

Regular practice will yield better and better results!

Why it Works

This is a state of concentrated, focussed attention. If you've ever found yourself intensely involved in a book, piece of music or television program, you might have entered a naturally occurring state of mind. Procedures for doing so typically involve moving away from the environment around us and turning our attention inward. The *Erickson Technique* accomplishes this by moving from actual environmental sights, sounds and feelings to imagined ones.

In many effective procedures, participants enter a trance and then give themselves suggestions via the conscious mind. However, a guiding principle of the *Erickson Technique* is that understanding by the conscious mind is unnecessary for change. As advocates of this technique have noted, if your conscious mind knew what to do about particular problems, you wouldn't need the procedure at all.

In fact, your conscious mind often gets in the way of change, saying things like "I can't..." or "I don't know how to...." The Erickson technique described above is designed to keep the conscious mind occupied so that it won't interfere while your unconscious mind is doing the work you requested.

The *Erickson Technique* takes full advantage of the power and resourcefulness of your unconscious mind, which has learned a tremendous amount during your lifetime(s) and can apply this knowledge for you in hypnosis. While your conscious mind can only process so much information at a time, your unconscious mind is not so limited. It can think holographically and is capable of finding better solutions for you than your conscious mind.

The reason why the *Erickson Technique* requires you to focus on things you see, hear and feel is not only to keep your conscious mind occupied, but also to help you enter an altered state. We process information (or think) in pictures, sounds and feelings. In Neurolinguistic Programming, these sensory modalities are referred to as representational systems: visual, auditory and kinesthetic (feeling).

Most of us have developed greater proficiency with one particular system, even though we each use all three of them. Therefore, the individual who thinks primarily in images wouldn't experience an altered state of consciousness simply by visualizing.

However, if that same individual were to experience a preponderance of feelings or sensations, this would be unusual - an alteration of their state of consciousness. An altered state simply refers to processing information in a different manner than usual.

I highly encourage anyone reading this page to give this technique at least several tries. It can change your life! You may find that the effects of the procedure in some areas (self-confidence, for example) wear off over time.

If you find results fading away sooner than you'd like, experiment with placing a time frame when stating your principal goal (for the next day, week, even year). Don't be discouraged. Just keep repeating the process until desired changes become a permanent part of your mind's programme.

The technique is also effective for short-term goals, such as being focussed on a particular project that you wish to let go of upon completion. You mind will know when it's time to shift into another mode. You're still in control.

In quick review, the process goes like this...

After making your statement of purpose, notice and focus on:
- Three things you see, three things you hear, and three things you feel.
- Two things you see, two things you hear, and two things you feel.
- One thing you see, one thing you hear, and one thing you feel.

Then close your eyes, imagining and focussing on:
- One thing you see, one thing you hear, and one thing you feel.
- Two things you see, two things you hear, and two things you feel.
- Three things you see, three things you hear, and three things you feel.

How your Reticular Activating System Helps You Achieve Your Goals

You've heard it time and time again — write down your goals as it will increase the chances of your achieving those goals. Some state that they can keep their goals in their head. However, there is research that shows that when you write your goals down and post them in visible places to remind yourself of those goals, you will be more able to achieve those goals.

The reality is that we only have a limited amount of energy and attention to direct toward our goals.

Evolutionary speaking, our brain is designed to conserve energy. We're either focusing on 1) dealing with threats in our environment and learning how to put out fires, or 2) focussing on ways to master our environment and work toward higher order goals that are important to our well-being.

Obviously with goal achievement, we are more interested in the latter, - learning how to master our environment by achieving our goals, because it brings us pleasure, rewards, life satisfaction and of course some degree of security as well.

A key factor that prevents us from staying focused on our goals, and achieving those goals is that it's hard to direct our attention on those goals *all the time* or often enough. There are so many distractions and demands in our every day life, that it seems almost impossible to stay focussed at times. Our RAS helps make this process of paying attention and being focused a little bit easier.

Specifically, research in goal setting and motivation states that our arousal systems help us focus on our goals. The reason we have arousal systems to begin with is that evolution has hard wired us to conserve energy, and we are only meant to be aroused when we have a concrete reason — protecting our safety in some fashion or increasing our resources in some way.

Our brain only gets super focused if and when it needs to, otherwise, just like a computer, one could argue that it goes to sleep and does the minimal amount of work needed. When a person has no clear goals, doesn't write their goals down and doesn't have plans to achieve those goals, their level of goal arousal, passion and overall enthusiasm is low. As a result, they do not recognise or identify the people, opportunities, situations or resources that could be helpful to them.

How do we increase our levels of arousal to help us achieve our goals? By learning how to activate your **Reticular Activating System (RAS)** which is part of your cortical arousal system, you can increase your chances of being much more efficient with your goals.

So what role does writing our goals down play in helping us to achieve our goals? By writing down your goals and your plans for achieving your goals, you learn to focus your attention on what really matters. Doing so gets your reticular activation system aroused and working in your favour.

How does this work? When you write down your goals, you make a point of being specific with a direction that is important for you to move in. You pinpoint specific destinations that you want to move toward, and the specific steps that you need to take to get there.

As you get in touch with what is exciting and rewarding to you, you increase your levels of arousal, and become crystal clear about what matters. As you are doing this, your reticular activating system in your cortex is aroused and promotes you being ready and alert to respond to cues in the environment that are relevant to your goals. When the RAS is activated, we can process and reorganize information much more efficiently in ways that support our achievement of goals.

A classic yet simplified example of your RAS working would be when you identify an article of clothing that you would like to purchase. You try on a beautiful blouse and you write down the size, brand, colour and store where you found it. In the mean time, as you are waiting for it to go on sale, you see other people wearing that blouse because now you are primed to spot it! You'll also recognize similar types of blouses perhaps by other designers. Your brain is automatically aroused when it notices this blouse because you have indicated that it is something important to you. The same thing happens when you identify a new car that you want to buy. You begin to notice that car everywhere, because you've signalled the importance of this car to your brain.

To learn strategies and tips on the how to activate your RAS to support your goal setting and achievement efforts, read these tips on visualisation!

Visualisation need not be complicated, artsy and all creative. Many people including myself find it too tedious to do the traditional imaginative exercises in our heads.

We lose concentration, we fall asleep, or for some other reason it just doesn't appeal to us.

So, here are some great ideas for the logical person who still wants the benefits of visual exercises, without having to imagine pictures in one's head.

Practical Visualisation Techniques

1. Print off a nicely organised list of your goals, or action steps for a particular goal, and then **put your goals in a nice picture frame!**

    Place this frame somewhere that you will see it every single day. How's that for a nice visual?

    Rather than having your goals written on some piece of paper or notebook shoved in a drawer, now you have them up on display! You can get as obsessed as you want with this technique.

    You might have several different frames up, each entailing a list of action steps for your various goal projects. Or, you might have several frames up, each with the big picture objectives of your various goal categories.

2. **Buy a really attractive or appealing greeting card** from your local store. Inside that card, write out all your goals, or again, the actions steps for a particular goal.

    Keep this pretty card sitting on your night table, on your desk, or even posted on your fridge, wall or bulletin board. Whenever you have a spare minute, read through your goals and action steps.

    By writing your goals and action steps in a beautiful card, it ensures that you don't shove the card in a drawer where it will get lost.

    So since you write your goals down on something that you paid several dollars for, you are more likely to keep that card in an easily accessible, visible location.

3. **Put your goals and actions onto your computer's screen saver or regular desktop background.** How's that for a constant visualisation reminder?

4. Program one of your big goals onto the **face-top of your cell phone!**

5. Forget showing off your driver's licence **picture in your wallet.** Instead, use that visual space to insert a printed version or a picture of what is most important for you to focus on completing right now! Maybe, you might even put a motivational quote or reminder in there.

Breathing Techniques

6. **Use Post-it sticky notes** to write down all the action steps needed for one of your current life projects. Post it right beside your desk where you work most often. This way, whenever you encounter a lull in motivation or a barrier, you will constantly be reminded of the steps that you need to execute to continue on with your goal.

    Often, when people run into barriers with their goals, they become foggy-minded, fooled, and disillusioned about their reality of what is happening. Soon, their fear and negative emotions paralyse them. Then, they forget what they need to do or try next to get started again. Don't let the bumps in the road cause you to forget what to try next. Have this post-it of action steps on your wall so you are always have a visualisation to remind you of what you need to do.

7. **Use the power of email!** Email yourself and in the subject title, simply write an action step or goal. Don't ever delete this email until you have completed the action or achieved the goal. Every time you log in to your email, you will be reminded of your goals or action steps!

8. **Create a vision board!** Buy a bulletin board from Walmart, and hang it somewhere visible. Then, cut out pictures that symbolize what you want to do, be and have in your life.

    You can even post real pictures of you that show you achieving your goals. Keep on the look out of inspirational pictures in magazines, the newspapers, etc. Clip them out and post them on your board.

9. **Use a whiteboard!** using the dry erase markers that easily are wiped off, you can write your to-do list on here for the day, week, or month. Organise it however you want, but keep it somewhere you can see every single day.

10. **Use a scrapbook!** If you want a more private medium, then you can store all your visuals in a book. However, keep this book right by your bedside table. In the morning and/or evening, pull out your scrapbook, and flip through all the pictures as reminders.

11. Buy a **hardcover, spiral bound journal of medium size — one that is really beautiful with nice designs on the pages.** Buy a nice bookstand or picture stand, and place your journal on it.

    As your goals or to-do lists change, simply turn the page, update your list, and put back on your display stand! I love this one, and I keep mine sitting right on my desk by my monitor.

    So, now you have a good handful of visualization techniques that do not involve lying down and listening to relaxational music. These are practical, and tangible strategies that are guaranteed to boost your productivity, keep you focused, and give you all the benefits of traditional visualization!

Here are Some Questions to Leave You With:

1. What other visual symbols or tangible items could I put in my environment to remind me of my goals and required action steps?
2. What visual strategies have motivated me, or kept me focused on my goals in the past?
3. What do I have the most difficulty imagining or 'seeing' in terms of my success? How can I find a real visible snapshot of this?

3 Quick Stress-Releasing Techniques for the Busy Professional

Technique #1: The Waterfall
This technique takes only a minute or less and is a powerful stress reliever. Take a deep breath. Imagine a relaxing waterfall of energy either in front or behind you (whichever feels best to you). Imagine this waterfall is flowing with healing, relaxing energy. You might imagine it as cool or warm water, as a stream of air, or simply soft, relaxing energy. However you want to imagine it is perfect. You might see it in your mind's eye, or feel it, or simply know that it is there. Now imagine that you step into this beautiful flowing waterfall of relaxing energy and it flows from the to of your head all the way down your body, flowing over your shoulders, your back, your stomach, your legs, all the way down to the bottoms of your feet, and down to the center of the earth.

The Waterfall Technique is powerful and helpful if you need a quick pick-me-up. You can flesh out the background, too. For ultimate stress relief, maybe you imagine you're in a tropical forest or on a gorgeous beach. You can imagine lush surroundings that are relaxing and comforting to you to round out your refreshing hypnosis experience.

Technique #2: Breathing
Another super quick and easy technique is (yes, you guessed it!) breathing. Simple deep breathing is one of the best starting points for any hypnosis technique (see technique #1). Begin by suggesting to yourself to just breathe. As soon as you give yourself this suggestion, you might notice that you take a deeper breath than your last one. Imagine that you can fill both lungs all the way to

capacity, letting the air reach even the bottom region of your lungs. You can also imagine that you can breathe into remote body parts, like your feet or your hands. Imagine that you can breathe into a sore spot in your body and revitalize that spot with the cleansing fresh oxygen. This is the easiest hypnosis technique of them all, and the best stress buster in you only have a few seconds.

Technique #3: The Mini Power Nap
This technique takes about 5 minutes or less, but the power in it is amazing. If you're feeling tired, run down, or generally lethargic, this is the technique for you! You'll need a quiet place to sit or lie down for just five minutes. If you're very tired, sitting might be better so that you don't fall asleep (The procedure is so very relaxing!).

Start by taking a deep, cleansing breath, and notice any tension in your body. Give yourself the suggestion that any and all tension can simply let go, and in it's place, direct a relaxing flow of energy to ease and relax your body. Bring you attention to your breathing, and imagine that you can bring yourself to the center of your being. You might imagine a beautiful garden or a powerful guide at your side or a safe cave at the center of your being. Anything that makes you feel good, safe, and centered is perfect setting.

Now give yourself the simple suggestion that you have five (or four or three) minutes for a super-charged hypnosis power nap. You might say to yourself, "I have this time here and now to allow myself a relaxing power nap to recharge and energize my mind, body, and spirit." Let your eyes close and keep following your breath down to the center of your being. Allow this self hypnosis technique to relax your eyes and your mind. Tell yourself that it's OK to let go and allow relaxation to flow through you for this short hypnosis power nap. Keep suggesting that this is a hypnosis power nap, and that when you are ready to open your eyes, you will feel refreshed, recharged and energized.

And there you have it! Three simple and easy to learn stress relieving techniques that you can do almost anywhere and any time. Use each technique as you are inspired for easy and quick stress relief.

Simple Steps to a Goal-Directed Relaxation
This is useful for boosting your confidence, encouraging yourself towards a healthier lifestyle and improving your performance. Follow these basic steps to help you move towards your desired goals:

1. Think about what you want to achieve or change, and state your goal in a single sentence.
2. Choose a place where you can be completely comfortable, whether sitting in a chair or lying down.
3. Set a time limit by mentally giving yourself the following suggestion: 'Exactly ten minutes from now, my eyelids open automatically and I feel calm, rested and refreshed.'
4. Close your eyes and take a few deep breaths. Progressively relax all your muscles, from head to toe, or toe to head, whichever you prefer.
5. Count down from ten to one and tell yourself that with each number you'll become more relaxed, both physically and mentally, and go deeper into trance.
6. When you're in a deepened trance state, start using the goal statement you devised for your session. Remember your single sentence goal statement, and make it as vivid as possible in your imagination. Then simply let go. Trust that you have handed it over to your unconscious mind, and that this wise part of you will now solve the problem.
7. Count yourself awake, up from one to ten, and tell yourself that you're no longer in trance.
8. A few minutes after awakening, you are still in a highly suggestible state. Use that time to reinforce how relaxed and calm you feel, and how pleased you are that your unconscious mind is helping you reach your goal.

Personal Growth Technique

This technique for personal growth is based on the principle that increased awareness leads to beneficial changes and increased integration of the individual. *The method combines ancient methods of meditation with modern techniques of psychology.*

PRELIMINARIES
1. **TIME AND PLACE**
   Select a quiet place where you can sit comfortably for a maximum of about 15 minutes once or twice daily. This is best practiced when the stomach is not full, early morning or late in the evening.
2. **POSTURE**
   Sit with spine erect as this facilitates awareness. The crossed-legged posture is best. Be flexible and not rigid(check this by swaying from side to side).

Breathing Techniques

3. **SELECTION OF A RELEASE-WORD**

    Select a word (or a combination of a few words) which puts you at ease and gives you a feeling of security. Do not change this frequently. For example, you may use the word, *peace, or release*. If you are religious, you can use the word God or the name of a god.

The Actual Practice

Step 1:

Become aware of external disturbances and how they affect you, particularly, listen to sounds.

Step 2:

Become aware of your body. Feel the sensations (tension, pains, heaviness, etc.) from head to foot. Become aware of how bodily sensations affection your mind. When you practise alone, initially, you can select each part of the body one by one, move that part, contract and release muscles in that area two or three times and also massage that area gently with your own hands, to increase awareness. This need not be done every day, especially after a few days of practice.

Step 3:

Become aware of your breathing rhythm. Feel the breath coming in and breathing rhythm and your present state of the mind. Deliberately take three to five slow and deep breaths, pausing for a comfortable period of time after each inhalation and each exhalation.

Step 4:

Become aware of your mind (thoughts and feeling). Observe thoughts coming and going in an associated sequence. Do not try to control or alter the *nature, content or speed of thoughts*. Recognise how thoughts keep coming and associated thoughts feelings arise, disturbing you. Do not deliberately start raking up or following any line of thought. Thoughts keep coming and get desensitised automatically.

Step 5:

Fix awareness on the Release-Word you have selected. You can repeat it a few (say, three to five) times in your mind, at a leisurely pace, gradually reducing the intensity and speed. This word (by auto-suggestion) will automatically pop up in your mind gently and bring your mind back to pure awareness when your mind starts going along any chain of thoughts in the next last step. You are strengthening a path from thoughts to pure consciousness.

Step 6:
>Here you do nothing. Let go totally. Do not desire, expect, deliberately look for, evaluate or try to become aware of anything. Do not try to control the mind. Do not use force or feel guilty of thoughts. When thoughts come, again the Release-Word, by association with the process of thoughts, will spontaneously appear in the mind, cutting the chain of thoughts. As the sequence of thoughts — Release-Word — stillness repeats itself, by gradual practice, and you will experience increasingly longer periods of stillness or pure awareness.

SEQUENCE OF THE SIX STEPS
There is no overlap of the six steps. For example, once you end step 1, after paying attention to external sounds, you do not have to pay any further attention to external sounds, and you do not have to pay any further attention to andy kinds of sounds. Similarly, once you close step 3 where you attend to breath and take a few deep breaths, you need not pay any further attention to how you are breathing during the following steps. Once you close step 5, where you attend to the Release-Word, you need not think of or intentionally take up the *Release-Word again*.

DURATION OF THE DIFFERENT STEPS
The total time for the whole practice need not exceed 15 minutes in one sitting. It is the quality which counts. Initially, the relative duration of the earlier steps have to be longer and day by day the duration of the earlier steps can be reduced and later steps can be increased (of course, keeping the total time 15 minutes or less). In step 6, stop if you feel increasing restlessness or that further sitting does not lead to further increase in the quality of pure awareness. By gradual practice, you will know how much time to spend on each step and how you can profitably reduce the time spent on earlier steps and increase the time on later steps.

PRECAUTIONS
If you have an improper lifestyle *(check physical, social and psychological aspects)*, you may experience increasing tension or feeling of disintegration when you practise this. If you experience any kind of distress, or you are in doubt, temporarily discontinue.

Take a *vegetarian diet with a high proportion of raw things*. Have p*roper, moderate physical exercise*. Avoid *intoxicants*. Correct any defect that you may have in your dealings with other people or in your value system. Take up the HIT practice again after you have attained the initial stability required for the practice.

Breathing Techniques

The Light Channelling Technique

"When a large number of people meditate, proven experiments state that it facilitates creation of peace," says Raghavendra Somayaji, who works at a study centre, researching spiritual realities at the Manasa Foundation created by Swami Krishnananda to enable individuals to achieve self-transformation via meditation. In this regard, Somayaji cites a research paper written on the worst of the Lebanese civil war in 1981 that showed that a small village in Lebanon was able to reduce war fatalities and bombing in the area after the village population began meditating.

Keeping that in mind, Swami Krishnananda decided to device a simple meditation technique called Light Channelling and introduced it in May 2008. When the brutal 26/11 terror attack struck India's financial capital, Mumbai, a few months later, Swami Krishnananda was inspired to take the "Light Channels World Movement" to a wider audience, assisting creation of peace.

Somayaji, who was in the IT industry for a long time, working in the UK until 2004, had begun practising meditation in 1995, under the guidance of Swami Krishnananda. When he returned to Bangalore in 2004, he continued working for an IT firm, but decided to quit in 2005 and joined Swami Krishnananda's Manasa Foundation, with the intent to serve in any possible capacity.

The Light Channelling technique, says Somayaji, is non-religious: "As air is around for everybody to breathe, light, too, is available for all, irrespective of religious or other affiliations." The intention is straightforward: To spread love, peace and harmony on this earth. "The impact is more when many channel the light, more so when many do it at the same time," says Somayaji.

Giving details of the technique, Usha Satishchandra, a light channelling expert who took voluntary retirement after teaching at various schools in the city for 20 years says, "It requires the practitioner to imagine light coming from the source of creation, descending and filling your body, and spreading gradually around you (your home/neighbourhood, city, country and the world at large)."

She stresses that 'intent' of the individual practising it is of utmost importance.

In an attempt to spread the word, Manasa Foundation's volunteers have been taking it to schools across the country. "Children are innocent, don't carry baggage and don't intellectualise the process and thus the impact is far more," says Somayaji. Convent schools,

Muslim ones, government and other schools have been forthcoming, making it possible for these light messiahs to aid healing of the earth. "Initially, we were apprehensive about the way they'd perceive us. Surprisingly, the response from schools has been phenomenal. We clearly state that it's completely non-religious," says Somayaji, "And we do it for free, though we incur costs on printing materials (freely distributed there) to enable easy practice at home."

Light Channelling Technique

Imagine an ocean of Light above you.
Imagine the Light descending and filling up your body.
Experience the Love and Peace of the Light for a minute.

Then, imagine the Light spreading around gradually to your home, locality, country and the whole world.

Golden Cock Stand on One Leg — Jin Ji Du Li

I got this information on e-mail from a friend of mine. It was all about some kind of self-help exercise which was a simple but very effective health exercise, very simple. The essence of the exercise is that your "Eyes Must be Closed" when you are doing this exercise. You must practise the *Jin Ji Du Li*"exercise with the eyes closed. This exercise was so simple and amazing that I thought I had to share it here.

Here is the exercise:

Stand on one leg while your eyes are closed. That is all. Just try it right now, stop reading and stand up, close your eyes and try standing on one foot.

If you are not able to stand for less than 10 seconds, it means that your body has degenerated to 60 to 70 years old level in other words, you may be only 40 years old, but your body has aged a lot faster.

I tried this exercise myself when I read the mail. I thought "oh, big deal, I'm sure I can do this easily" I was fooling myself, I'm glad I tried it because I discovered much to my surprise that while I could stand easily on one foot with my eyes open, trying the same thing with my eyes closed was another story! I just could not keep my balance for more than two to three seconds before I started wobbling and hopping around and gave up altogether.

You do not need to lift your leg high, if your internal organs are out of synch, even lifting your leg this bit will make you wobble.

Now this was quite scary because it told me that my body was almost 60 years old and here was me, barely into my forties! These Chinese are really very advanced in their knowledge of the human body. It was very heartening to know that frequent and regular practice can help you recover your sense of balance. In fact, the Chinese specialists suggest daily practice of *Jin Ji Du Li* for 1 minute, which helps prevent *dementia*.

You can try slightly closing both your eyes, while practising *Jin Ji Du Li*, instead of completely closing them; in fact this is what the health specialist *Zhong Li Ba Ren* recommends.

Daily practice of *Jin Ji Du Li*, can help in healing many illnesses or diseases like

- Hypertension,
- High Blood Sugar or Diabetes,
- Neck and Spinal Diseases,
- It can also prevent you from getting Dementia.

Zhong Li Ba Ren has written a book titled 'Self Help is Better than Seeking Doctors' Help', which is a best-selling book that has been the best-seller health book in China since it was first published. Its success can be measured by the fact that it has been reprinted 12 times within six months, with more than 1 million copies sold. The book is a hot-seller because it teaches many simple practical health tips.

It is said that according to the understanding of Chinese physicians, diseases appear in the body because the coordination between the various internal organs encounter problems and that causes the body to lose its balance. *Jin Ji Du Li* can read just this interrelationship of the organs and how they function with each other. Zhong Li Ba Ren stated that many people can't stand on one foot with their eyes closed for even 5 seconds, but later on as they practise it daily, are able to stand for more than 2 minutes.

As you gain ability to stand for longer time, the feeling of "head heavy, light feet" disappears. As benefits or practising *Jin Ji Du Li*, you will experience that the quality of sleep improves, the mind clears up and memory improves significantly. Most importantly, if you can practise *Jin Ji Du Li* with your eyes closed for 1 minute every day, you will not get *dementia*. (I think this also means the brain will remain healthy).

Zhong Li Ba Ren explained that there are six important meridians passing through our legs. When you stand on a single leg, the weak meridian will feel sore while getting the necessary exercise, and as this happens, the corresponding organs of these meridians and their pathways, start getting the necessary tuning. This method can focus or concentrate the awareness, and channel the body's *qi* to the foot. The beneficial effects of practising *Jin Ji Du Li* on various illnesses associated with *hypertension, diabetes, neck* and *spinal* diseases are quick to be seen and felt. *Jin Ji Du Li* can also prevent gout.

Jin Ji Du Li helps to strengthen the body immunity rapidly.

Jin Ji Du Li it is suitable for everyone generally. It is the basic cure for "Cold Feet Disease" and it can also strengthen the body's immunity. You do not have to wait until you have any illness to start practising Jin Ji Du Li. It is especially beneficial for young people, when they practise it daily, while they are healthy, so that their chances of contracting the various illnesses associated with ageing is comparatively lower.

Please note that it is not suitable for people over 70 years old, or those old people, whose legs are not strong and cannot stand steadily.

How To De-Stress Fast

How To De-Stress Fast Technique
1. Lightly place your finger tips on your "O' My God!" Points (the Neurovasculars), one inch above the eyebrows. You can also put your elbows on a table and 'hold your head in your hands.'
2. Place your thumbs on your temples next to your eyes.
3. Breath and notice the blood (pulsing) returning to your forebrain, enabling you to think more calmly and clearly. This can usually be done in less than five minutes.
   You can of course hold other peoples Neurovasculars to help them de-stress fast.

Some Suggested Uses:
Decision Making: Holding 'the points' is a good idea before making any big decisions you need to make because you will keep the blood in the forebrain, enabling you to think things through more clearly.

Before Exams: Most people have some anxiety when giving an exam. Hold the neurovasculars before the exam for five minutes, while thinking about actually being sitted in the exam room.

Before A Date: Got a hot date that's making you a bit nervous?! Before you go out, maybe in the bath or shower, do the *How To De-*

Stress Fast Technique for a few minutes, while thinking about the date.

Before Phone Calls: Do you have to make an annoying phone call, maybe a billing mistake or something. Sit down and hold 'your points' for a few minutes before picking up the phone.

Before Sleeping: This is a great idea, that I personally use every night. Simply lay in bed and hold your neurovasculars, allowing you a more settled mind before sleeping.

Before Meditating: It's a really good idea to hold 'the points' before you meditate because it calms you down and balances your brain hemispheres giving rise to an easier meditation.

Before Paying Bills: Bills can be stressful, especially when there is a pile of them! Sit down and do the Stress Fader, while thinking about the stack of bills.

At The Airport: Airports have become more stressful in recent times due to the sheer volume of people and of course, the stringent security and safety checks. While waiting, why not hold your neurovasculars to help remain calm and balanced. You could go in the rest-room for more privacy.

Before Work: Hold 'your points' before you go to work. You could think about certain stressful aspects of work to re-program your response to them. If needed, you could also rebalance yourself during breaks.

Instant Peace of Mind Is Now In Your Hands! (Well, Within 5 Minutes.)

So now you know how to de-stress fast. Be sure to give it a go because once you've experienced the results I'm confident you'll wonder how you ever managed without it before. It's a remarkably simple and effective technique. It could be easy to dismiss it. Please check it out because I and many others have found it to be very useful in situations where nothing else was working. Remember when, blood is back in your forebrain, you have access to much more of the mind's resources!

How To Solve Relationship Problems With A Jedi Mind Trick

Wouldn't you agree that in any interaction between two people, there are two points of view, right? Well, yes, that's true and there is also a third point of view: Imagining the two of you over there interacting with each other.

These points of view can be called 'Perceptual Positions:'

1st Position (Associated or Self-Perspective)
Seeing the situation through your own eyes. You are primarily aware of your own thoughts and feelings.

2nd Position (Other Person Perspective)
Imagining what it is like to be the another person in the interaction. Imagine stepping into their body, seeing through their eyes, hearing through their ears, feeling their feelings and thinking their thoughts.

3rd Position (Disassociated Perspective, Neutral or Meta Position)
Take a detached viewpoint. Imagine you are looking at yourself and the other people in the situation, 'over there'. Try different 'camera angles' to gain new understandings. You could also take the perceptual position of God, Infinite Intelligence etc. for an interesting angle.

You actually shift between these points of view already at an unconscious level, but with conscious intent and practice you can learn how to solve relationship problems more quickly by gaining empathy, insight and rapport with the other person.

Have you ever had the experience of being in an argument with someone and found yourself dumbfounded by the other persons reaction?

Go ahead and think about one of those situations now and run through the following 'Jedi Mind Trick.' I think you might be surprised by what revelations come up!

How To Solve Relationship Problems With *A Jedi Mind Trick*

Think of a time when you were in a situation with other people and you didn't and still don't understand their perspectives on whatever issues were discussed. (Examples: A meeting, an argument with someone etc.)

Now run through this situation from 1st Position. This means looking at the situation through your own eyes and hearing through your own ears. Notice your feelings and any thoughts you have about it.

Next step inside one of the other people present (2nd Position). Literally imagine being in their body looking out of their eyes. So of course you will be able to see yourself. Notice your feelings as you see and hear from this perspective. Become aware of any new learnings!

Now move to the 3rd position. Remember, this is the 'neutral position.' It's kind of as if you are a camera observing everything. See/hear yourself and the others and notice any new learnings you can observe.

Try changing 'camera angle.' You can get almost limitless, new perspectives. How about, "Getting above it all?", "A birds eye view?"

If you've gone through the process, you'll have new insights into yourself and you will have a better understanding of others too! Sometimes this technique can be quite a revelation, seeing yourself as others see you enables you to change your behaviour to something more appropriate, if necessary.

Keep in mind - If you want another person to change, it's better and easier to change your own behaviour!

Enhance Well-Being With 5-Minute Practices

Your Thoughts--Simple Mindfulness Exercise

Try this experiment, whether for an hour, a day, a week or more. I think you will find it interesting.

Be mindful of your thoughts and take note of every time you are focussing on something you don't like or want. When you catch yourself focussing on what you don't like or want, immediately replace it with what you do like or want. It is akin to brushing off a red hot cinder before it burns.

You'll be surprised on how often you think of the things you don't like and/or want. The good news is, being aware is the first step to changing the pattern.

Top Ten Relaxation Techniques Exercises For Busy People

Practising relaxation technique exercises is essential these days if you want to keep your sanity. But with the hustle and bustle of daily life, it can be difficult to find the time to chill-out. However, the following relaxation techniques only take a few minutes to do and will enable you to experience more peace of mind:

One: Part of You is Relaxed now...
A. Close your eyes and become aware of where the most relaxed part of your body is?
B. Imagine spreading this feeling throughout your body, from the top of your head to the tip of your toes.

C. Enjoy cycling through these relaxing feelings by starting again at step A.

Two: Slow Down Your Internal Voice

We often stress ourselves with internal critical voices. A simple and effective way to reduce the suffering caused by inner voices is to slow them down.

A. Pick one of those critical internal voices that annoy you from time to time.
B. Notice it's location in space and what it says to you.
C. Now hear what it says again except this time slow it's delivery down. Way down. Repeat the sentence and slow it down even more.
D. Do this a few times until it's really slow and notice how you feel more relaxed!

Three: Re-Access Relaxation

A. Have you ever felt relaxed or at least at ease, maybe, it was on a beach or in a beautiful woodland.
B. Re-access the peaceful state by remembering what you saw, what you heard and smelt and allow those relaxing feelings to arise again.
C. Just sit with those pleasant feelings for a few minutes, and that will serve the purpose.

Four: Relaxing Music

A. Where do you want to be more relaxed? Notice what you see and hear just before you would want to feel a wave of relaxation. eg) The office door
B. If I were to ask you what some of your favourite relaxing music was then what would it be?
C. Hear that relaxing music, nice and clear inside your mind and allow those pleasant feelings to arise.
D. Now think of the trigger you choose in Step A and while hearing the music in your mind, imagine walking into the situation.
E. Do this a few times to 'wire it in' and you could even do this on a few other situations, where relaxation would be useful.

Five: Spinning the Movie Backwards

Our peace of mind can get disturbed by memories. Here is technique that enables us to neutralise negative emotions associated with troublesome memories.

A. Remember an occasion where you got annoyed. Maybe, somebody made a remark that did upset you a bit.

B. Imagine re-viewing it from the beginning to the end. Freeze-frame it at the end.
C. Pick some funny music. Cartoon? Circus or music?
D. Now reverse the movie: That is play it backwards from the end to the beginning with the funny music playing.

When you play the movie backwards, make it so as it's faster than normal reality because it adds to the humour!

Six: *A Walk in Nature*

This one's a simple, time-tested gold nugget. Get yourself out into nature. It may just be a park in the city with some trees. Observe nature. The sounds, the smells, etc. Become curious at the wonder of it all. Is it possible to be aware of all your senses at once?

Seven: *Shapeshift into the Wind*

A. Step outside and become aware of the wind.
B. As you notice its presence and shifting patterns, allow yourself to 'shapeshift' into the wind. Simply imagine you have become one with the wind.
C. Close your eyes and indulge yourself in this moment now.

Eight: *Imagining Your More Relaxed Self*

A. If you were more relaxed now what would that look like out there in front. It's OK if this is only 5% of the relaxation you need because this is about going in a relaxing direction, isn't it?
B. Notice what that you look like, your posture, your breathing, your facial expression, etc.
C. Now imagine stepping into that more relaxed, 'you'.
D. Repeat from step A.

Nine: *Hakalau*

This a really interesting technique that comes from the **Hawaiian Shamanism, Huna**.

A. Look out in front of you at a 20 degree angle upwards. Become aware of objects/movements in the horizontal part of your peripheral vision.
B. Become aware of objects/movements in the vertical part of your peripheral vision. (eg., your shoes and the sky.)
C. As you notice, more and more of your peripheral vision allow it to spread out and around you so that you can imagine what is behind you too.
D. Now you can do this with your other senses. Spread your hearing out and around and then do the same with your *kinaesthetics*.
E. Stay in this state for several minutes and you will become very relaxed. This technique *switches on your parasympathetic nervous system*.

Try closing your eyes and doing it!

Ten: *Simple Breathing Meditation*

Meditating on the breath is probably the most widely used and ancient of practices for relaxing the mind. It's very effective.

A. Sit down with your back straight.
B. Close your eyes and simply breath through your nostrils and out through your mouth.
C. Just observe the breath going in and out.
D. Try pausing for a second before the out breath, focussing on the heart centre.

Repeat for 10 minutes or more if you can!

So there you go! Why not experience one or two of these relaxation techniques exercises now and discover how much more relaxed you can become in just a few moments...

THOUGHT CONTROL

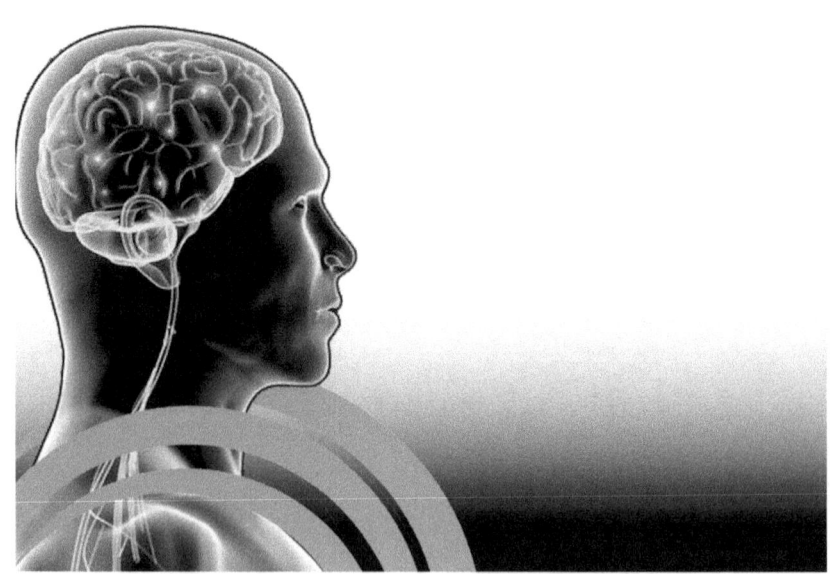

Thought Control

Be a Spectator To Your Own Thoughts

By Ray Chambers, *United Nations Special Envoy for Malaria*

So often, we find ourselves emotionally caught up in everyday conflicts. If we could only step back and watch what is going on, even thought we're in the midst of the scene, we would be able to objectively determine what our reaction should be and how to deal with our emotions.

Many times we are angry and feel justified in our anger. The outcome for the personal relationship and for our subsequent internal feelings never turns out positive when we act in anger. If we could step back and be a 'spectator', especially, after we've begun to have an emotional reaction, that process would almost immediately break the cycle of our angry response.

We have tried this approach with inner city youth in Newark, New Jersey. We've taught them that once they are feeling an angry reaction to whatever is the provocation, to just take a deep breath and picture themselves trying to help or hug that person. Invariably, taking the breath, stepping back and witnessing what is going on, almost always prevents the young person from exercising a negative physical or verbal response.

I recall being in a Board of Directors' Meeting when another Board member viciously attacked the CEO verbally. I rushed to the defence of the CEO and the other Board member then criticised me. My immediate reaction was one of being angry. I then pictured this man as a six-year-old boy in short pants cowering from his father (who he had told me that had been a strict disciplinarian) and my angry feelings dissipated. My response was then measured with he calmness.

Let's think about stepping back and being a spectator my our thoughts, whenever possible, especially after we've begun to experience a negative emotion.

Take Your destiny In Your Hands

Brahma Kumari Sister Shivani is a popular motivational instructor and lecturer, whose regular television programmes and lectures have inspired thousands of professionals, youth and even children to change their perceptions of religion, spirituality and their way of life.

After graduating as an electronics engineer, she went on to start up her own software company, including one to teach children *robotics*.

Her *practice of meditation* for the past 12 years has enabled her to explain to her audiences how values and spirituality can be used naturally in daily life. Shivani is also a regular presenter on the *Aastha.*

Channel with a viewership of *over 200 million.* She also appears regularly on *Sony TV, Sanskar* and *Zee Jagran Channels* which are socio-spiritual-cultural networks.

"It is your choice to decide what destiny you create for yourself,"

Brahmakumari, sister Shivaniben stressed during an address in Mumbai.

She was speaking on **Destiny:** Is it a matter of chance or choice?

She started the session by asking her listeners to sit silently for a minute and ask themselves what they would like to change in their lives. Then she asked them to ask what came to their minds concerning destiny. "Who feels that God writes our destiny?" There was a show of hands followed by a discussion with various participants presenting their points of view.

She asked them to imagine themselves writing their children's destiny.

Wouldn't they do a better job than their present situation? *There is no perfect destiny*, she said. We could write a better one than the one they are having to go through. Would you create such an unequal world?

So God himself says: I don't write your destiny. Parents can give knowledge, love, support and freedom to implement the right thing, but the child does what he/she chooses to. You can give your child support but he/she has to face the consequences for what he/she chooses to do.

Once you create this thought, it is immediately followed by a feeling, *All feelings determine your attitudes which determine actions and then habits. All your habits determine your personality. The energy it creates will come back to you and create your destiny,* she clarified.

We all want to know our destiny, get our palms read, follow *feng-shui, vastu, astrology,* etc. All they can do at best is to give you information based on your present parameters. *But they are not reality, only predictions.* Based on your parents' health and your own present condition, your doctor can predict whether or not you will contract diabetes and when. But it all depends on how you react to the prediction.

An astrologer gives you a ring to change your destiny. It will work only if you believe in it. If you believe everything is fine, you will be fine and you will save on consultation fees. *The highest energy is your thought.* And all thought is free. The more you are dependent on outside influences, the less you use you own power, and you lose that power.

How often do we take and appointment with ourselves to enquire how to change your destiny? If you are conscious that you are taking your destiny in your own hands, you create your own destiny. Let us say you do something and someone takes credit. How do you react? It's never about the other person. It's about how you react. Adapt. The more I adapt, the more use I make of my own power to mould my own destiny.

From a young age, you get used to and demand appreciation from others.

Addiction to appreciation follows. If I have a craving for appreciation I will never be stable. *If you become immune to appreciation, you also become immune to criticism.*

Look at everyone with whom you have an undercurrent of problems.

Then, (1) stop blaming them; (2) exercise your own choice and rise above ordinary thinking; (3) forgive yourself for giving up your power. It's as simple as choosing a dress you are going to wear.

Are you ready to forgive yourself? Then accept responsibility for whatever happens to you. No more ill-feelings, resentment, hatred towards anyone. Are you ready to do it now? Send love and compassion to all. Meditation gives you the power to act on this knowledge.

Otherwise, you'll only be reflecting other people's behaviour and lose you own personality. Show sweetness to everyone and soon everyone will reflect your sweetness. Use it everywhere, every time, with everyone.

The more you use it, the more it will increase. Don't reflect others. Be original to the best of your capacity. Learn from the hospitality industry in their training to be sweet to every client, however rude they may be. *They do it for their salary; you should do it for your happiness.*

Getting started on Brahma Kumari Meditation

Make an appointment with yourself for 10 or 20 minutes each morning or evening.

Find a quiet place and relax. Soft music, though not a necessity, can create an appropriate atmosphere. Sit comfortably upright on the floor or in a chair. Keep your eyes open and, without staring, gently rest them on a chosen point somewhere in front of your room.

Gently withdraw your attention from all sights and sounds. Become the observer of your own thoughts.

Don't try to stop thinking, just be the observer, not judging or being carried away by your own thoughts, just watching.

Gradually, they will slow down and you will begin to feel more peaceful. Create one thought for yourself, about yourself for example, "I am a peaceful soul."

Hold that thought on the screen of your mind; visualize yourself being peaceful, quiet and still. Stay as long as you can in the awareness of that thought. Don't fight with other thoughts or memories that may come to distract you. Just watch them pass by and return to your created thought, "I am a peaceful soul."

Now think of the Supreme Soul, who is the ocean of peace, bliss, love and so on. Soul receives all these virtues from Him.

Acknowledge and appreciate the positive feelings and other positive thoughts, which may spring directly from this thought.

Be stable in these feelings for a few minutes. Be aware of unrelated thoughts. Finish your meditation by closing your eyes for a few moments and creating complete silence in your mind.

Raja Yoga Intensive

Transcript of a lecture by Brahma Kumari Sister Shivani Verma

The word "meditation" comes from "medivate" (to heal).

[An unexpected loud screeching noise on sound systems...]

Situation comes, situation goes, what is left behind is the impact. Was the situation worth it for us to be disturbed? It was a trivial disturbed 30 seconds. Add the 30 seconds and one can become disturbed beings.

- In a crisis, in order to come up with the right solution, the mind has to be stable. If the mind is disturbed, it will not be able to see the solution. You can be stable with the earth shaking below you.
- When we were in Pakistan, there was an earthquake, but we got together to meditate for 1 minute without the thought of the earthquake. We stayed calm, so others stayed calm.
- Irritation. Is one born with this or is this cultivated? When a child wants something, he cries and throw tantrums to get what he wants. If he gets it, he learns that this is how he can get things. Instead, if the adult gives the child only if he asks politely, then we teach him that love, courtesy and respect is the way to get things.
- What does **'Raja Yoga'** mean?

'Raja' means highest.

'Yoga' means connection, communion or link.

It is through meditation that I become the ruler of myself. A self-ruler over my mind and over my sense organs.

- Who am I?
  The consciousness which I sit on brings about the next series of thoughts.
- Ego. What is that? Anyone? (asking audience)
  (Suggestions from the audience)
  To protect ourselves.
  Attachment to the self.
  Body consciousness.
  I am right you are wrong... etc
- These are attachments to the wrong image/belief about myself.
- Who are you?
  Are you your name, designation, qualifications,...etc. Your name is your label, not your identity. Your titles and roles are also not your identity even!

- When we hold on to something that we have to let go, there will be pain. We are then going against what we know is the truth. By doing so, we didn't enjoy the moments when we have that something. Everything is absolutely going to go one day. Fear of losing, fear of death,...etc.
- Say "I" and some of us may picture our body. We say, my body is aching, or I body aching ? We don't say, "I body acheing", because it is not 'I' that is aching, but our body.
- One wrong consciousness can make everything go haywire.
- **Human Being.**
  'Human' is matter.
  'Being' is energy.
- 'I' decide what to think, and what to see.

He/She is the one who expresses himself herself through his her body. I think, I create and speak through this body. My 'consciousness' or my 'body'. Any difference?

I am the 'programmer' (of my body).

The programmer has the power of the choice of instructions to feed into the computer that runs the robot.

In the morning, when you reach the office, you saw the security guard and you spoke to him, then you see the receptionist, and you spoke to him; then you spoke to your boss; then you spoke to the CEO, etc.

- Now, which of the four conversations comes from your real, 'you'? (from audience)

The conversation with the security guard?

None?

If the conversations were made from your actual nature, it wouldn't have changed.

- I am a pure being walking into the office, I meet another pure being playing the role of a security guard, then another pure being playing the role of a receptionist...etc.
- When a person got out of a car, are you speaking to the person or the car?

If you establish relationships based on what you have acquired in your lifetime would be doing it on temporary foundations.
- It'll be more peaceful if you are the same to all four of them. Be yourself. You'll stop wearing masks and stop having to be polite. Soul consciousness helps us to connect to the other person. We seldom talk about the 'soul' in our daily life. It seems the word 'soul' only comes up in a spiritual discourse or in a funeral.
- When you see the person as a spiritual being, that's the highest respect you can give to that person.
- Respect = re-spect.
- If you live a life believing that you are a body-mother-wife, it'll be difficult to leave this body. It is akin to children who got attached to the dress.
- What's the 'art of dying'? We speak about the 'art of living' more, but what's the 'art of dying'?
  If you understand the art of dying, then death won't be painful. Detachment is living with the consciousness that you are a pure being.
- We spend to much time on things that are not important.
- At the time of dying, then do we realise that they are not taken care of. The rest which we have spent much time and taken care of, we will leave behind when we die.
- Say if a few of us go around India in a train in our white saris. After a few days, the saris will be stained, but each sari is stained our own way. Same in life, though we started as pure beings, we developed differently and have different personalities. But the sari despite being stained, is still white. The soul despite having developed personality, is still pure. If you keep focusing on the stain, it will become worse. Focus on the white. That's the vibration we are going to send out.
- I create thoughts which is the mind.
  The mind evaluates, discriminates and decides (using the intellect). This will lead to action, and frequent actions form habits that will create personality traits.
- Our personality traits are affected by:
  Parents
  Environment
  Past
  Own Will power
  Our original nature.
- Our original nature is peace, love, happiness, power, purity, knowledge of who I am and bliss.
  Bliss is the pleasure beyond the sense organs.

- Shift from body consciousness to soul consciousness. Try to remember who we are. After each hour, pause for one minute to remind who we are.
- Medical science is trying to prove the presence of the soul through out-of-body, 'near death' and past life regressions.
- If our mind is stable (strong), we are not vulnerable and we are taken care of. Be soul conscious. Astrology...etc, doesn't have power over you. For instance, an astrologer may ask you to wear a stone, but that'll only work if you believe. So, who's doing the work? You or the stone?
- From the audience: How about the Year 2012, Dec 23?
- Yes, what about? Whatever that time means, what can you do about it? Just enjoy now. *laughter*
- I can remember everyone, even people I don't like, but I can't remember Him. Why when I quieten to remember him, the mind starts to wander? That's because we don't know who is the Supreme Power. He himself will give his introduction which will be accurate. Others give the introduction based on their own experience. God resides in us. God is omnipresent. We are all Gods.
- What is said of God is heard, read and passed down from generations to generations. We have to experience it for ourselves. When was the last time you experience divinity?
- In entropy, order will turn to chaos. There is then an external supreme intervention that is accepted by everyone.
- From the symbol of light, we build a stone, then a temple of deity, then men worship nature and then worship human beings, like Mahatma Gandhi.
- Therefore connect to Him as He is, not as the person I connect in the middle.
- I am a peaceful soul. I am in an ocean of peace.

Think Your Way To A Better Life

Life's slings and arrows is Harvard-educated neuroscientist Richard J. Davidson's phrase for the events we spend our days ducking, sometimes unsuccessfully. Losing out on that promotion. Getting dumped. Navigating a cocktail party of boors (or bores). The stuff that conspires to keep us in a foul mood, despite our best intentions. And Davidson argues that our response to such events - and even to full-on tragedies, such as the death of a loved one - is as much a part of our identity as our fingerprints.

"Each of us is a colour-wheel combination of the resilience, outlook, social intuition, self-awareness, context and attention dimensions of emotional style," he writes in his new book, "The Emotional Life of Your Brain" (Hudson Street Press), "a unique blend that describes how you perceive the world and react to it, how you engage with others and how you navigate the obstacle course of life."

Unlike our fingerprints, though, our emotional style can be altered. "We have the power," Davidson contends, "to live our lives and train our brains in ways that will shift where we fall on each of the six dimensions of emotional style."

That may sound more like your yoga instructor than a guy who has spent the past three decades studying brain chemistry. But study brain chemistry he does, which makes his findings all the more compelling. (And he did spend three months during graduate school in India and Sri Lanka studying meditation, therefore he's entitled to sound a little like a yogi.)

So, the six dimensions. Davidson, a professor of psychology and psychiatry at the University of Wisconsin-Madison, identifies them as such, based on activity he has identified in specific brain circuits:

Resilience: How slowly or quickly you recover from adversity.

Outlook: How long you are able to sustain positive emotion.

Social intuition: How adept you are at picking up social signals from the people around you.

Self-awareness: How well you perceive bodily feelings that reflect emotions.

Sensitivity to context: How good you are at regulating your emotional responses to take into account the social context you find yourself in.

Attention: How sharp and clear your focus is.

The book offers exercises to help assess your emotional style, mostly from true-or-false statements. ("When I go to a museum or attend a concert, the first few minutes are really enjoyable, but it doesn't last." "Often, when someone asks me why I am so angry or sad, I respond or think to myself, 'But I'm not!'")

Answers yield a score that places you on a spectrum for each of the six dimensions. Scoring 1 in resilience, for example, means "fast to recover"; a 10 indicates "slow to recover."

"There's no single optimal emotional style," Davidson said. "Emotional diversity is crucial for the successful operation of society. It's good, for example, that we have people who prefer to interact with machines over people.

"Neither end of the spectrum is necessarily better or worse than its opposite."

Still, he contends, certain emotional styles make it harder to lead a meaningful, productive life. Which inspires both the bad news and the good news from the book. A person who is self-opaque in the self-awareness department, puzzled in the social intuition department and unfocused in the attention department will likely struggle at dinner parties. (Bad news.) But, according to Davidson's findings, the brain is malleable enough to kick your scores up or down each spectrum a few notches, paving the way for future social success. (Good news!)

"It's best to regard your emotional well-being as a skill that can be trained," he says. "In many ways, it's no different than learning to play the violin. If you practice, you'll get better."

Essentially, Davidson argues, our brains - and therefore, our personalities - are hybrids of our genes and our environment.

"We can't do anything about our genes per se," he says. "We're all born with a complement of DNA that's just not possible to change. But our brains are constantly being shaped by the forces around us, and we can take more responsibility for the optimal shaping of our brains by engaging in certain, deliberate behaviors."

The extent to which certain genes are expressed, he notes, is largely affected by our environment - whether it's stressful or safe, perilous or nurturing.

"The decades-old neuroscience dogma that the adult brain is essentially fixed in form and function is wrong," he writes.

The final chapter is devoted to specific exercises for adjusting your emotional style - rewiring your brain, if you will.

To change your outlook: Write down one positive characteristic of yourself and one of someone you regularly interact with. Do this three times a day.

For social intuition: To enhance your sensitivity to vocal cues of emotion, when you are in a public place such as a subway, a busy coffee shop, a store or an airport terminal, close your eyes and pay attention to the voices around you.

Tune into specific voices; focus not on the intent but on the tone of voice.

Describe to yourself what that tone conveys: serenity, joy, anxiety, stress, etc.

"One of the central messages of the book is that different things work differently for different people," he says. "I encourage people to try things, to have an inquisitive curiosity and a playful attitude to see what works."

Think Yourself Out of Illness Into Health

Healing is that process of allowing for our return to wholeness, this mending of our brokenness.

First, experiment with being in the moment. Be in this very moment as you read these words. Not in the next moment, not in the past moment. Not in your thoughts of the future, worries, or reflections on the past. Just be here in this moment.

Being with the breath can be the easiest way to experience being in the moment.

Experiment with meditation. It's not about not having thoughts or quieting the monkey mind. It's just another experience of being in the moment. Take a class.

Try journaling. Write off the top of your head whatever you are thinking and feeling. Journaling can be a good way to slow down and be present with what's going on for you.

Then try writing about your dreams and desires. Don't limit yourself. Don't let any circumstances of your present life inhibit you: finances, relationships, health concerns, work, or geography. Write in the present tense.

Be intimate with yourself. Love, accept, and cherish yourself unconditionally. All of you. Your blemishes, your tarnish—all of you.

Your fears, your insecurities, your anxieties, and your upsets. Accept and cherish them all. Be gentle with yourself as you would with a child or a beloved pet.

Be even gentler with yourself. Delete "should" from your vocabulary.

Feed your inner child. Dialogue with a picture of yourself as a young child, real or imagined. Ask the little one what he or she needs. Try to give yourself some of that.

Explore intimacy with another: the intimacy that reveals your true self, that self that you allow yourself to love and cherish—

unconditionally. Blemishes, tarnish, fears, insecurities, and anxieties. All of you. If this notion is a hard one for you, or it feels scary or stressful, then just consider becoming friends with a pet. Or a child.

And speaking of children, take time to watch them play. Feel their spontaneity, their unselfconsciousness. Breathe some of that in. Experiment with being a little childlike, a little bit, every day.

Experiment with faith. Experiment with surrendering. If you're a non-believer, then pretend. Pretend that you are not in charge. Experiment with surrendering to something greater than yourself, even if it's just the weather.

And consider that this very moment, whatever is going on for you, is perfect, no matter what—no matter what is your mental, emotional, or physical state. Don't try to change it, resist it, make it go away, or make something come to you.

Mind Powering Made Easy

Thoughts are powerful vibrations that can keep us well or make us sick. Negative thoughts can make us sick and keep us sick. Positive thoughts can heal us and transform our lives. These concepts do not come from the realms of pseudoscience. In fact, there is a tremendous body of scientific research that can support these principles.

Researchers in physics and engineering have been conducting experiments that suggest the profound effects of consciousness on the material world—how our thoughts can affect us.

1   For over 25 years, scientists at Princeton University's Princeton Engineering Anomalies Research (PEAR) Laboratory have demonstrated powerful correlations between human intention and machine behavior. They have shown that untrained individuals can influence the output of random mechanical and electronic number generators, just by thinking in which direction the numbers should go. These effects were found to be independent of space and time. Effects also occurred when the individual was thousands of miles away.

2   These ideas are millennia old and have roots in many of the world's ancient traditions. However, Western allopathic medicine usually ignores these concepts. Most doctors did not study advanced physics in undergraduate or medical school.

Some examples of how our minds can affect our health include the following: positive thinking lowered blood sugar levels in diabetics, lessened asthma attacks, reduced colitis symptoms and improved immune function in HIV-infected individuals. Not only can our thoughts affect our bodies, but also our thoughts can affect others. Numerous studies have demonstrated the clinical efficacy of prayer, most notably the positive effect of prayer on patients in a coronary care unit.

In addition to this concept of the inherent connectedness of mind and body, as suggested by both ancient wisdom and modern science, is the existence of some ineffable source-entity, energy, connectedness—which embraces all and affects us all. Healing traditions around the globe draw on this source as a conduit to healing.

Our thoughts and emotions can get us well and keep us well, or get us sick and keep us sick—practical tools for harnessing the power of intention.

Our thoughts and feelings affect us. They can affect all aspects of our lives: our health, relationships, even finances. What I come across most often in my work is the impact that thoughts and feelings have on health. Negative thoughts and unexpressed feelings can create energy blockages, which become foci for disease.

Many of us spend our lives not even knowing how we feel, let alone being able to express feelings. Instead, we may medicate ourselves with activity to avoid feeling uncomfortable feelings. Workaholism, food, alcohol, addiction to exercise, dependence on pharmaceuticals and relationships are some of the ways we can avoid knowing our feelings and ourselves.

Feelings are normal and natural. Anger, sadness, fear, whatever you are feeling, is completely normal and natural. It's what we do in response to our natural feeling state than can become harmful to us. Keeping uncomfortable feelings inside can make us sick.

When we learn to feel our feelings, and "just be" with them, rather than keeping them stuck inside our bodies, we can harness the amazing inherent power that each one of us holds.

The following simple writing techniques will help you to get in touch with feelings and transform negative thoughts and uncomfortable feelings.

Get a notebook that can serve as a journal. It helps if you can commit to this daily practice and start your day with it. If your schedule doesn't permit, any time will do. Soon you will miss it when you don't do it! If you can take your journal around with you, you'll find it can be a source of comfort when situations arise that bring up uncomfortable feelings.

1. Stream-of-Consciousness Technique: Write down all your thoughts and feelings, including fears, resentments and anxieties. If you are not certain, then just write that. Even if you are feeling that you don't want to write, write that down! Be "in the moment" with whatever is going on. Do not censor or judge what you are writing. Take your feelings to the limit. For example, if you are worried about money, write why, what might happen—your innermost and deepest fears. If you are having a hard time with a spouse, significant other, or co-worker, write about this. As you are engaged in this process, your mind will naturally have reflective thoughts in response: Difficult feelings will transit to positive responses. Write these too. If more feelings come up, continue with these until you can write no more.
2. Non-Dominant-Hand Response Writing: After you have written your feelings down, write with your non-dominant hand: If you are right-handed, use the left and vice versa. Do not censor, and don't worry what your penmanship looks like. Just let your hand do the writing. Just write whatever comes to mind. See what happens—you will probably be surprised!

What follows are two additional simple writing techniques to help transform negative thoughts and feelings. The first involves releasing resentments; the second involves the power of affirmations.

Resentments

Resentment keeps us stuck or blocked more than any other emotion. In Chinese medicine, anger is a source of many physical diseases. A specific writing exercise to release resentment is as follows: Make 3 columns on a page. In column 1, write down the names of all the people you have ever felt angry or resentful toward, as far back in your life as you can remember. In addition to people include institutions, organizations and even social injustices that you may feel angry about. In column 2, write down what circumstances made you feel that way. In column 3, write down how this situation made you feel. Be specific: not just angry or resentful, but, for example, not honored, not respected, not taken seriously and so on. In the process of writing, you will discover that these feelings will transit.

Affirmations

In list form, write down all that you dream of and desire. Limit yourself in no way whatsoever. Your present personal, financial, employment, or geographical circumstances are irrelevant. Do not allow any of these situations to limit your creative imagining. Write about your ideal partner, job, home, vacation activity, financial needs. For example, if you dream of a new job, describe your ideal job: what you do, location, co-workers, how much money you make. And, most importantly, write in the present tense, as if you have all these desires now. Imagine how you feel in these circumstances. Write these feelings down.

And finally, if you are without pen and paper, and are feeling stuck in a negative mode of thinking, or feeling uncomfortable feelings (like fear, anxiety, frustration or anger), you can shift these thought/feeling patterns just with your intention to do so, and a simple technique. Imagine the scenarios you wrote about above: your specific dreams and desires. With your eyes closed, slow your breathing down, breathe fully and deeply into your abdomen, and imagine these ideal circumstances. Visualize them if you can, note the feelings you have about them, feel any sensations you may have. Note how the negative feelings have shifted. The point is to turn on positive thoughts, and turn off the negative ones. And remember, you can do this anytime, anywhere.

DIET-CONTROL

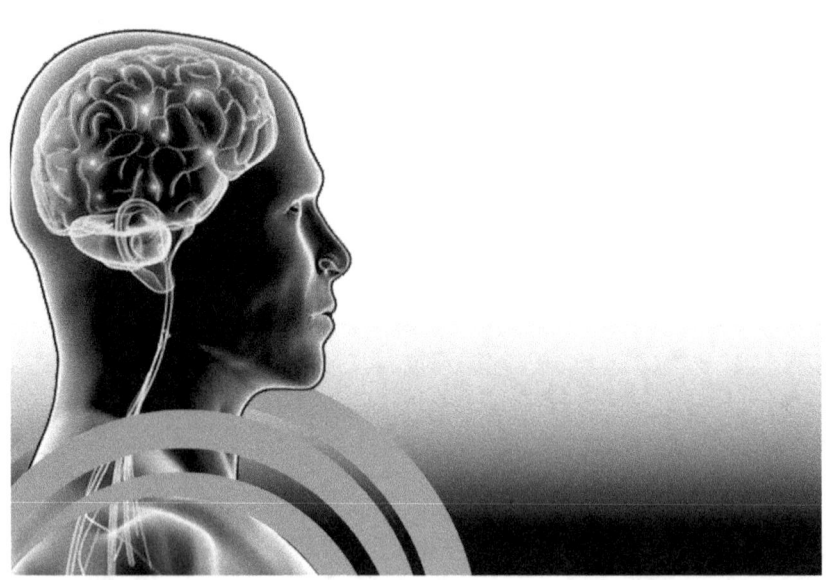

Diet-Control

Use your Kitchen Pharmacy

While each of us has unique nutritional needs, the following are general guidelines. How each of us responds to specific foods is unique. While a certain food substance in one individual maybe curative, in another it may aggravate symptoms or a condition.

Some of us are more sensitive to certain foods than others, and individual constitutions may be more or less tolerant to some of the suggestions below:

Make changes gradually. Your body has all the wisdom it needs to heal itself, but it also needs gentleness. Cravings for foods and/or substances considered unhealthy are merely signs that on one or more levels (body/mind/spirit) you are not getting what you need.

Our bodies recognise the nutrients in food that are closest to their natural form and that have not been chemically or mechanically altered.

Try to eat fresh cooked food that is in season whenever possible.

Try to avoid frozen food and leftovers. Food that is cooked and then refrigerated or frozen not only has little nutritional value but also can be toxic. When we eat food that is lacking in nutritional value, we may develop cravings, and may overeat to compensate for inadequate nutrition.

If you eat animal protein (beef, poultry), make sure it is organic. Non-organic sources contain HGH (human growth hormone) and antibiotics. HGH can affect endogenous hormone activity and should be avoided especially if you are dealing with male or female reproductive organ issues (breast, uterine or prostate problems). Antibiotics can interfere with the natural flora that live in our intestines, causing digestion and absorption problems. Also, they can interfere with our immune function.

If dairy products are part of your diet, make sure these are organic. Non-organic sources contain HGH and antibiotics.

If you include fish in your diet, make sure it is fresh, not farmed, and local. Farmed fish is often fed growth agents and antibiotics.

The best dairy products are made from raw milk (milk that is not pasteurized). Raw milk products contain all the necessary enzymes and nutrients needed for proper digestion. Pasteurization destroys these natural enzymes. Foods that lack these natural enzymes can contribute to malnutrition and overeating as the body tries to compensate for the lack. See www.realmilk.com for sources of raw milk by state.

Try to eat produce that is organic and in season. Our bodies are sensitive to the change of seasons, and recognize most optimally the nutrition from foods that are local.

Regarding grains, avoid all processed white flour and grains. Eat only whole grains.

If you eat at restaurants and are eating meat or fish, try to choose a source that you are certain of, unless the restaurant is reputable and uses organic sources. Fresh, unfarmed, local fish would be safer than poultry or beef.

GLASS JARS: Storing food in glass avoids the problems of food stored in plastic, which can result in compounds in the plastic being absorbed by the food. These compounds have estrogenic effects, which may upset the endocrine balance of the consumers. (Photos.com) How we prepare and store our food can affect how our bodies digest and absorb nutrients. How much we eat and in what combination affect these functions as well. In Part 2, we describe what cooking practices to avoid, how best to store food and beverages, suggestions on portion size, and food combinations.

Food Preparation and Storage

Do not use a microwave for any purpose (cooking, reheating, thawing, or boiling water). This form of electromagnetic radiation alters the chemical nature of food and water, severely reducing its nutritional value. Our bodies will experience malnutrition in response to eating microwaved foods, and we may experience cravings and overeat to compensate.

Try to avoid storing food in plastic wrap and plastic containers. Plastics are hydrocarbons that can modulate endogenous hormone activity. If you must, use paper or unbleached parchment paper to separate the food from the plastic.

Try to avoid bottled drinking water in plastic bottles, for the same reason.

Avoid aluminum foil for storing food and cooking. This heavy metal has been found to be associated with Alzheimer's and other chronic neurologic conditions.

Avoid aluminum cookware for the same reason.

Avoid all cookware made of synthetic materials, for example, Teflon.

Glass and ceramic are good materials for cooking. Heavy-gauge stainless steel and cast iron are good choices also, but make sure they aren't coated with Teflon, graphite or other substances.

Food Combining and Portion Size

If animal protein is part of your meal, eat this first, before eating complex carbohydrates, such as potatoes and pasta. To digest protein, the stomach needs concentrated digestive juices, which become diluted as we eat.

If you are eating animal protein, eat between two and four ounces at a meal. Make sure a meal of animal protein has adequate fat. For example, including the skin on the turkey or chicken is actually healthier than eating only the meat.

With the exception of bananas, fruit should be eaten alone as a separate meal or snack. Combining fruit with other food types (especially grains) can result in improper digestion.

Our bodies are happiest with small meals more frequently, rather than large meals many hours apart. Going without meals for too long actually puts our bodies into starvation mode; our metabolism will slow down and we will be in a fat-storing mode. However, each of us is unique with regard to portion size and frequency. Some of us need to eat as frequently as every two hours; other constitutions can space meals four or sometimes even five hours apart.

Each meal should be able to fit into the palms of your two cupped hands; more volume will not be digested.

Sugars and Sweeteners

Avoid all artificial sweeteners. These can confuse your body into thinking it is getting sugar. It will respond by increasing the insulin level, increasing fat storage and increasing sugar cravings.

Avoid refined sugars: cane sugar, brown sugar, fructose, glucose and corn syrup. When shopping, check labels for these hidden sources of sugar. Frequent consumption of refined sugar can lead to obesity and diabetes.

If you use honey as a sweetener, make sure it is raw honey. It contains all the necessary enzymes for digestion and will minimize the insulin effect.

More body-friendly sweeteners include rice syrup, barley malt syrup and Stevia liquid or powder.

Fats

Use high-quality fats and oils that are unrefined, cold-pressed and organic. Refined oils may be processed at high temperatures, which can cause the beneficial effects of these oils to be lost.

Avoid all hydrogenated and partially hydrogenated oils. They contain trans fatty acids, which have been shown to have adverse effects on blood fats.

Avoid margarine and any other "fake" butters and oils. These also contain trans fats.

Avoid "non-fat" and "low-fat" products. These are not necessarily better for you than full-fat products, and, in fact, can contribute to nutritional deficiencies. Low fat frequently means high carbohydrate, which can make losing weight difficult.

Raw butter is best. It contains more vitamins, minerals and a better quality fat than standard butter. These advantages are enhanced when it is made from raw milk from range-fed cattle. See www.realmilk.com for sources.

Fat does not make you fat. In fact, eating too little fat can keep you fat or make you fat. It is an essential nutrient, and if you don't have enough in your diet, your body will experience malnutrition. When we don't get all the nutrients we need, the body tries to compensate by overeating. Also, the body will hold onto any "extra" body fat when in a stressed state.

Beverages

Try to avoid all iced drinks. Iced drinks inhibit the digestive fire. If you crave these, it is a sign of excess heat in the body. This craving will lessen as energies become balanced.

Avoid carbonated beverages (sodas). These inhibit digestion, absorption and elimination.

Avoid concentrated fruit juices. These have unnaturally high concentrations of sugars. Room temperature water is the optimal drink.

Do not drink with meals because this dilutes digestive juices. At most, two or three sips of room temperature water are okay, but cold beverages inhibit the digestive process.

Discontinue all caffeinated beverages, including green tea, decaf coffee, decaf tea and decaf sodas. Caffeine is an irritant to the nervous system and can lead to mineral imbalances. Decaf coffee and decaf tea do contain some caffeine.

To ease caffeine withdrawal, try grain coffees, kukicha and bancha teas, but these teas do contain caffeine.

Alcohol is really a poison and toxic to the body. If you find yourself enjoying regularly drinking alcoholic beverages, it's a sign that your body/mind/spirit needs something you're not getting.

Desserts

While desserts are very much a part of our dietary culture, our bodies don't do well having dessert immediately after a meal. The food we have just eaten will not be properly digested.

If you are craving dessert after a meal, it is best to wait for at least an hour. Then ask yourself if you are still hungry for that food. Often you will not be. If you are, ask yourself if it is true hunger, or habit hunger.

If it is true hunger, by all means, have it. Depriving our bodies of what we are craving can be more harmful than having a particular food.

Over time, as your body/mind/spirit gets into balance, such cravings will lessen.

SWEET CRAVING: If you find yourself craving this kind of food, it may indicate a systemic imbalance or an emotional need. (Photos.com) Cravings and taste preferences are helpful clues about a person's nutritional and energetic balance. It is not only an issue of what we eat, but also how we eat. In this part, I will discuss cravings and mindful eating.

Cravings

Sweet, salty, sour, spicy and bitter are the five principle tastes we experience. If you have strong cravings for one or more of a particular taste, it is a sign of an imbalance.

Cravings for sweets and carbohydrates are very common. Sometimes the cause is physical, digestive or metabolic problems or fatigue. Sometimes the cause is emotional. Sadness or lack can cause us to crave these tastes and food types.

Cravings for other tastes, such as spicy and salty, indicate other types of imbalances in body/mind/spirit.

Try not to deprive yourself when you have strong cravings. This can be more harmful than avoiding the desired tastes.

How to Eat

How we eat is just as important as what we eat. The physiological mechanism of digestion is affected and inhibited by our eating habits. Indigestion can lead to cravings and overeating, because the body's nutritional needs are not being met.

Make time for each meal. Always eat sitting down. Eat mindfully. Before your first bite take time to pause and breathe gently and deeply.

Diet-control

Just eat. Don't read, watch TV, work, or talk on the phone. Digestion and absorption will be inhibited if you are doing anything in addition to eating.

Eat when you are in a relaxed mood. Avoid unpleasant thoughts and stressful conversations at mealtime. These will inhibit the digestion and absorption processes.

Eat slowly, and chew each bite until it is a mushy liquid consistency. Digestion starts in the mouth. By giving our salivary enzymes time to do their job, we can optimize our digestion. Otherwise, food will not be digested or absorbed, and we may become malnourished, have cravings and overeat to compensate for what we are lacking. If eating slowly is a challenge, try putting down your utensils between bites.

If you have tendencies toward emotional overeating, try to do deep abdominal breathing before you eat. Also, it can be helpful to keep a journal where you write your thoughts and feelings in a stream of consciousness style before meals. Pause to get in touch with what you really need, what you are really hungry for. Is it food, or is it something else? Part of my practice is helping patients get in touch with that "something else."

Most importantly, honour yourself with gentleness and patience. All the suggestions above are just that--suggestions. Don't berate or judge yourself if the suggestions feel difficult and hard to follow. As your body/mind/spirit comes more into its natural state of balance, all will come naturally, without effort.

POWER OF POSTURE

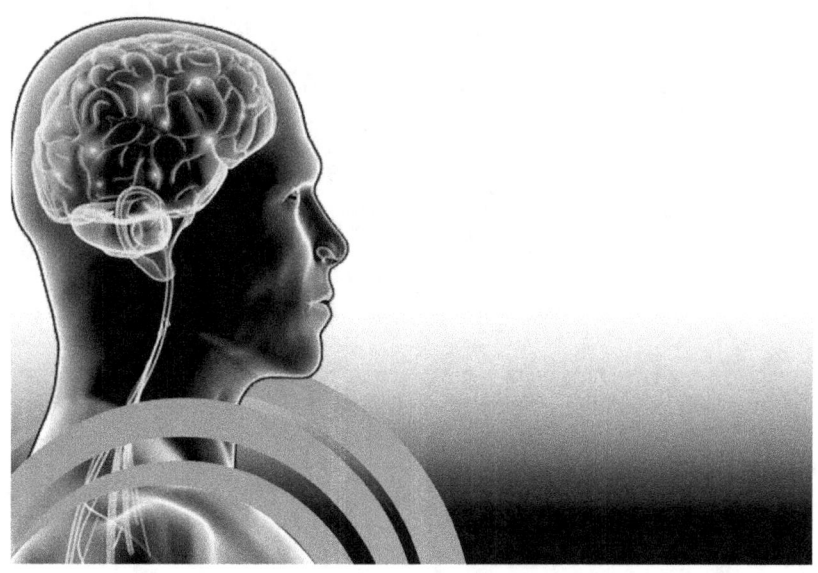

Power of Posture

It Only Takes Two Minutes In A 'Power Pose' To Completely Boost Confidence

[Pin it] [Pin it] The feeling of being in control is very powerful. It makes you more confident, and is something others can sense. The same can be said for feeling nervous or intimidated.

Harvard Business School's Amy Cuddy and Columbia's Dana Carney recently published research about the effects of body posture. They found that by **holding oneself in a "power pose" for as little as two minutes makes people feel measurably more powerful and willing to take risks.**

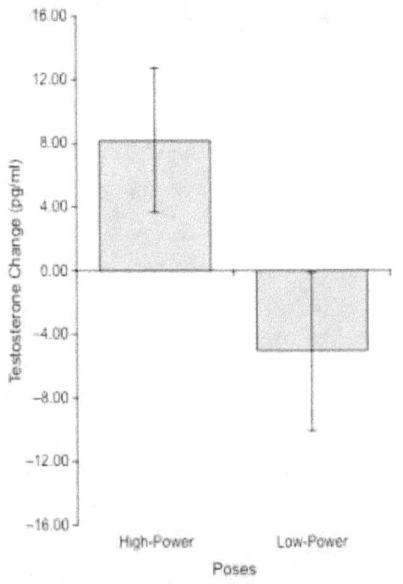

Fig. 3. Mean changes in the dominance hormone testosterone following high-power and low-power poses. Changes are depicted as difference scores (Time 2 – Time 1). Error bars represent standard errors of the mean.

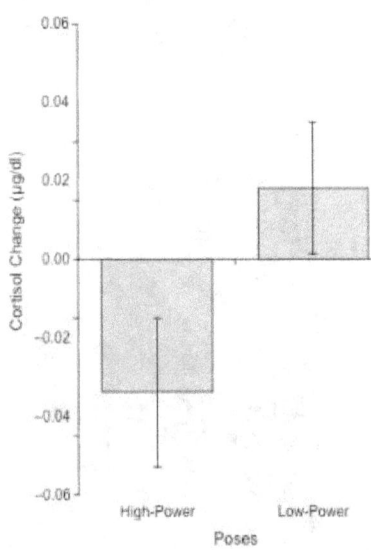

Fig. 4. Mean changes in the stress hormone cortisol following high-power and low-power poses. Changes are depicted as difference scores (Time 2 – Time 1). Error bars represent standard errors of the mean.

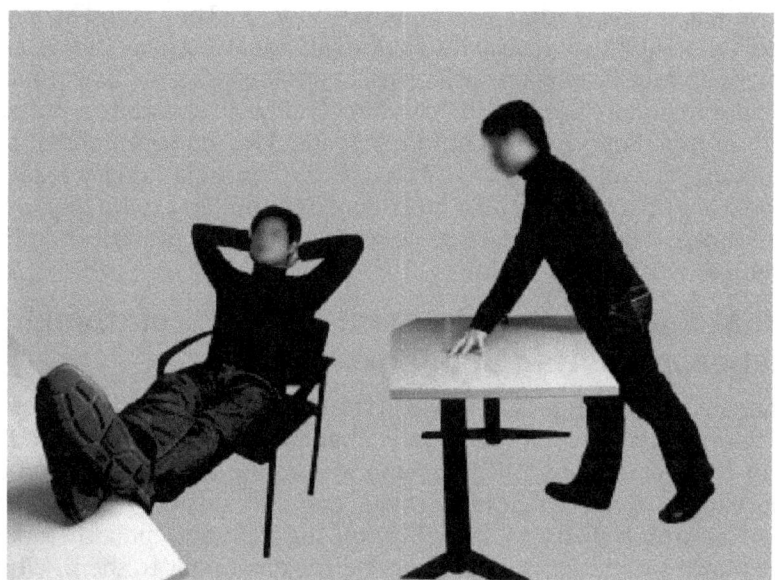

Fig. 1. The two high-power poses used in the study. Participants in the high-power-pose condition were posed in expansive positions with open limbs.

It's not just in your head. As the chart below shows, holding a power pose actually changes your hormones, increasing testosterone, a hormone that makes you feel dominance, and decreasing cortisol, a stress hormone:

Dana R. Carney, Amy J.C. Cuddy, and *Andy J. Yap*

So what does a power pose look like? The authors include this photo in their research:

Dana R. Carney, Amy J.C. Cuddy, and Andy J. Yap

Those two examples are perhaps a bit aggressive for daily use, but the study found other expansive poses had similar effects. Next time you find yourself slumping into a meeting, take a few minutes to stand tall and confident. Even better, make a conscious effort to pose confidently throughout the day.

You might be surprised at the results.

Leadership Advice: Strike a Pose

Want to become an effective leader? Watch the way you sit, stand, and posture, says a Harvard B-School professor.

We know how leaders are supposed to look. They stand straight and tall. They are physically expansive, radiating confidence and power. In fact, taking on such physical attributes can actually make people feel more leader-ish, says Amy Cuddy, an assistant professor at Harvard Business School. Cuddy and two co-researchers are studying "power posing"--an exercise for charisma-hungry leaders who want not only to appear more confident but also to be that way. She spoke with editor-at-large Leigh Buchanan about mastering the physical side of leadership.

What Led to Your Interest in the Relationship Between Posture and Power?

There's often a gender grade gap in the M.B.A. classroom in the sense that men appear to outperform women. And one thing I noticed is that the women don't sit the same way as the men. They're much more likely to have their legs crossed and their ankles wrapped. The men are more likely to sit with their legs spread, their shoulders open, arms sometimes draped around the chair next to them. When they want to get in there, they lean forward and stick up their hands. We've known for a long time that the postures assumed by many of the men are associated with power.

So Your Posture Reflects how Powerful You Feel.

I wondered what would happen if you forced students to change their posture. Would that lead them to participate more? Can you fake it until you make it? There's evidence from social psychology and research on facial expressions that suggests it's possible. When you force people to smile and to contract the muscles in the face that are involved with smiling, it makes them happier. That's called the facial feedback hypothesis. But what happens below the neck conveys a lot of information, too.

Is There a Known Physiological Basis for That?

We looked at testosterone, the hormone associated with dominance, and cortisol, a hormone that is released in response to stress. In primatology, the belief is that individuals born with the highest testosterone become the alphas. But it's also true that if an individual is forced to take over the alpha role, within a few days, his testosterone has gone up, and his cortisol has gone down. And if you get pushed to the bottom of the hierarchy, your testosterone goes down, and your cortisol goes up. That makes you much less disease resistant and more likely to get picked off.

Some social psychologists at the University of Texas have found that the most effective leaders have both *high testosterone* and *low cortisol*. You don't want *high-testosterone, high-cortisol* leaders. That person is going to be defensive and very reactive to stressful decisions. *He or she will be less likely to make good decisions.*

How Did You Test Your Hypothesis?

We brought people into the lab and had them split into a little vial to get baseline testosterone and cortisol levels. Then some of them would do high-power poses for two minutes and some would do low-power poses for two minutes. Then we gave them $2 and the chance to roll a die and win $4. And we had them answer questions about how powerful they felt. After 15 to 17 minutes, we'd take a second saliva sample.

And The Results Were?

The high-power poses caused a decrease in cortisol of about 25 percent and an increase in testosterone of about 19 percent. The low-power poses increased cortisol about 17 percent and decreased testosterone about 10 percent. On the gambling task, 86 percent of the high-power posers chose to take the risk, compared with 60 percent of the low-power posers.

Was it the Same for Men and Women?

Both showed the same pattern of changes.

Is there a minimum amount of time people need to power pose in order for it to take?

We advise people to do this before they go into a situation where they need to appear confident. Normally, what people do before they give a speech or go into a sales meeting is sit in a chair, hunching over their notes or their iPhone. That's the opposite of what you should be doing. You're making yourself tiny. Instead, you should be walking around the hallway, putting your arms up. Sit at your desk and put your feet up on it. Stand on your tiptoes with your hands in the air. When you go into a sales meeting, you want to be as squared off and tall as you naturally can be. If you're sitting down, you might consider not crossing your legs. If the chair has arms, rest your arms on those arms. That will help prevent you from crossing your arms or wrapping them around your torso.

How long does the effect of power posing last? Can it get you through a sales meeting? A morning? A whole day?

That is an empirical question we will be trying to unravel. At this point, we can say pretty comfortably that the initial effects seem to last 15 or 30 minutes. I think the more interesting question is whether or how it becomes self-reinforcing. You pose powerfully; you perform better; you feel more confident and powerful; then you perform even better. At the same time, people respond to that confidence and performance boost and give you feedback that further elevates your feelings of confidence and power.

Are the effects of power posing cumulative? In other words, the more regularly you do it, the longer the effect lasts or the easier it is to achieve? Does there come a point, if you maintain the poses long enough, that testosterone and cortisol simply assume the optimal levels?

I'm not the best person to answer that, because I'm not an endocrinologist. But I don't think it's likely that your hormone levels are going to change permanently. What might be more likely is that once you learn that feeling, you can achieve it mentally without doing the poses. It would be interesting to answer the question: Can you close your eyes and picture yourself in one of those postures and get the same effect?

How important is the physical sensation of confidence or power in being a good leader?

It gets into this idea of embodiment. For example, people who hold a warm cup behave more warmly. When you hold a cold cup, you behave more coldly. That was in a paper published in Science a few years ago--it's good science. So feeling yourself in a position of power and confidence can give rise to behaviors that reflect that. You fake it until you make it.

What is the effect of power poses on risk tolerance? Is there a concern that people might experience irrational exuberance postposturing and make unwise decisions as a result?

It does increase risk tolerance. But for the average person, it's still well within the normal range. Only a small, pathological percentage of the population might be pushed over the edge.

I suppose that people naturally have different levels of testosterone and cortisol. Is that what underlies the argument that some people are born leaders?

It may be partly that.

Is this something that should be taught in leadership development programs?

It should be part of leadership development. But the people who could benefit the most are not necessarily the people who end up in an M.B.A. classroom. It's the people who are powerless and suffering because of it. Two days ago, someone invited me to talk at a women's shelter about this. That's my greater hope.

If a leader's problem is the opposite of a lack of confidence--if he or she is arrogant and impatient and tends to steamroll people--can assuming postures of submission help?

I'm sure it could. But how would you convince someone like that to actually do it?

What Does Dominance Look Like?
We asked Amy Cuddy to describe *four classic power poses*:
- **The Performer**: *Mick Jagger* --"This is a classic expression of feeling powerful in the moment-it causes you to physically expand."
- **The CEO**: *Oprah Winfrey*--"The body language naturally projects dominance. It's unusual to see a woman in this position."
- **The Classic**: *Wonder Woman*--"She's really opening up. The feet spread, the hands on the hips. She's taking up space."
- **The Loomer**: *Lyndon Johnson*--"Johnson was 6'4", and he used his stature very thoughtfully-to both intimidate and seduce."

LONGEVITY

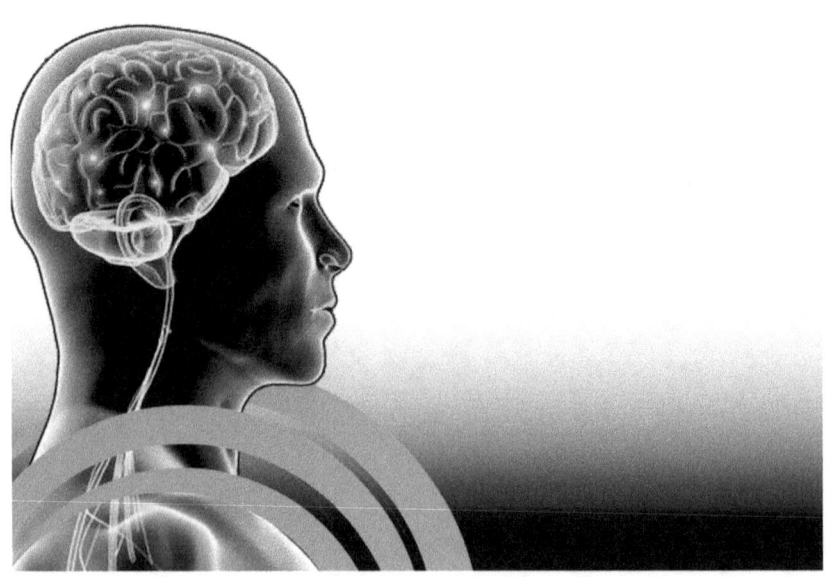

Longevity

Inner Peace Can Make You Look Younger

Cutting edge scientific research shows that the way we think and live can have a massive impact on the way we age. New research focussing on longevity hotspots around the world, found that small lifestyle changes can add up to 10 years to most people's lives. Aging is 10% genetic and 90% lifestyle, the research found. Using practices to shed stress and boost relaxation can have a massive impact on not only how you age but how long you live. Let's do it!

Be Kind

Scientists now believe that ageing is actually like a disease and that the possible lifespan of the human body far exceeds what we currently live to. They believe that inflammation is a primary cause of ageing. Scientists have discovered that the vagus nerve – the longest nerve in the body that is stimulated by acts of kindness and compassion serves as a 'brake' on inflammation in the body. "We have far more control over the ageing process than we think," says Dr David Hamilton, author of Why Kindness is Good For You. 'Being kind is better than botox!" says Dr Hamilton.

Slow Down Your Brainwaves

Our brain waves are measured as micro-electrical charges per second. The one we are most familiar with is beta - at 13-30 cycles per second, known as our waking, conscious mind. Then there is the alpha state, measured at 7-13 cycles per second. This is known as our meditative or contemplative mind. Theta is 4-7 cycles per second. Delta brainwaves are considered the most relaxing brainwave frequency range. Delta brainwaves are commonly associated with the deepest sleep and a state of unconscious awareness: ranging from 0 – 4 cycles per second.

One of the associated benefits of increasing your delta brainwaves is the release of 2 powerful anti-aging hormones - melatonin and DHEA. The delta brainwaves are also associated with decreased levels of cortisol – a hormone linked to stress that has been scientifically proven to speed up the aging process. We get delta waves when we are in a deep sleep. Click here (See Below Michelle) for 10 tips on how to get a good night's sleep and up those anti-ageing Delta Waves.

Learn to Meditate

Dr. Robert Wallace was one of the first scientists to study the effects of meditation on aging. He found that subjects with an average chronological age of 50 years, who had been practicing Transcendental Meditation for over 5 years, had a biological age 12 years younger than their chronological age.

If meditation isn't your bag, don't panic.

William Bloom, one of Britain's top holistic teachers and author of The Endorphin Effect, studied and taught meditation for years but was thrown when people in his meditation classes said they felt just as good stroking their cat (or riding their motorbike/going for a lovely walk) as they did meditating. This led Bloom to research what is now known as the 'endorphin effect' – how relaxed, loved-up and peaceful you feel when your body is flooded with endorphins. Bloom's research has shown that there are five ways you can trigger these endorphins – without meditating.

1. Think about someone you like or do something you like. (Make a list of things you genuinely enjoy and do more of them – this will naturally trigger a flood of endorphins.)
2. Make napping your greatest skill. Or at least allow your body to slump and your body language to sink into napping body language. A 3- or 4-minute slump will release that flood of feel-good hormones.
3. 20 minutes of movement – it doesn't have to be aerobic; any sustained movement for 20 minutes or more will release endorphins.
4. Connect with nature – be it staring at a blade of grass or going for a walk in the woods. This is proven to release endorphins in the body.
5. Monitor how your body feels and give it a break – treat it as you would a hurt animal or child – gently relax and think loving, kind thoughts about your poor old body. Apparently, every time we do this, endorphins flood to the rescue.

Four Skills Necessary:
- Pause (when stressed OR experiencing pleasure, put on the brakes and take a mental pause)
- Notice sensations (notice the actual sensations and feelings in your body)
- Absorb (if the sensations are pleasurable, chill a bit more and absorb the good feeling)
- Hold (if the sensations are tight, painful or distressing, turn your focus toward them, use the inner smile and 'hold' the feelings of discomfort)

Walking: The Easiest Way To Live Longer

Did you know that every minute you walk can extend your life by 1.5 to 2 minutes? In addition, many studies show that people who walk regularly live longer, weigh less, have lower blood pressure, and enjoy better overall health than non-walkers.

Ready to lace on your shoes? If you want to add to the amount of walking you do, just clip on a pedometer. That simple action actually increases your physical activity by over 2100 steps per day, a review that pooled data from 26 studies found.

Here's a look at the ten major benefits of walking:
Walking Increases Your Lifespan
Walking more than an hour a day improves life expectancy significantly, a 2011 study showed. The researchers looked at 27,738 participants between the ages of 40 and 79 over a 13-year period. Surprisingly, their lifetime medical costs did not increase—even though they lived longer.

"An increase in walking time at the population level would bring about a tremendous change in people's health and medical cost," the study authors wrote.

Walking Wards Off Diabetes
Just thirty minutes of walking a day can prevent diseases such as type 2 diabetes, a 2002 study looking at both overweight and average weight men and women in a population at high risk for the disease showed.

If you already have diabetes, walking is helpful for you, too. A mile or more daily cuts your risk of death from all causes in half, according to a 2007 study.

Walking Keeps Your Mind Sharp
Walking 72 blocks a week (around six to nine miles) helps increase grey matter, which in turn lowers the risk of suffering from cognitive

impairment—or trouble with concentration, memory and thought, according to a study which looked at 299 seniors over a nine-year period.

Furthermore, walking five miles per week can provide some protection to the memory and learning areas of the brains of those already suffering from Alzheimer's disease or mild cognitive impairment, and lead to a slower decline in memory loss.

Walking Helps Lower Blood Pressure
Walking just 30 minutes a day, three to five days a week—even when the 30 minutes are broken into three ten-minute increments—has been found to significantly lower blood pressure.

Walking is Great for Bone Health
Putting one foot in front of the other for about a mile a day led to improved bone density in post-menopausal women, and slowed the rate of bone loss from the legs, according to a 1994 study. "It takes walkers four to seven years longer to reach the point of very low bone density, study leader Dr. Krall told the New York Times.

Walking Cuts the Risk of Stroke
Walking about 12.5 miles a week or more cut the risk of stroke in half, according to a study looking at over 11,000 Harvard University alumni with an average age of 58.

Walking Improves Your Mood
If you're feeling down in the dumps, walking is a quick and easy solution. Just thirty minutes on a treadmill reduces feelings of tension and depression, according to research published in the British Journal of Sports Medicine. In fact, the study found that walking lifted moods more quickly than anti-depressants did (and with fewer side effects).

And the more people walk, the better their mood and energy, says California State University Long Beach professor Robert Thayer, based on a study looking at 37 study participants over a 20-day period.

Walking Torches or Burns Calories
Just 20 minutes of walking a day will burn 7 pounds a year. The effects are even more dramatic when you add in some dietary changes as well.

23 Diet Plans Reviewed: Do They Work?

Walking Improves Insomnia
Having trouble sleeping at night? Try taking a brisk 45-minute

walk in the morning five days a week, and your sleep may improve significantly, according to research from the Fred Hutchinson Cancer Research Center in Seattle, which looked at women from the age of 50-74. (Walking in the evening, however, sometimes has the opposite effect—so keep an eye on when you're exercising and what your sleep patterns are.)

Walking is Good for the Heart
Women who took brisk walks for three or more hours per week reduced their risk of heart disease by 30-40 percent, according to an analysis of over 72,000 women aged 40-65, who were enrolled in the prospective Nurses' Health Study. As I reported recently, heart attacks kill more US women than men annually. However, the benefits of walking aren't limited to one gender. A different study showed that walking can cut the risk of coronary heart disease in half for men between the ages of 71 and 93.

Five Types of Behaviours that Promote Healthy Living in old Age

The Five Types of Behaviour to Live Past 90
A regular exercise routine may reduce your risk of death by 20-30 percent!

1. **Don't Smoke**
   Smokers had double the risk of dying before 90 compared with non-smokers.
2. **Keep a Healthy Weight**
   Obese men were 44 percent more likely to die before 90 than non-obese men.
3. **Avoid High Blood Pressure**
   Men with high blood pressure were 28 percent more likely to die before 90.
4. **Exercise Regularly**
   Men who exercised regularly reduced their risk of death by 20 percent to 30 percent, compared to men who never did.
5. **Avoid Diabetes**
   Men with diabetes were 86 percent more likely to die before 90 than men without the illness.

What Do These Factors Have in Common?
They are all things that you can modify in your life right now, largely by choosing to not smoke, eat healthy and exercise regularly.

"The take-home message," said the study's lead author Dr. Laurel B. Yates, a geriatric specialist at Brigham and Women's Hospital in Boston, "is that an individual does have some control over his destiny in terms of what he can do to improve the probability that not only might he live a long time but also have good health and good function in those older years."

Living tO 100: What's the Secret?
FROM HARVARD MEDICAL SCHOOL
Trusted advice for healthier life
Starting in the year 2012, 10,000 people a day will start turning 65. We are aging differently than previous generations, however. Physically and mentally, the health of today's 70-year-old now equals that of a 65-yearold in the 1970s. In that period, deaths from heart disease and many cancers have dipped. And while most older adults have at least one chronic health problem, disability has slowly but significantly declined.

Our life expectancy continues to inch upward, a happy trend, although some wonder if we could be doing better, since the United States has been slipping downward in longevity rankings compared with many other countries. Infectious disease and acute illnesses, once the leading causes of death, have given way to chronic ailments and degenerative illnesses— like heart disease and Alzheimer's disease— that people often live with for decades.

How long are you likely to live? Will your later years be blessed by healthy aging or marred by a host of illnesses? Certainly, the answers to those questions rest partly with the genes you've inherited. Yet at the turn of the millennium, more than a third of deaths in America were tied to smoking, poor dietary choices, and inactivity.

This report attests that the actions you take today matter. Simple lifestyle choices have an enormous impact on your longevity and quality of life.

What is essential for healthy aging? Full engagement with life. People who are curious, open, and eager to make connections with the world most enjoy the last decades of their lives. Even in the face of disabilities, these people seem to thrive and find joy despite their challenges. Depressed, anxious, or grumpy people in good health can also live long lives, but take far less pleasure in them. No magic pill, no secret potion can make us long-lived and healthy. But if you bring to your life appreciation and respect, and embrace aging with good humor, grace, vigor, and flexibility, you will— at the very least— be happy to grow old.

How long do we live?
Nowadays, life expectancy at birth is nearly 78 years in the United

States. This is a great leap forward from 1900, when the average newborn couldn't expect to reach age 50. Indeed, in the 20th century the life span of the human species — in developed nations— expanded more than it had in any century since the birth of mankind. When the numbers are crunched more carefully, though, there are obvious differences between men and women and people of different races. A newborn boy born in 2004 or after can expect to live a bit more than 75 years, while his sister can expect to live to slightly more than 80. Life expectancy measured from birth is more than five years shorter for a black person than a white one, although the gap narrows to less than two years for those who survive to age 65. If you live to celebrate certain milestones of age, your life expectancy stretches (see Fig. 1). In other words, the longer you live, the longer you're likely to live. Because many people who have chronic ailments or engage in behaviors that raise the risk of accidents or illness get cut from the herd much earlier, the oldest old are often remarkably healthy.

Increasing the Lifespan of People

As you grow older, your average life expectancy stretches. For example, while the life expectancy of a newborn in the United States is nearly 78, a 65-year-old can expect to live 19 years longer, and a 75-year-old for another 12 years. Why did life expectancy increase so much in the 20th century in developed nations? Whether individuals develop a particular disease is usually determined by three things: their lifestyle (including diet and exercise), their environment (such as exposure to infectious microbes or toxins), and their genes. Increased life span surely has nothing to do with genes: our genes today are the same as they were a century ago. Instead, changes in lifestyle and environment are responsible.

Changes in the environment—such as better sanitation, the use of antibiotics, and many other improvements in medical care—can claim much of the credit. As for lifestyle, in developed nations, nutritional deficiency diseases largely were eliminated in the last century. Still, not all nutritional changes have been entirely for the better. In the United States, at the turn of the 20th century, most Americans lived on farms or in rural communities. We ate fresh, unprocessed food every day, and we worked hard physically. Today, our diets are less healthful in many ways, and we exercise less.

The secrets of centenarians Each year more Americans drift into the upper age brackets on census forms. According to the 2000 census, there are more than 330,000 people ages 95 and over in the United States, while 85- to 94-year-olds number 3.9 million.

Studies of people who reach the century mark note that their health is surprisingly robust despite advanced age. Once decline does set in for these centenarians, death follows fairly quickly. That's an attractive prospect for those who fear a drawn-out loss of health and independence in their waning years.

What's the centenarians' secret? Not surprisingly, genes play a role. A study of Swedish twins ages 80 and older attributed about half of the changes in mental function to genes. Other twin studies suggest genes are responsible for up to 35% of the physiological changes of age and that longevity itself is 25% to 35% inheritable. But don't start viewing your genetic inheritance with rue or glee. Genetics is only part of the equation. Simple math tells you there's plenty of room left for the role that other factors — such as your diet, exercise routine and regular exams for illnesses— play in how you age.

Extending your life It's all very well to pile up statistics on average life span and speculate about factors in the aging process and the biological limits of life. Yet what does this tell you about your own life? Not enough. Clearly, more work needs to be done to crack the code of aging. But you don't have to wait until the final answers are in to take steps that may extend and enhance your life right now.

How well you age will help dictate how long you stay alive and how happy you are to do so. Whether or not your family is long-lived, the answers lie less in your genes than in your actions. Do you smoke? Do you eat well or poorly? Do you stay active? Are you a healthy weight? What ailments do you have now and, judging from family background and your current lifestyle, which ones are you likely to get? If your answers seem discouraging, take heart. It's not too late to make changes. A 2007 study in The American Journal of Medicine focused on adults who adopted a healthier lifestyle during middle age. The researchers followed 15,700 adults (ages 45 to 64) for a decade and noted that 970 of these people embraced a healthier lifestyle by the sixth year of the study. These individuals ate five or more daily servings of fruits and vegetables, worked out at least two and a half hours per week, didn't smoke, and avoided obesity. Benefits appeared quickly. Just four years later, the group of individuals who made these four changes had a 40% lower rate of death for any reason and 35% fewer cases of heart disease compared with the participants who made fewer of these changes.

No matter what your age or stage of life, you have the power to change many of the variables that influence disability and longevity. With these 10 steps outlined below, you can learn how. Optimism and survival It's obvious that healthy people live longer than sick people. If optimism actually improves health, it should also boost longevity — and according to two studies from the U.S. and two from the Netherlands, it does.

The first American study evaluated 839 people in the early 1960s, performing a psychological test for optimism-pessimism as well as a complete medical evaluation. When the people were rechecked 30 years later, optimism was linked to longevity; for every 10-point increase in pessimism on the optimism-pessimism test, the mortality rate rose 19%. A more recent U.S. study looked at 6,959 students who took a comprehensive personality test when they entered the University of North Carolina in the mid-1960s. During the next 40 years, 476 of the people died from a variety of causes, with cancer being the most common. All in all, pessimism took a substantial toll; the most pessimistic individuals had a 42% higher rate of death than the most optimistic.

The two Dutch studies reported similar results. In one, researchers tracked 545 men who were free of cardiovascular disease and cancer when they were evaluated for dispositional optimism in 1985. Over the next 15 years, the optimists were 55% less likely to die from cardiovascular disease than the pessimists, even after traditional cardiovascular risk factors and depression were taken into account.

The other study from Holland evaluated 941 men and women between the ages of 65 and 85. People who demonstrated dispositional optimism at the start of the study enjoyed a 45% lower risk of death during a nine-year follow-up period. Blue skies

More study is needed to clarify the link between optimism and good health. It's likely that multiple mechanisms are involved. Personality is complex, and doctors don't know if optimism is hardwired into an individual or if a sunny disposition can be nurtured in some way. It's doubtful that McLandburgh Wilson was pondering such weighty questions when he explained optimism in 1915:

> "Twixt the optimist and pessimist
> The difference is droll
> The optimist sees the doughnut
> But the pessimist sees the hole."

Today's doctors don't think much of doughnuts, but they are accumulating evidence that optimism is good for health. As you await the results of new research, do your best to seek silver linings, if not doughnuts.

Ten steps toward a longer healthier life
1. Don't smoke.
2. Build physical and mental activities into every day.
3. Eat a healthy diet rich in whole grains, vegetables, and fruits, and substitute healthier monounsaturated and polyunsaturated fats for unhealthy saturated fats and trans fats.
4. Take a daily multivitamin, and be sure to get enough calcium and vitamin D.
5. Maintain a healthy weight and body shape.
6. Challenge your mind.
7. Build a strong social network.
8. Protect your sight, hearing, and general health by following preventive care guidelines.
9. Floss, brush, and see a dentist regularly. Poor oral health may have many repercussions, including poor nutrition, unnecessary pain, and possibly even a higher risk of heart disease and stroke.
10. Discuss with your doctor whether you need any medication—perhaps to control high blood pressure, treat osteoporosis, or lower cholesterol—to help you stay healthy.

SELF IMPROVEMENT/PERSONALITY DEVELOPMENT

All books available at www.vspublishers.com

QUIZ BOOKS

ENGLISH IMPROVEMENT

OTHERS LANGUAGE

ACTIVITIES BOOK

QUOTES/SAYINGS

BIOGRAPHIES/CHILDREN SCIENCE LIBRARY

COMPUTER BOOKS

All books available at www.vspublishers.com

STUDENT DEVELOPMENT/LEARNING

POPULAR SCIENCE

PUZZLES

DRAWING BOOKS

VALUE PACKS

COMPREHENSIVE COMPUTER LEARNING	SECURE A JOB	QUIZ TIME	सम्पूर्ण शख्स-विकास	व्यक्तित्वयोगी	गुरुर्मत्यगोयी	ज्योतिष का खजाना
(124105)	(06005)	(023125)	(002235)	(140015)	(105055)	(122115)

Contact us at sales@vspublishers.com

www.ingramcontent.com/pod-product-compliance
Lightning Source LLC
Chambersburg PA
CBHW070312230426
43663CB00011B/2103